Chase
The
Dream

Janice Knight

Chase The Dream

Constance Colson

PALISADES

Also by Constance Colson
Cherish

This is a work of fiction. The characters, incidents, and dialogues are products of the author's imagination and are not to be construed as real. Any resemblance to actual events or persons, living or dead, is entirely coincidental.

CHASE THE DREAM
published by Palisades
a part of the Questar publishing family

© 1996 by Constance Colson

International Standard Book Number: 0-88070-928-6

Cover illustration by Bill James
Cover designed by Kevin Keller
Calligraphy by Bill McConaughy, Portland, Oregon
Edited by Paul Hawley

Printed in the United States of America

For information:
QUESTAR PUBLISHERS, INC.
POST OFFICE BOX 1720
SISTERS, OREGON 97759

96 97 98 99 00 01 02 — 10 9 8 7 6 5 4 3 2 1

To Dad and Mom
With much love, respect, and gratitude.

For your sacrifice, encouragement, support, honesty,
protection, and unconditional love…
For Kittens in lunch boxes, surprise car trips west, and
advice to take another look at the man
I almost passed by —
and later married…

For teaching me to "run like the wind," reminding me to
keep my head on straight, and assuring me that
your love would only increase with each tomorrow…
I thank you.

May Mark and I be the blessing to our children
that you were and are to me.

God keep you.

"So then it *does* not *depend* on the man who wills
or the man who runs, but on God who has mercy."

ROMANS 9:16 (NASB)

PART I

Childhood Dreams

CHAPTER

1

WUMPF!

Young Sterling Jackson Jr. watched his eleven-year-old son land on the ground spread-eagled, the dust from his fall billowing around him. "Naw, not like that, Forrest! You rode that calf like a sack of feed."

As he strode into the fog of debris and sunlight hovering near Forrest, Sterling released a stream of expletives. "How many times I got to tell you, boy? Keep up on that rope. Don't let a little ol' calf throw you off balance!" He slapped his son on the back, a customary form of cowboy encouragement that discharged another cloud of dust from Forrest's filthy shirt and toppled the rising mini-wrangler.

"Biggest calf I ever saw." Forrest spat, returning the dust to whence it came. He sat on the ground and gathered his legs close.

The ride had gone badly, but Forrest was beyond caring. He wiped his hand across his gritty, sweaty forehead and matted blond hair. His tongue worked his dry mouth, and he tried not to think how good a plunge into Mancos Lake would feel. A swim was beyond hope this afternoon, a still greater calamity because the rash of hot weather was unusual for Colorado in September, and the lake would soon turn cold. "Can we go back to the broncs now? Or maybe take a break?"

His father's hands slid to his hips, resting on a thick black, tooled leather belt fastened by a dazzling golden trophy buckle. "How do you expect to ride in the National Finals Rodeo someday if you can't even handle an itty-bitty calf, Forrest?" Sterling stalked off to recapture the bawling calf, who was trotting nervously near the catch pen where other calves waited.

"I don't like bulls. I don't ever want to ride 'em. I like horses. An' roping. They got those in the NFR, too, don't they?" Forrest muttered, but his father, busy herding the calf back into the chute, didn't hear. Just as well. He'd probably get a tanning for using such language around a man who prized bull riding above everything else in life.

Though not large, Sterling was imposing, in the prime of life and built solid as the beefsteaks he rode. His Nordic looks — blond hair, blue eyes, and disarming smile — camouflaged a personality as warm and pliable as steel.

As Sterling bullied the squalling calf into the chute box, Forrest's own blue eyes watched him with a mixture of love, and other emotions. Forrest knew he was old enough to quit being scared of his father, but the man's superiority cowed him more than anything except his grandfather's icy rule.

"All right, now. Let's try 'er again." Sterling hung over the chute rails to hammer the calf's rump, leaving his own sticking up vulnerably in the air.

"Need some help?" Forrest swiftly scaled the rails just as his father righted himself.

"Naw, I'm only givin' your mount a little incentive. Gotta keep 'em mad, Forr. They give you the best bucks when they want to get even. It don't work for broncs, but for bulls, the madder, the better." Sterling seized his son by the shoulders and lowered him bodily into the iron confines of the chute, throwing the bull rope to him. The bell tolled as Forrest wrapped the rope first around the calf's belly and then around his gloved hand.

"Now pull the wrap snug, an' don't go bailin' off this time. Show some style! Broncs ain't the only fancy ride, ya know. Keep at it, an' you're gonna love ridin' bulls. No feelin' like it in the world."

Forrest merely nodded. He would gladly face a thousand bucking broncos before he ever wished to climb on a bull. But he had quit trying to explain that to his father. The bull rider reacted by making their practice sessions longer and more intolerable. Fortunately, rodeo kept Sterling away from home most of the year, except when the season began winding down before the NFR, as it was now.

"You ready?" Sterling bellowed, jumping from the chute railing and preparing to open the gate.

Forrest nodded again.

Sterling hopped on the gate rails and pounded Forrest on top of his head, anchoring his son's hat more securely and adding another dent to the beat-up crown. "Say something, boy. Give a whoop or a ki-yi or somethin'! Show some try!"

"Let 'er buck!" Forrest shouted, trying to rupture his father's eardrums but losing focus, so that when the gate swung open and the calf bolted, Forrest almost immediately dragged from the calf's side, his hand stuck in the bull rope.

"You got to be ready when they blow from the chute!" Sterling yelled, jogging after the runaway calf.

"I'm hung up!" Forrest screamed. The ground seared him from the waist down as he was towed. He could feel his skin ripping away even through his Wranglers, and his arm suffered agonizing jerks with each of the calf's frightened bounds.

"Help!" Forrest's legs skittered back and forth on the dirt, perilously near sharp hooves.

"Daddy! Daaaaa-aaddddy!" Forrest yanked frantically on his hand, fumbling with the tight wrap. He found the end and released it just as the calf trod the side of Forrest's heel, missing his flesh.

"You're all right. Get up, Son," a voice said above him, but Forrest didn't even breathe in response.

"Wind knocked out of ya, huh? We all been there."

Despite his pain and shock, Forrest perked up. He'd never been placed among the ranks of other bull riders before, and although his legs throbbed and burned even worse than his strained riding arm, a stab of pleasure shot through him.

"I'm okay," Forrest said rustily, squinting to hold back tears that would certainly dissolve this new bond with his father. Cowboys didn't cry; it was a rider's first lesson. Forrest hoped he could hold out.

"C'mon." Forrest felt himself being lifted, and his limbs cried out against the motion. "Let's go on back to the house. That's enough for today." Sterling rubbed his stubbled chin. "Maybe the problem's simpler than I think. You're gettin' too old for calves, too leggy. One of these days, we're gonna put you on somethin' bigger. Maybe that'll help."

The short man hoisted the boy to his feet, and Forrest staggered toward the sprawling mansion that was the living quarters and business offices of Colorado's great Jackson and Son Cattle Company. Neither Sterling Jr. nor Forrest saw the thin man on horseback who watched their retreat, fingering a tuft of silver protruding from his cowboy hat. His mouth ejected a dark stream that curved through the air and landed in the dust like some unspoken but critical comment.

❦

Color, music, and swirling movement surrounded Alison, and as the nine-year-old leaned forward to enter into the pageant more deeply, she felt a rough, restraining hand on her bare arm, pulling her gently back.

"Not so close," Harvey Austin told his daughter, the merriment in his hazel eyes negating the warning in his voice. "You're apt to fall right out of your seat and land smack in front of some cowboy's horse."

"Not cowboy," Alison corrected, flipping her streaked curls aside to watch the racing riders, now forming two companies to approach an invisible obstacle course from opposite directions. They carried brilliant flags and wove in and out, creating a string of figure eights, barely missing each other at each apex. "These are cowgirls, Dad. They'd catch me. They'd put me on their saddle, right up in front of them, and I'd tell them to ride like the wind!"

"Sounds like she's coming down with rodeo fever, Harvey," said a woman's voice on Alison's other side. "Just like my Jenny. It's too bad Eileen couldn't get off work to be here. I'm sure it would bring back memories."

"Yep. It's too bad, Virginia," Alison's father answered, but when Alison glanced at him, she saw worry dulling his expression.

"Dad?" Alison forced herself to concentrate on him, even though tantalizing new sounds were coming from the loudspeakers. Some shift, some change in the rodeo was happening. Alison longed to see what fantastic sight it would bring, but she kept her attention on her father. "I'm sorry." She placed her hand on his shoulder. "I won't lean anymore."

"Thanks." He smiled slightly, and Alison's gray eyes flew to the dirt arena, skimming over the puzzled look on her aunt Virginia's face.

Instead of the graceful flow of women on horseback, Alison saw only one flag-bearing rider. The woman's horse stood in the arena's center, an enormous flag lapping its flank.

Disappointment hit Alison like a punch in the stomach. Where were the speed, the snap of the flags, and the hooves stirring melodic sprays of gravel against the metal fencing?

"Stand up, Al," her father urged, tapping her shoulder. "Didn't you hear your uncle Barney? Put your hand on your heart and face the flag."

Alison surveyed the rising crowd around her. "Are we all going to say the pledge?"

"No, honey," her aunt replied. "We're going to sing."

"What song —" Alison began to ask, but a multitude of voices drowned her out. She peered at a raised announcer's box in the arena's corner, where several figures inside looked down upon the crowd. "Is Uncle Barney crying up there? He sounds just like Mom when she cries. Her words get all stuck, too," she said, but in the crescendo of "the rocket's red glare," no one heard her.

"When's Jenny going to race, Aunt Virginia?" Alison demanded when the anthem's strains ebbed.

"First Uncle Barney's going to introduce everyone who works hard to make the rodeo run: the judges, the pickup men, the clowns who protect cowboys from the bulls —"

"Will Jenny race after Uncle Barney quits talking?" Alison asked, noticing that Aunt Virginia's green eyes turned even prettier when she smiled. "Jenny's lucky to have her own horse. Someday I'm going to have a whole ranch of 'em. I've been saving up since I was little. I've got two hundred dollars in the bank now. How much did

14

Jenny's horse cost? Is it a long time until she races? Does she have to wait for more kids to get here first? Is she fast?"

"Jenny's going to race when all the other barrel racers do. She won't go as fast as the adults. She's practicing, getting used to riding in front of people and doing what she's learned in rodeo school. She'll get faster in time."

Alison puckered one side of her lips. "If I was Jenny, I'd go fast right away. With the adults, too. No one would beat me."

Aunt Virginia looked ahead of her again, and Alison saw more men walking and riding into the arena. They wore bright western clothing and waved their hats at the crowd, but they were nothing like the women who had ridden with the flags — women almost as beautiful as those in her dreams, on horses nearly as fast as those she imagined. More than anything, Alison wanted to be like them — a beautiful woman on a fast horse.

"Aunt Virginia, if I don't like racing, I'm going to carry the flags. That way I can race and get a flag, and I still get a horse."

Alison saw Aunt Virginia open her mouth to laugh, but instead the redheaded woman nodded. "You have always loved horses, haven't you?"

"Always."

"And you really have two hundred dollars in the bank that you've saved up to buy a horse with?"

Alison poked her father's arm. "Tell her."

A noncommittal stretch tightened his lips, and he scratched the lower fringe of his right sideburn. "She's right, Virginia. Two hundred dollars at Madison Municipal Bank. In pennies." He pointed at the nearest end of the arena. "Look, Al. They're going to ride the bucking stock now."

Alison whooped. "More horses!" She lowered her voice. "I don't think it'll be as good as racing, Aunt Virginia. But some horses just like to buck, even more than they like to race. I'm glad they can do what they want. I'm glad no one hurts them to make them buck."

"You sound like you know all about this," Aunt Virginia replied, but the child did not answer, and her fingers tightened around the rodeo program in her fist.

2

"YOU TOOK ALISON TO THE RODEO without Eileen knowing?" Virginia asked, glancing behind her to the back seat where Alison and her own daughter traded excited chatter.

"I'm not saying Eileen doesn't know," Harvey hedged, gesturing with one big hand as he drove. "I'd just appreciate it if you wouldn't mention anything about us going today."

Virginia stared at him. "I told Eileen when I called last night that if we were going to have any time to visit, Jenny and I needed you to give us a ride after the rodeo. Do you think Eileen would ever believe that you'd miss the show beforehand? What's more, how do you intend to keep that one quiet?" She crooked her finger toward the back seat.

"Don't worry about Al. She can do about anything if it's got horses involved, even keep quiet..." Harvey's face turned pallid, setting off his black, sixties-style sideburns. "You told Eileen? You called last night?" His forehead bore creases that seemed even now to be deepening.

"I'd hoped that you'd reached an understanding, as Barney and I have. I thought that with Alison's interest in horses —"

"The horses Eileen doesn't mind anymore. It's everything else she's scared of."

"Racing?"

Harvey nodded as he flipped on his turn signal. "I don't even say the word when Eileen's around. Or rodeo, either. I never mentioned them to Al before today." He cast red-rimmed eyes at his sister-in-law. "Virginia, Eileen even makes me hide my issues of *Rodeo News*. It's like I have to conceal some kind of criminal past."

Virginia cocked an ear, but the girls could hear only each other. Her niece's voice dominated, and words like "barrels," "rate," and "win" peppered her rapid sentences. With a sinking feeling, Virginia knew the words, in their present context, were probably extremely recent additions to Alison's vocabulary. Already her niece used them fluently.

"I think I know how Eileen feels, Harvey. I'm well aware of the dangers, the drawbacks of a rodeo life. As a young Christian, I used to see only the benefits: the discipline of competition, the fun, the patriotism. When Jenny finally came along, I hoped Barney would find a job close to home or centered in Wyoming, at least. He tried, but he had to go back. He loves rodeo. Soon I saw that Jenny did, too."

Virginia listened to the conversation in the back seat, feeling a mother's constant guilt. "Sometimes I worry about Jenny, wonder if she's missing something vital by growing up on the road. But I think the Lord's given us this way to be a family, together. I shelter Jenny from what I don't like, teach her what I believe is right. When she falls behind in her schoolwork or gets too tired, we go home to Gillette or stay in Oklahoma with Eileen and Barney's sister. Then we rejoin Barney." Virginia looked at Harvey compassionately. "I pray you and Eileen can work things out between you, too."

Harvey's shoulders sagged. "I've tried to talk with Eileen." He neared a yellow traffic light and applied the brakes. They caught in uneven jerks. "She's not satisfied with the way things are for us. She wants us to do better, get ahead more." Squealing, the car stopped at last. "She's had it with riding in rattletraps, she says. She wants a house of her own instead of an apartment. Wants to forget about rodeo and lead a normal life." He sighed wearily. "Normal. Any idea what that is?"

Virginia shot up a prayer, then asked her brother-in-law, "And what is it that you want, Harvey?"

His eyes focused for a minute far past the light. "I'm not even sure I know anymore."

As Virginia weighed her response, youthful voices drifted to the front of the station wagon.

"You did a good job racing, Jen. You didn't win, but you're still learning. Someday, when I get my horse, I'll practice with you, and we'll be...winners of the world!"

Jenny's doubtful voice contrasted with her cousin's impassioned certainty. "You think so, Al?"

"Yep! Soon as I get my horse. But until then, you've got to tell me everything you learn, so I won't be behind. We need to be winners together. I wasn't sure until I saw it, but now I am: I want to barrel race, too. And after we win, we'll have a horse ranch and race whenever we want."

"That sounds real good. I always wanted to have a ranch house someday. And a big yard. With a fence all around to keep everyone home."

"Harvey," Virginia began, when Alison went back to planning her and Jenny's grand racing future, "perhaps you don't know what you want, but I think your daughter does."

"I think you're right," he answered dismally, but Virginia saw

19

pride in his face. "Al said 'horsie' almost 'fore she said 'Mama.' I figured she'd end up in the arena. She'll be a world champion, too.
Her mother nixed the horse idea for the longest time, but she gave
in when she realized Al never would." Now Harvey made no
attempt to disguise his pride. "I don't put anything past Al, once she
sets her mind. And I'd say it's set."

"If that's true, what about Eileen? What's going to happen when
she finds out her daughter plans to be a barrel racer? What's going
to happen to all of you?" Virginia asked, remembering all she and
Barney had suffered before finding their compromise.

"I'll break it to Eileen one of these days. She'll understand, just
like she did Al's hankering for horses. I've already got something
going on that score." He looked ahead, as if into the future. "Rodeo's
getting bigger, better, more organized every year. Who knows what
opportunities Al'll have? Ones we never even dreamed of."

"You're talking about that rodeo circuit that gets everyone excited
every decade or so, aren't you? The Rodeo Olympics or Exposition
or whatever they're calling it nowadays."

"Maybe I am. Maybe Al'll be the first barrel-racing Olympian."
Harvey let that thought linger. "I'll tell you what, Virginia, if my
daughter wants to take a shot at racing, I'm behind her. She'll get
her chance. No matter what."

Harvey's decisiveness left Virginia speechless.

"First off…" he said, using a tone Virginia had heard only when
men were talking to themselves or gripped by some all-consuming
thought, "first off, Al needs a horse."

A cool wind blew over the field grass, bending it in tan waves and
reminding Forrest of his granddad riffling through papers in a full

file drawer. The stock pond's surface broke into ripples, distorting the mirror image of the sky that Forrest had been contemplating.

"No swimming today, Tom. Not even in the pond. No more for the year, probably." Forrest reclined, feeling the rough welcome of the rangy grass against his cheek.

"Aren't you too sore to go swimming anyway?"

Forrest glanced at his companion. "Pretty sore," he agreed, "but I wouldn't let it stop me from a swim. Was all I could think of yesterday, but Daddy didn't go 'til this mornin', an' I had a time before Granddad'd let me leave the ranch. Did you go?"

"Swimming? No. We had church today, and yesterday I was helping Mama with the chickens. We've got forty in the freezer now. Mama says that'll keep us until we get more next year. It'll be good to have beef and chicken both. And with wintering a few hens, maybe we'll get some eggs, too."

Forrest put his hands beneath his head. "Daddy said he was takin' me to the Palace next month, Tom."

The other boy sat up. "The Cow Palace?"

"Yeah."

Tom gave a breathy whistle. "For the whole thing?"

Forrest couldn't hold back a grin. He plucked a dry stalk and sucked on it like a pipe stem. "We-ell, I don't know about the whole thing, but I'm goin'," he said, speaking around the grass.

"I thought you hated to see your daddy ride."

"Comes a time a man's got to face his fear." Forrest looked skyward. "I'll be ridin' bulls myself soon."

Tom's brown eyes bulged. "I thought you hated bulls!"

Forrest shrugged, his flannel-covered elbows spearing the air. He stuck out his lower lip. "I'm not sayin' they're as good as broncs or ropin', but I figure I should give 'em a try. Maybe I'll be the World

All-Around Champion someday, if I can learn to do three events instead of just two. Yeah, I think I'll give those bulls a whirl."

"That's great, Forr. Maybe we can practice together!"

"Maybe, 'cept when my daddy's home. You know how it is." Forrest realized he could learn a lot from his friend, but getting himself shown up in front of his father was not in his plans. "Your daddy been workin' with you?"

Tom shook his head. "He tells me stuff, sometimes, when he's home and in a good mood, but mostly I've been learning from books and practice. We've got one cow that is so mean —"

"A cow? You're ridin' an ol' cow?"

"Well, I try the steers when I can, and I've got a barrel hooked up in a tree I use sometimes, but I need someone to pull the ropes to make it buck, and Mama's so busy —"

"You mean she don't want you ridin'." Forrest screwed up his lips. "That's women for ya. Sure glad I ain't got no mama stoppin' me from doin' what I want."

"You've got a mama. She just isn't around here."

Forrest said nothing.

"I don't mind my mama, Forr," Tom said in a more conciliatory tone. "She does worry some, but mostly she says she just gives it over to the Lord, same's she does everything else. Since my riding's okay with Daddy, she says she's not going to argue."

Forrest lowered his elbows and rolled on one side, looking toward the weathered yellow building that served as Tom's home. "She in there now?"

"Probably. Cooking or cleaning or something."

"Maybe we should go give her a hand." Forrest threw his pipe to the ground.

"You want to help her work?"

Tom was bewildered, and Forrest enjoyed the moment. "Yeah. I want to help her with the cookies. She always makes cookies on Sunday, don't she, Tom? You tryin' to keep 'em for yourself?"

Tom giggled his relief and smacked his forehead, disturbing his brown bangs. "You had me going, Forr. Yeah, she made the cookies, to warm up the house when we got back from church."

"Let's go, then." Forrest began to sprint the quarter mile toward the house.

"Wait," Tom said, running after him. "You have to listen to her Bible story first, before you get to eat the cookies, remember? You said last time you'd never do it again."

Forrest waved at Tom to hurry him. "Who wants to hear about a princess?" As Tom drew alongside, Forrest began running again. "I like those stories about lions and giants, though. You tell her that, Tom. Go first."

"Tell her yourself."

Forrest's face blanched. "No, you tell her."

"Come to think of it, you never do say much around her any-more." Tom grinned wickedly. "Are you scared of her?"

Forrest guffawed. "Your mama'd never hurt a thing, 'cept chick-ens, I guess." Still, he felt uneasy. Fear wasn't it, but he did feel something around Tom's mother, something...indefinable. Nice, but...unsettling. "An' she's so small, an' always smilin'. Who's scared of that?"

Tom put a hand on his friend's shoulder, his mischievous look gone. "Then why don't you talk to her, Forr? She'd like it if you did."

"I do. Some. I'll try more." Forrest shook off Tom's hand. "I guess...I guess I just like...to hear her talk instead."

Tom nodded. "You still miss your mama, don't you?" As Forrest fumbled for an answer, Tom continued. "You can pretend my mama's yours, too, like you used to. She doesn't mind. I think she misses you calling her 'Mama.'"

Forrest sucked in his breath. "She say that?"

"No, but —"

"Forget it." Forrest raced away, suddenly conscious of every bruise on his body.

Betty Rawlings looked across her Bible at the two boys devouring her gingersnaps. "It's good to see my reading didn't affect your appetites." She tousled Forrest's hair, then smoothed it and did the same for Tom.

"Yes, ma'am," Forrest replied, and Betty was glad to see him grin. So often the child flitted about like a somber little ghost, desperately in need of love and attention to make him materialize.

"And you, Tom?" Betty asked her son. "Were you able to hear the story over your own chomping?"

"The story was about a boy who ran away from home with lots of his father's money, spent it all, then got hungry feeding pigs, so he came home and ate," Tom recited, biting his cookie.

Betty stifled a sigh. Despite her efforts, Tom always seemed to miss what she tried to teach him. He got only the basic facts. "Did you like the story, Forrest?"

The young boy fingered his collar, a habit of his grandfather's. "Yeah."

"What part did you like?"

"The pigs!" Both he and Tom roared, sending cookie crumbs all over her floor, try as they did to belatedly cover their mouths.

Betty knew she should have expected the response. Forrest generally went for a laugh before he went deeper. "Anything else?"

Forrest set down his cookie. "Where...the boy comes home, an' his daddy's waitin' for him, happy to see him."

Her heart ached for the child, raised by two men who prided themselves on being tough and unemotional. It was the cowboy way, she knew, but she dreaded the thought of either Forrest or Tom becoming as hardened as their fathers. She paged through her Bible and read Psalm 23 to her cookie monsters, all the while praying for the Lord to protect and care for them as she could not.

The Valley. As she often did, Betty envisioned the two boys on a dangerous journey, all on their own. She could see them making their way past hulking, craggy mountains, terror on their faces as they wound through the dark valley road they walked. *Lord, keep them. Keep them safe through the Valley of the Shadow.*

CHAPTER

3

"I LOVE VA-CA-TIONS! I love va-ca-tions!" Alison sang for the umpteenth time.

Feeling crimped as the new curls in her strawberry-blond coif, Eileen turned to confront her daughter. "Alison, if you yell in this car once more —"

The girl seemed to be weighing the punishment against the suspense of not knowing it.

"If you scream again, we won't take you along the next time we travel. I can't bear screaming," Eileen said, knowing she'd never carry out her threat. "How much farther is it, Harvey?" Eileen whispered, drumming her fingernails on the armrest. Alison, now singing for her Barbies, didn't hear the question she herself had asked countless times.

"Not too far." He answered her exactly as he had Alison.

Before Eileen could demand a proper response, Harvey moved his hand in a wide circle. "Look at that landscape, Eileen! The trees on the hills look like —"

"A huge box of Crayolas," Alison said helpfully from the station wagon's back seat. "But just the golds and oranges and yellows and reds. No blues, except for the sky."

"Fall colors," Harvey agreed. "I forgot how they could glow. Just like you say, Al, like rows and rows of crayons. This change of scenery is what we all needed. Nothing like fall in the country. I remember once when I climbed up a fire tower in Perkinstown —"

"How far, Harvey? In exact miles." Eileen twisted the top button of her tweed pantsuit in agitation.

Harvey laughed. "Miles? Oh, Perkinstown's around twenty or so miles from —"

"How far until we reach your mother's place!" Eileen burst out, nearly snapping her button's threads. She released the button and resumed her drumming.

"'Bout seven miles," Harvey answered quietly.

No one said another word until the car drew into the outskirts of a small Wisconsin town. A railroad crossing interrupted the pine trees lining the roadway. On one side of the tracks were a truck yard and garage; on the other, a handful of businesses. Young maple trees, planted in open dirt blocks of the sidewalks, brought the burnished autumn hues of the hills to the town's main street.

"But you've gone too far, Harvey," Eileen said, assessing the sight in one glance. "We're already in Gilman."

Her husband made a left-hand turn without using his signal. "Mom's moved into town, Eileen. I told you she sold the farm."

"I knew you went to help her, but I didn't know she'd moved completely out." Eileen looked down the residential street at the houses on unmowed lawns with unbagged leaves. "Surely she's not in this neighborhood?"

Harvey made another left turn.

"Will you please use your signals, Harvey? I don't relish getting into a collision just because you forget all good driving practices once you step off your job."

"Nobody uses signals here, Eileen. I'd probably scare some poor soul to death if I did. 'Sides, I don't want to act like an outsider in my own hometown." He pulled into a curved driveway and parking lot, deep black from recent resurfacing. The tar made a perfect backdrop for the many-colored leaves blowing slowly across it, and for some reason, the scene lodged in Eileen's mind as a personal portent of change.

"Here we are," he said, turning off the engine.

"When are we going to the farm?" Alison unfastened her seat belt and looked out the window.

"We'll go there later, Al," Harvey said, opening his door.

"Promise?" Alison looked skeptical.

As well she might, Eileen thought. She left the car and walked with her daughter past Harvey to the building's entrance. "Which room is your mother — never mind, there's a directory." She pushed Janette's buzzer and the security door of Senior Manor beeped and unlocked.

Alison scanned the entrance. "Where's Grandma?"

"*Grandmother* is in her new apartment," said Eileen. "She doesn't have to come to the door anymore. She'll have a much easier time in town than she has on the farm since Grandfather died."

"What about her animals? Her cats and dogs and —"

"I don't believe they allow animals here, Alison."

"Then I don't think Grandma will like it."

They passed several rooms, stopping at one with Janette's name mounted on the door. The entire surface, even the doorknob, was decorated with knitted, painted, and sewn crafts and keepsakes, evidence of Janette's fondness for pink.

Alison reached for the knob. "This must be Grandma's."

"Wait —" Eileen said, but the door opened, pulling Alison into

28

the room, to the waiting hug of a woman who didn't look nearly old enough to reside in a place called "Senior Manor." Gray hardly touched her brown hair, and age hadn't dimmed her hazel eyes. She wore a pink shift more stylish than practical.

"Blessed child! You're nearly grown up!" Janette kissed Alison, drawing her near again. "Harvey, Eileen," she said as Alison moved aside to give them room to enter. "Come in, come in."

Janette dispensed lavish hugs and kisses, then ushered everyone past a small kitchenette and into a living area, decorated in pink. Underneath three large windows, a narrow table was spread with Janette's beloved plants.

"How I've waited for this day!" Janette said after she saw everyone seated. "I only wish you had acted in time to get the farm, but maybe it will be nicer having your very own place to fix up just as you wish. Let me know if you find yourselves in any need. I know, farming has many unforeseeable expenses, particularly when you're just starting out." Janette beamed. "We haven't had much opportunity to come to know each other well before this, Eileen. Now at last we'll have that chance."

Has she lost her mind? Eileen flashed Harvey a troubled look. *Is that why he's been so quiet lately, so taciturn about his mother's moving?* Her husband's face gave Eileen no direction, so she hazarded a cautious smile. "Yes, of course. Just as you say, Janette," she replied, nudging her husband.

"Yeah, Mom," Harvey said, standing. "No more of that for now, though. How are you coming along here?" He walked a tight circle around the room, his hands thrust deep in his pockets. "Meeting any new friends?"

"One rarely meets new friends, Harvey." Janette laughed. "One generally earns them. Most of the ladies are much older than I, of course, but that doesn't seem to bother..."

Janette chatted while Alison explored the room. Eileen's mind strayed from the conversation as she watched her daughter handle plants, knickknacks, books, picture albums. Little escaped Alison's inspection.

As the scent of baked chicken became stronger, Janette moved to the kitchen. Eileen rose despite her mother-in-law's protests and with Alison's help began setting the table, which she asked Harvey to pull away from the living room wall.

Eileen didn't think it strange that Harvey said little to his mother as the meal progressed. He answered her questions, but in the brief way so like him. She didn't begin suspecting, until after the dishes were done and they had said their good-byes and promised to return in time for supper, that he was up to what would be his worst scheme ever.

It occurred to Eileen midway down a gravel road, while enduring Alison's chants of "We're going to the farm, the farm, the farm," that both he and Janette had referred several times to her farm as sold. Why, then, were they going to visit it? Wouldn't the new owners object? And why hadn't Janette come with them?

"Harvey, how long ago was your mother's place sold?"

He quit humming. "Few weeks back. Little more, maybe."

"So when you came down here to help her, you moved her into her apartment? The farm was already sold then?"

"Yep." He took up his quiet tune again.

"I imagine the new owners were eager to settle in."

Harvey nodded his answer, his tune decreasing in volume as he slowed the car and turned down a dirt lane.

"Then why on earth are we going to barge in on them? I know Alison enjoys seeing farm animals, but we simply can't —"

"We're not going to Mom's farm. We're going to another farm."

Eileen raised an eyebrow at that, but continued her questioning as the car climbed a hill and leveled out, revealing the most ramshackle farm she could recall ever having seen — not that her knowledge of farms was extensive. "So that's why you took this roundabout way? Just so Alison could risk being kicked by some cow or horse?" Eileen shook her head as Harvey turned into a curved driveway and parked outside an old farmhouse. "She'll be a positive mess if she ventures out there. It's a good thing you didn't tell me about this beforehand."

Harvey didn't look at his wife as he shut off the engine and opened his car door. "Yep, it's a good thing I didn't," he said, and climbed out.

The musty scent of old hay thickened the air of the barn, and Alison inhaled deeply. "Mmm. Barns smell so good, Dad," she said, scooping up another armful from the cracked concrete floor and tossing it above her head. She danced underneath it. Hay and dust particles floated around her, more visible because of the shaft of sunlight showering through one of the barn roof's holes. "Don't you love the smell of hay?"

"You like this place, Al?"

"I'd like it better if there were animals. Not one horse or cow. Or even a kitten." She had already checked every enchanting cranny she could think of, but no furballs rewarded her search.

Harvey removed a piece of hay from her streaked blond hair.

Alison began picking out fibers from her tangles. "I'll have to clean up before I go back to the car and see Mom. But why aren't there any animals? Doesn't anyone live here?"

"Nobody has for a while." Her father stood and counted roof holes aloud. "Seven big holes. Who knows how many little ones. Cheap place, but it's going to take a lot of work." He rubbed his back and stuck his head out the open barn door before returning inside. "Think your mother could ever be happy here?"

Alison answered from a darkened corner she had missed earlier. "She doesn't like farms much." She ran back to her father. "But I love farms! If I had one, I'd get cows and kittens, and —"

"Horses?" her father asked.

"Dad! Of course horses! Are there any here? Behind the barn? Or in the other room? I haven't checked there yet."

"If there was a horse, would you listen to me tell you how to ride her?"

"I'd race!" Alison sang, bolting around the corner to the next room. "There is a horse here, isn't there? Hey, horse, I'm coming!"

"Al."

His commanding tone brought her back. "Yes, Dad?"

"If there was a horse, would you listen to what I said about how to ride her? Would you wait until I said you could race before you did it?"

"Is there a horse?"

"Would you, Al? Would you listen to everything I told you?"

Her mouth twitched as she thought about it. "But I could race, when you said I could? It would happen?"

"Yep. But not until I said. It might take a year or even longer."

"All right." She breathed deep. "I promise."

Her father's smile was faint, but definite. "Okay, Al. There's a horse here. Your horse."

"M-my horse?"

"Yours."

"Where!"

"I'll show you." He caught her arm. "But you can never forget your promise, Al. Promises are...hard to keep, sometimes." He looked back toward the car. When he turned, his face was deadly serious.

Alison put her hand in his. "Dad, you don't have to give me a horse if it'll make Mom mad." The words dragged from her, but she said them tearlessly, having done without that form of precipitation even as a small child.

"What?" Her father touched her shoulder. "Don't you want a horse? Don't you want to be the best barrel racer in the world? Didn't you tell Jenny you would be?"

"Yes, but if Mom doesn't like —"

"No."

Alison never forgot his expression. He had decided, and he would see it through, no matter what the cost. His look was one that, in time, she came to have also.

"If you decide to be best in the world, Alison, you can never go back. No matter how much pain or practice or time it takes, and even if it means leaving your friends, your home, your family to do it, you've got to do it...if that's what you decide."

"I did decide. I want to race, to be...the best." *A beautiful woman on a fast horse.* Alison's head filled with visions of dream riders. "The best in the world."

Her father nodded and stood. "Then let's go show your horse her new home. And yours," he said, walking away without a backward glance. "I'm sure your mother will like the horse and the farm just as much as we do...after she's had some time to think about it."

CHAPTER

4

EXCEPT FOR THE NFR AT OKLAHOMA CITY, San Francisco's Cow Palace was Sterling Jackson Sr.'s favorite rodeo arena. Though he had never qualified for the Grand National, his son seemed to ride for him.

Always before the performance, the gaunt, silver-haired rancher would take a tour of the city or its environs. He might stop at Fisherman's Wharf, to watch the boats come off the Pacific Ocean and smell their exotic cargoes. Or else along the sandstone headlands, where the waves invisibly eroded the soft cliffs, reminding Sterling of his business conquests. Or through the tangle of trails winding among the redwoods, great trees that had withstood time and unknown enemies to rise high and proud. Perhaps Sterling loved this area most of all.

But now he was saddled with his grandson, who wanted nothing more than to sit in the grandstands and watch everything that went on in the Palace — never mind that the Grand National wouldn't start until 8 P.M.

When they had set out from the hotel that morning, the old man thought it entirely natural that the first thing Forrest asked to do was to go to the Cow Palace. But after walking around the entire building, examining the grandstands, rest area, chutes, arena, rest-rooms, and every other inch the boy could think of, Sterling Sr. was hoping he could leave his grandson with the rodeo secretary or some other custodian.

It was a fine thing for Forrest to be so absorbed with the Palace, except that it cramped his grandfather's style. And his back, and legs, and nearly everything else. When the performance did begin, the old man wondered if he would be in any shape to sit through it. And still Forrest wanted to keep his grandstand perch.

Sterling Sr. stood cautiously, working the hitches out of his joints. "Stay put until I get back." He walked down the aisle without giving the boy a second look, knowing he would obey.

In the rodeo office, papers fluttered and exchanged hands, and ringing phones interrupted hurried conversations, but Sterling Sr. passed through the atmosphere like a bull through a grain field. "Hey, Mary," he said to the middle-aged head secretary. "Your mama still living in the City?"

Several pens stuck out of the woman's yellowish-blond pile of hair, and she grabbed one to scribble some message she was receiving from the phone held to her ear.

"Mary!" Sterling Sr. leaned over the counter and gestured with his thin arm. "You don't answer me this minute, I'm going to make this nice white floor of yours a different color. Where's the spittoon, woman?"

Mary mouthed, "O-ver there," her pen pointing behind the door. She had finished her phone conversation when Sterling Sr. turned back to her. "You're sassy as usual, Sterling, but a little grayer, I think." She smiled and walked to the counter, extending her hand. "Good to see you."

"Don't go in for handshakes 'less it's business," he grunted. "But you can plant one here." He presented his grizzled cheek.

Mary laughed. "But it is business, isn't it? What else do you want with my mother?" One painted eyebrow lifted. "Or are you trying to start things again?"

"Not starting anything." The old man tapped his cheek. Mary kissed it. "That's better. No, I just thought maybe she'd look after my grandson 'til the National gets going. She's not busy, is she?"

"She's been spending her time knitting since she last saw you. She's got her own business, Sterling, remember?"

"The souvenir shop down at the wharf?"

"That's right." Mary walked back to her desk.

"Call her."

"What?"

"Go ahead. And tell her it's worth a hundred to me."

"I'll tell her two, not including expenses." Mary picked up the phone. "Maybe you'll have a chance, then." She paused before dialing. "I'm not sure I should be doing this at all."

"I'm sure enough for us both," the old man said. "Tell her it's only for today. I'm packing the boy home tomorrow. Either that, or his daddy can worry about him. Don't get away from the ranch too often, and I mean to have some fun my own size."

"Mother will be glad to hear that, anyway," said Mary, placing the call.

Forrest didn't mind his granddad going off and leaving him with a stranger. That was nothing unusual. But the clucking old hen now attending him was. Forrest couldn't concentrate with her filling the deserted grandstands with chatter. He couldn't do what he needed to before the performance began. For despite what he had told his best friend, Tom, Forrest hadn't faced his fear.

What would happen when his daddy climbed on his bull? Forrest had never been allowed to attend his father's performances, and he wasn't sure what his reaction would be. The scenes on television were bad enough. Forrest watched them in his bedroom, where he could gasp and scream and hide his eyes all he wanted.

He had thought, now that he was older and soon to ride his own bulls, that he'd love coming to the Palace. He'd planned to dream of his own perfect ride, to fix the place so indelibly in his mind that wherever he went, he'd be part of its glory. He'd thought that when he saw his father ride, somehow Forrest himself would ride with him, no longer the son of a six-time world champion, but a champion himself. Somehow, the crown would be passed to him.

But that had changed after the initial excitement of being in the Palace. When he had thoroughly checked it out, Forrest found it was just an arena. Bigger and with more seating than he had ever personally seen, but common dirt made up its floor — dirt that his daddy might be thrown onto, that might suck up his daddy's spilled blood. Or, eventually, his own blood.

"Forrest!"

He felt a withered hand stroke his wrist.

"How'd you like to run over to Candlestick Park? You might see a Forty-Niner or two if we go now. We'll be back in time for the show."

Forrest shook his head.

The woman tried again, still touching his wrist. "There's a mint not too far from here that your granddad used to like visiting. Plumb full of money." She smiled, evidently sure that gold ran in Forrest's veins, too. Forrest let her know it didn't.

"Listen, son. Your daddy's busy gettin' geared up for his ride. You won't see him 'til the show begins tonight. That's a long time off. Ain't you hungry? A little shop I know sells the best jerky in —" She stopped herself as Forrest turned away. "And an ice cream parlor, with thick malts and hamburgers this high." She spread her fingers wide to illustrate. "Got to get used to fast food if you're gonna rodeo, son. Best start now."

Forrest swallowed, and the woman hauled him off victoriously.

After dispatching one burger and a heap of fries, Forrest slurped his chocolate-banana malt in contentment.

"That's better, now, ain't it? See, Lorna knows what you need. Glad you came?"

"Yeah." Forrest ignored his spoon and poured the malt straight from its frigid metal tumbler into his mouth. He enjoyed the sugary shock of ice cream sliding down his throat.

"I've known your daddy since he was a little older'n you," Lorna said, and Forrest was more inclined to give her his attention now. "I thought I might be his new mama for a while there, but things… well, sometimes life don't work out like you figure."

"Yes, ma'am. You knew my daddy pretty good?"

"Sure did. Felt like he was my own little boy, almost. I used to come see him lots, bring him presents, teach him songs —"

"You taught him that song?" Forrest set his malt down.

"Well, now, which one you talkin' 'bout?"

"The one he was singin' last night. I liked it." Forrest cocked his head to one side, remembering the scene. Forrest's granddad had stretched out on the couch in their hotel room, and Forrest had sat on the soft corner of the bed across from him, his daddy off to the right but between them like the top point of a triangle. The hotel was quiet. Forrest's father's voice didn't break that stillness but moved with it.

The song was slow, accompanied only by strums of Sterling Jr.'s guitar. While it didn't seem sad, it made Forrest feel that way. The words talked about a cowboy's life, about going down the road, about saying good-bye and moving on, always moving on. Forrest remembered the chorus and the melody holding the words, yodely and solemn, like his daddy's voice:

Fol-low the ro-de-o star....

Don't matter much where you are,

One town or the other, so much like another....

Just fol-low the ro-de-o star.

"Now that was nice. But no, I didn't teach your daddy that song." Lorna sipped from her glass.

Forrest hadn't realized he was singing aloud. He looked around him, dazed.

"Haven't heard it on the radio, neither. No, I bet your daddy made that one up." Lorna smiled and crumpled her napkin by poking her face with it. "I think we'll go to the beach now, and then the zoo." She leaned over the table to squeeze Forrest's shoulder. "That should make the day go by quick enough, shouldn't it?" Lorna dug through her purse for her billfold. "We can get a bite to eat later on, so you won't be hungry again when it's your daddy's turn to ride."

To ride. Your daddy's turn to ride. The words clanged in Forrest's head, and an old, sick feeling rose from the depths of his stomach.

"I'll be right back." Lorna went to pay for the meal, leaving Forrest to deal with his renewed terror by himself.

From the best seat in the Palace, Sterling Sr. crowed, blending in with the tumult around him. "Did you see that move, boy? Blast Off's calling card: a few straight-out jumps and then a killer right reverse. Sure tumbled ol' Hank Dixon!" The old man hooted as the fallen rider sought refuge behind the arena rails. A big black Brahma-cross bull took a stab at one of the bullfighting clowns, then ambled off to the catch pen.

"Dixon's safe, but he's out," Sterling jeered, turning to his grandson. "Ever think of that? You'd never see that happen in no baseball game now, would you?" He didn't wait for an answer, but thumbed at a loaded chute, only yards from where he and Forrest were sitting. "Rawlings is up next. He's a good rider. Might even get hisself another world-champion buckle if your daddy messes up some year. Not likely that'll happen, though, is it?" He pummeled his grandson's shoulder.

Sterling Sr. watched Bob Rawlings climb the back of the chute, flexing his gloved hand in the air as if he were a surgeon prepping for an operation. Sterling's son was near the chute with Rawlings, helping him slip the bull rope around the massive red brindle, who rammed his horns against the rails. The cowboys jumped back reflexively.

"There's your daddy, Forrest!" Sterling shook his grandson's arm. "Soon's Rawlings's done, your daddy's going to show this Palace how royalty rides!"

Sterling Jr. handed the end of the rope to his traveling companion, and Bob Rawlings straddled the chute. He bent over to make adjustments, then lowered himself. Only from the shoulders up was he visible above the chute rails. The crowd quieted as he tied himself to his beast.

"Okay!" Rawlings gave the signal and the gate tender threw the gate open.

In one motion, the brindle emerged, swinging just as the gate had. The bull bellowed and made a spin to the left, then a rocking lunge backwards, another spin, then a reverse. Dirt flew in all directions with the bull's thrashing. The crowd strained to keep up with the whirlwind of power, movement, and sound.

And Rawlings stuck to the brindle. He even managed to spur out the beast, busy as he was with changing directions and shifting his weight to avoid being sucked into the spin's well, thrown off balance, pushed into his riding arm.

"Well." Sterling caught his breath, unable to believe someone other than his son was making the remarkable ride. He calculated how long it had been since the gate opened. The crowd raged, the seconds evaporated, the brindle skittered and arched and sidestepped and tossed, but Rawlings kept his seat.

Sterling Sr. saw Rawlings reach down and loosen the wrap around his riding hand before the old man realized he had made a qualified ride. His tobacco nearly dropped from his mouth when he glanced at the scoreboard.

The old man sat down and rubbed his hands on his thighs to wipe off the sweat. Idly, he watched the unharmed bull make a run at a colorfully dressed bullfighting clown, who herded the brindle to the catch pen while his partner in greasepaint kept between the animal and Rawlings.

"Eighty-eight, Granddad." Forrest looked worried. "Tom's daddy got an eighty-eight."

"I know!" Sterling Sr. bellowed.

His grandson cringed, but Sterling Sr. paid him no mind. "Come on, Son," the old man began coaching softly as Sterling Jr. finished his wrap and settled onto his bull. "You drew Sky High. You can make the ride. You got to make it." Sterling Sr. rose from his seat. "Let 'er buck, Sterling!" he shouted, his voice louder for the tension weighing on the crowd, smothering them to silence.

Sterling Jr.'s face jerked up, and his fist punched the air above his head.

"That's right, that's right." The old man sank to his chair. "You can pull an eighty-nine out of him. You can pull a ninety," Sterling Sr. breathed.

Beside him, his grandson's voice piped up, "You can do it, Daddy. But be careful!"

"Careful!" Sterling nearly slapped Forrest. "Ain't no time for care. Your daddy knows that. He's got to ride all out. And he will."

No echo doubled his words.

"Do it," Sterling urged, seeing his son signal.

The gate opened and the black bull charged, churning dirt and covering ground with leaps that brought it near the stands, drawing shrieks of horror and pleasure from the spectators. Sterling Jr. raked the Brahma-crossbreed with his spurs, leaving no mark but making an impressive sight.

"That's it, Son. Play it up!"

The bull advanced, maddened by the stimulus all around him. His jumps grew higher, his rocking wilder. And Sterling Jr. rode as if on a bubble, spurring the Brahma out, twisting with the bull's gyrations.

Sterling Jr. leaned hard ahead, saving himself from the bull's latest backward lurch. His head dropped just as the Brahma's thrust upward, grazing Sterling Jr.'s cheek but failing to connect with full force.

"Ride him, ride him!" Sterling Sr. screamed, and then the scream locked, and went on and on. He saw his son's stunned look, heard the blast that signified the end of the ride. But Sterling Jr. did not free his hand and leap clear of the bull as he always had. He slid, hanging from the bull's side as the monster reached to hook him.

The bullfighters rushed in for the save, but the Brahma straightened and plowed into the rails, crushing the young cowboy between iron and bone.

Sterling Jr. made a weak grab to undo the rope. The bullfighters tried to aid but were driven back. The Brahma again slammed into the rails, and the cowboy's body slipped under the beast's back hooves. A ton of bovine came down once, twice, then, ironically, the force of the blows loosened Sterling Jr.'s wrap. He slumped to the dirt and did not move.

Forrest's scream replaced his grandfather's, a childish howl rising over the confusion of bullfighters, spectators, announcers, cowboys, and paramedics. The sound became the hallmark of the old man's dreams.

PART II

Young Riders

5

"JEN! I THINK THAT'S HIM ON THE BRONC IN CHUTE FIVE!"

Jenny O'Neill leaped to her cousin's side, and the two young women pressed against the arena railing, Al to see better, and Jenny to get closer to the cowboy who had filled her thoughts since she'd seen him take the senior boys' honors at a Little Britches rodeo. She'd been only thirteen then, and though she'd raced well that day, she hadn't attracted the notice of Forrest Jackson. Now, at sixteen, and a competitor at the illustrious National High School Rodeo Association's finals rodeo, Jenny was determined to win his attention.

"I see why you like him," Al said as the young cowboy rose out of his chute to stretch his riding arm. "Blond hair, great smile, terrific build, just like you said. Blue eyes, I suppose?"

"I think so. Talk quieter, Al," Jenny replied, her face as red as her hair. She glanced behind her to see if anyone was looking their way, especially her parents, who had not yet found her in the crowd.

"He is kinda near. Not near enough to tell about his eyes, though." Al turned to her cousin. "Relax, Jen. Everybody's involved in the rodeo. It'd be pretty hard to hear us over all this racket. Forrest is gorgeous, all right. Maybe he just wears blue contacts, though. Maybe they're really brown." She grimaced.

"Contacts? I don't think so," Jenny said, crestfallen that Forrest might have a flaw, but hoping this imperfection might make him attainable after all.

"You never know, Jen. He's a cowboy. There's got to be something wrong with him." Al tapped her head. "Up here, probably. I wouldn't be surprised if —"

"Knock if off, Al."

"Okay." She sighed, but teasing still lit her gray eyes. "He rides perfect, of course?"

"He'll be this year's National High School Rodeo Association Champion Saddle-Bronc Rider." Jen savored every word of Forrest's future title.

Al grinned. "You're only saying that because it's just the first go-round. By the next go, you'll be predicting that he'll be the NHSRA All-Around Champion, too. Am I right?"

"He will be, Al. For the third year in a row. Look, he's going to ride." Jenny started as the gate opened and a solid white bronc shot out like a spring. "He's still on!" Excitement made her voice race. "Forrest knows this horse's first two jumps are the toughest. He has to stay tight, centered, or he'll buck off in the next few."

Jenny watched Forrest absorb the bronc's heaves and run his regulation-dulled spurs from the horse's neck to his saddle cantle. "He knows Cloudburst comes down hard with her forefeet and kicks up hard with her back. He's taking a beating, Al, but he's got a chance of scoring in the seventies if he can hold —"

The whistle sounded and the two pickup men drew alongside the white bronc, who continued bucking. Forrest released his rein and grabbed at the waist of one of the pickup men, sliding smoothly from the bronc onto the arena. He stood and raised his hat, flashing a smile as everyone clapped and the announcer gave his score:

seventy-three. Outstanding for high school rodeo.

"You really called that, Jen. Sure can tell your dad's an announcer. Jen? Jen?"

The petite redhead didn't answer. From the middle of the arena, Forrest Jackson walked toward the rails, each step bringing him closer. He halted, looked as if he might change direction, then continued to advance.

Suddenly Jenny didn't wonder anymore if his eyes were blue. She knew they were blue as a summer sky in Montana, blue as a motionless geyser pool in Yellowstone that plunged to the center of the earth. Forrest Jackson's eyes were the purest, deepest blue Jen had ever seen. And they were looking straight at her.

"What did you think of those two girls by the rails, Forrest?" Tom asked his traveling partner. They were behind the empty chutes, each cleaning the grime of the morning's ride from their equipment, checking it as they had before the go-round to make sure no parts were damaged or weak. The chore was one of habit as well as duty, and eased the descent from performing.

Forrest yanked on his stirrups. "What two —"

"Give it up, cowhand. I saw the look you gave the one when you finished riding Cloudburst." Tom scraped old rosin off his bull rope, enjoying both the sound made by the action and his friend's discomposure. "What I want to know is, what kind of look did she give you?"

Forrest's wide grin completely ruined the tough image he tried so hard to project. Even without the smile, though, Tom was pretty sure he knew his friend's real feelings.

"The redhead? Why, Tom? What do you know about her?"

"Plenty. Should I fill you in?" He knew Forrest was wondering whether the girl who had stopped him in his tracks this morning would be worth the risk of getting to know. Tom could almost see the inner working of his friend's mind. Forrest approached new ideas like an unseasoned bull did a Wrangler bullfighter: charging, then feinting, then running away only to charge again. Eventually Forrest might completely lose interest — unless Tom raised the stakes.

"Okay. Your loss. Everyone's going to want to know her by the end of this rodeo." Tom went back to scraping.

Forrest looked over at him. Tom caught the motion but didn't let on that he did.

Forrest shook out his saddle and began rubbing off the remaining dirt with his hand. "What's her name, anyway?"

"I don't know."

Forrest snorted and drew his brows together. "If you don't even know that —"

"Jenny O'Neill."

"Jenny...." Forrest sat still. "You said there were two girls. What about her friend?"

It was Tom's turn to become irritated. "What about her?"

Forrest's grin returned. "Oh, I get it. You're after her friend. Should've guessed. Must be the loyal type: won't date unless the other does, too. That right? What's she like, Tom? A bleached blond, wasn't it?"

"Not hardly." Tom couldn't keep back a snort of his own, although he knew Forrest was needling him. "You don't even know the color of her hair, you were so busy looking at Jenny."

"No, I remember now." The cocky look Tom hated appeared on Forrest's face. "She had black hair. Yeah, I could go for her."

"A dark blond!"

"What, Tom?" Forrest asked innocently.

"Al has brownish-blond hair, not black. Or bleached!" Tom gave his bull rope a good, strong wrench. "You talk about going for her and you don't even know what she looks like!"

"Well, I know she wasn't cuter than Jenny," Forrest said in a low voice.

Tom turned, wondering if he'd heard right. "You think Jenny's better looking than Al?"

"Sure. That should make you feel better. Your new girlfriend's in no danger from me." Forrest shook his head and began working on his own ropes. "Al. What a name. No wonder I didn't see her. Probably one of those macho cowgirls who tries so hard to act like a guy that she looks like one. You really can pick 'em, Tom."

"Forr." Tom dropped his rope and stood over his friend. "I'm not saying I've picked *Alison*. I don't even know her. But just like you noticed Jenny today, I happened to notice Al. I heard them talking during this morning's go, and I was having a good time listening, too — until you got done with your ride and made me practice for our roping run." His anger subsided as he thought back to their victory, then to Alison. "I don't know if this changes your mind about Al any, but she didn't seem so impressed with you, either."

"After what I did on Cloudburst? Doesn't she know anything about riding?"

Tom met the jab with one of his own. "What's to know? Anyway, Jenny announced your ride. She pointed out Cloudburst's bucking style, your reaction, everything. She sounded like a pro. I heard her say that Jenny's daddy is an announcer, so I guess it figures."

"No." Forrest sounded horrified. "Not 'Blarney' O'Neill's daughter. On the International Pro Rodeo Association circuit?"

"Could be. Doesn't he have red hair, too?"

"That's great." Forrest threw his coil back into its box. "An IPRA announcer's daughter. She's probably a loudmouth just like her daddy."

"I don't think so."

Forrest gave Tom a scornful look. "Didn't you say she spent my whole ride acting like she was an announcer?"

"Yeah, but —"

"There you go." Forrest stared at his rope box morosely. "Such a beautiful face, too. Oh, well…"

"Since when did a loudmouth ever stop you? What about Felicia Newcastle?" Tom asked, feeling he had one last chance to make the double date come off.

Forrest chuckled. "You got me on that one. But Felicia's a fantastic racer, Tom, with a face pretty as any rodeo queen's, including her sister. And she's not bad in other areas, either."

"Did I mention that Jenny's a fantastic racer? Be interesting to see who gets the barrel racer's buckle on Sunday. Don't bet all your money on Felicia." Tom unhooked his rope from the fence rails.

"Jenny's that good?"

"You'll see. She's racing tonight." Tom noticed that Forrest couldn't keep a smile from his face.

"Felicia's racing tonight, too. She's already celebrating her win." Forrest paused. "Might be fun to see someone give her a run. Tell you what, Tom, if Jenny O'Neill even comes close to taking the victory lap, maybe I'll let her be my partner for a couple of songs at tonight's dance, just so her friend'll give you a chance."

"Sounds like a good idea," Tom said. "Especially since I ran into Jenny and Al after we finished our roping run and told them we'd meet them at the dance. You can tell Jenny what a good racer she is then — if you can get in a word edgewise." Tom hefted his equipment to his shoulder and walked away before Forrest could reply.

"You sure they're going to be here?" Jenny looked at the couples already dancing, wondering if she should go back to the hotel and quit while she was ahead.

"Relax, Jen." Alison appeared as calm as a timekeeper. She sipped the Pepsi she had just bought from the concession stand and smiled at several cowboys who appeared to be searching for partners. "You heard what Tom said. They'll meet us here."

"Yeah. I heard." Jenny toed the ground with the tip of her boot. "But what if Forrest doesn't come? What if he doesn't want to?"

"I've got a bigger worry for you." Alison jerked her head to the right. "What if that hotshot barrel racer you blew away tonight beats you up?"

Jenny raised her eyes just enough to see a lovely but enraged blond glowering at her from where she stood, circled by a pack of four or five cowboys. Still revved from competing, the cowboys' attention shifted in quick, repetitive bursts from the music drifting from the portable bandstand, to the dancers kicking up their heels on the groomed arena, to the motionless Felicia. But the bleached-blond's attention was all on Jenny. No doubt about that. "I'm going, Al." Jenny spun on her boot.

Her cousin caught her shoulder. "Jen! You can't."

"Al, I've heard about Tom. He's a nice guy. A little on the tame side, for a bull rider, but you'll survive." Jenny glanced at Felicia, who had moved a pace closer. "Me, I'm not sure about. I'll see you at the hotel —"

"Hey, you're leaving? Thought I was meeting you here."

Jenny knew it was Forrest's voice before she turned around. Slowly her eyes swung from Felicia's to his, locking on their blue depths.

"Want to dance?"

Jenny nodded, and the hand that he'd put on her shoulder took her by the waist and drew her toward the loudspeakers.

Then she was close to him, her cheek resting on his warm, solid chest and her arms barely able to meet around his neck. She couldn't recall if he'd pulled her near first, but she hoped so. His arms felt so good around her, his hands resting above the small of her back. Their bodies weren't wedged against each other like some of the other couples around them. Nor were they dancing awkwardly apart, as if waiting for the song to end so they could separate completely. Jenny and Forrest were just...together. And no race or victory lap had ever felt so wonderful.

"Nice run tonight."

His voice, so near her ear, startled her. "What?"

"You beat Felicia." His face lowered, and Jen could feel him smiling against her cheek. "She giving you a rough time now?"

He was so close that if she pulled back and turned her face slightly to the side, she'd run right into his lips. The thought took away her power of speech.

"I know how Felicia can be sometimes. Dancing like this with me isn't going to help, either. You mind?" He brought one hand to her chin and coaxed her face upward. Their lips were so near that a misstep by either dancer would cause a glorious collision. Jenny almost prayed to stumble.

His smile faded as he stared at her, and a strange intensity invaded his eyes. Jenny felt she had to look away, and she did, jerking her chin free of his hand. She hadn't realized they had quit dancing, and now she feared he would leave the dance completely. Though she knew she should say something, not a single word came to mind except his name. "Forrest."

"Yeah, Jen?" The way he said hers made it sound as if he said it often, had said it for years. His hand went around her back again, and she felt him moving both their bodies to the music's slow beat. "What is it? You want to stop dancing?"

"No! I...I...just don't want to talk about Felicia, if it's okay with you."

For a minute he said nothing, and Jenny felt sure he was deciding how he would get away from her. The only reason she herself didn't leave was that along with her brain, her feet had forgotten how to function.

When she dared to glance at him, she saw his brilliant smile.

"S'all right with me, honey," he said, nestling his close-shaven cheek against hers. "Never was much for words anyhow."

CHAPTER

6

FORREST TUCKED HIS LARIAT LOOP UNDER HIS ARM and gripped his saddle horn, holding coils of rope in his other hand, ready to react, ready to race. Atop his horse in the three-sided box next to the steer chute, Forrest watched his team-roping partner back his mount into his box on the other side of the chute, eye the arena, take a steadying breath, eye the imprisoned steer, and nod.

The chute opened. The steer rushed ahead, and Tom rode full speed out of his box after him. Forrest held his horse in check an instant to keep from crowding Tom's throw, then dug his heels into his own mount and hurtled after his partner.

Switching into a mode of instinct and practice, Forrest anticipated Tom's head catch. Tom's loop went snug around the steer's horns, and with his taut rope, Tom headed the animal into position for Forrest's throw. The steer's body responded, and the animal fought the rope, turning and showing good heel action.

Moving in behind the steer's left hip, Forrest tried to pick up the rhythm of the animal's gait. Forrest leaned forward, standing in his stirrups and swinging his rope faster over the steer's back, waiting until the bovine's heels extended.

In time with the steer, Forrest swung his lariat and gauged his target. Then he threw his loop, roping the steer's heels in midair.

Yanking up the slack, Forrest wrapped his rope repeatedly around his saddle horn in a swift dally while signalling his horse to stop. He kept the rope tight so the steer wouldn't pull his legs out of the loop; Tom spun his horse to face Forrest's, momentarily immobilizing the steer between them.

The catch was complete, header and heeler showing the folks in Shawnee, Oklahoma, how boys from Colorado did ranch work — in 6.8 seconds.

The time had been good enough to keep them in the lead for the NHSRA championship, but it hadn't caused Forrest to cancel his and Tom's practice session the afternoon of their final run.

Tom made another throw at his dummy, and Forrest was glad to see the rope slide around the horns with precision. "Nice one. You're all set for tonight, aren't you?" Forrest wound up and threw a loop at his own target, a replicated pair of steer's raised hooves.

"All set for what? The short-go or the dance?"

Forrest knew what he would see if he looked at his friend's face, so he didn't. "The go."

"Yeah, sure." Tom flipped his lasso in the air. "I wish I was as ready for the dance as I am for team roping."

"Still having trouble with Al?"

"Let's just say we're not the couple you and Jenny are turning out to be."

Forrest sauntered toward the dummy and retrieved his lariat. "Okay, buddy. Let's just say that."

"You have no mercy, do you?" Tom asked, coiling his rope and putting it away. He came to the fence post Forrest was leaning against and did the same.

"You were right about Jen, Tom. She's fantastic. And I'm not only talking about her riding."

"What, then?" Tom asked with no enthusiasm.

Forrest folded his hands and took in a deep, thoughtful breath. "I don't know." He laughed. "Can you believe that? Every day I think I'm finally going to put my finger on it. Every day I keep wondering."

"Mmmph," Tom replied.

"It's like...she listens to me, Tom. Doesn't just sit there like a — a dummy," he finished, looking back at the practice area. "And when she talks, she thinks about what she's saying. She thinks about what I'm saying. And it's almost like it really matters to her." He glanced at Tom before continuing in a soft voice, "Reminds me of your mama, Tom."

Tom studied the ground and gave it a listless kick.

"I'm sorry, Tom. Maybe I shouldn't have mentioned your mama. I know how you felt about her." Forrest fingered the handkerchief at his neck. "I never told you this, but when she died, it was like I lost my mama, too. Like I didn't have a daddy or a mama anymore."

"You've still got a mama."

"Do I?" Forrest felt bitterness rising inside him. "Want to take a stab at telling me where?"

Tom didn't answer, and Forrest let a fair amount of time pass before he spoke again.

"Anyway, Tom, what I was trying to say was, I feel like I finally met a girl who —"

"Yeah," Tom interrupted. "I guess I should be happy, all the work I did getting you two together."

"Tom," Forrest said quickly, "you'd never tell Jen what I said... before?"

Now Tom appeared more animated. "Let's see. It was something

about her being, what was it, a loser? No, no…a lemon. Oh, wait…
a loud-mouthed, loose-lipped, long-haired —"

"Cut it out." Forrest gave him a shove.

"Not funny? You always laughed when I said things about
Felicia —"

"I don't want to talk about Felicia," Forrest said, suddenly hearing a sweet echo of his words.

Tom resumed his position on the post, shouldering his friend a
bit. "Uh-oh. Not getting dreamy again, are we?"

"Why are you hassling me so much about this girl? You never
did before."

"You never cared before," Tom shot back. "And maybe I'm jeal-
ous."

Forrest straightened. "You like Jen, too? 'Cause if you do, buddy,
just remember you had first pick. And you picked Al. You just stay
in your own corral from now on."

"I'd love to. But I don't think there's a corral that could keep
Alison Austin in, though that's not what I'm trying to do to her. I
just wish she'd give me…a little time, Forr. She's always moving so
fast that even when we're together it seems like she's already past
me, way ahead of me somewhere. And then I look at you and
Jenny.… Well, I won't have to worry about that much longer."

"What do you mean?" Anxiety stripped Forrest's words of
expression.

"Jenny's still in high school." Tom shrugged as if what he had
said made sense.

"Yeah?" Forrest waited. "What? You know something you're not
telling me? Jenny got a boyfriend at home or something?" Forrest
racked his memory. "She never said anything about it. Course, she
doesn't say a whole lot —"

"No, Forr. We just won't be moving in the same circles. We'll be starting the IPRA circuit now, and Al and Jenny probably have two or three more years before they go pro."

"But?"

"But what?"

"There's got to be something we can do about it. Or else you wouldn't have said anything, right?"

"I don't know. Do you have any ideas? I'm out."

Forrest slammed his heel into the post, propelling himself forward. "Why'd you get things going, then, Tom? I was doing fine without her."

"It's only been a week. Less than a week. It's not going to alter the course of your life." Tom put a friendly hand on Forrest's back. "Maybe in two years, when Jenny joins the IPRA, if she does...." He brightened. "Hey, maybe Al will change by then."

"Or maybe Jen will." Forrest moved toward his equipment, which lay on the ground. But when he reached it, he kept going, leaving it behind.

"You're not saying anything." Jenny removed one hand from around Forrest's neck and touched his face, delighting in its smooth, handsome contours. That he would allow her to be so near him still amazed her, still made her feel off-balance.

"This's almost our last dance, Jen."

She couldn't tell from his words or the tone of his voice how he felt about it. "I know."

"So..."

Jenny forced herself to let him finish his sentence. So he was thinking about it, too.

"So...isn't there anything we can do about it?"

She slid her hand around his neck and leaned on his chest. "I don't know, Forrest. You've probably got a lot more ideas about it than I have."

"What does that mean?"

"You know." Jenny pressed her cheek closer to him. "You've had other girlfriends."

She felt his breath catch before he answered.

"And you haven't, Jen?"

"Well..." She looked up and smiled. "Just Al."

His chest moved with his laugh, but it was a while before he spoke. "You've got nobody at home, then? Waiting for you?"

"Home?" She raised her head. "Where's that?"

"You telling me you live on the rodeo circuit?" His voice sounded strangely hopeful.

"We've got a trailer in Wyoming, where my mother's from, but we're usually on the road. I home school. My mother teaches me. It took some talking from my daddy to get NHSRA to let me compete." She smiled broadly. "Good thing Daddy's a professional talker. Most weekends, Mother takes me to race in some NHSRA or Little Britches rodeo. Otherwise, we go see Daddy wherever he's announcing, then travel together." She stopped talking as she felt him pull her close. "Was that the right answer or something?"

"Very right." He kissed her cheek, then nudged her forehead with his lips, and when she leaned back, he lowered his mouth onto hers.

Though the music still played, Jenny didn't hear it again until he drew back, his breathing as unsteady as her own.

The song faded and was replaced by a fast tune, but Forrest didn't quicken his steps. Moving with deliberate leisure, he held her and kissed her again, longer, pausing only to put one hand on the back of her head and pull her still closer, his fingers probing the depths of her hair.

"Forr...For-rest..." She could hardly get the word out, so relentless were his lips. The music throbbed in her ears, his grip around her tightened, and his kiss became unbearable.

With all the strength that he had not yet drained from her, Jenny unclasped her hands from his neck and put them on his shoulders. And pushed.

The link broke.

Jenny turned and ran, bumping into several dancers before she found freedom, space. Despite the arena lights, Jenny couldn't see clearly. She could hear better, away from the loudspeakers, but she couldn't see. And she couldn't think.

"Jen?"

She felt his hand on her, and she twisted away. Her tears fell, blinding her, but she kept running, fighting the hand that returned to her shoulder and held her back. "Let me go!"

"Jen, what —"

She turned, her eyes fiery with salt and anger. "Get out of here, Forrest! Leave me alone!" What more she planned to say was washed away. Through her private rain, she felt him drawing her toward him and prepared to fight.

"Easy, Jen. Easy. I'm sorry." His touch was light, and the hand that brushed wet strings of hair from her face no longer demanded what she wasn't ready to give. "I'm really sorry." He kissed her cheek, but made no move toward her lips. "Would you...come by me again? I just want to hold you," he hurried to say. "I won't attack this time."

She stood a moment, looking at him with hurt and suspicion

before she moved into his arms.

His embrace was an apology, and as her tears dried, slowly Jenny relaxed. She felt so exhausted that she was grateful for the support of his arms, though still wary of them.

Forrest put his cheek against hers and spoke softly. "I can't figure you out, Jen. I thought you wanted —"

"Forrest," she said, looking him straight in the eye and trying not to fall into the fathomless blue, "I know what you're used to, but I...I'm not...Felicia."

Surprise registered on his face, mixed with — what? Jenny wasn't sure until he smiled.

"I'm glad, Jen," he said, hugging her, then releasing her carefully. "I'll try to remember." His smile widened. "But I bet you'll remind me if I forget."

Jenny placed his hands around her waist and hugged him back. Relief flooded her, sweeping away the tear stains. "You bet I will, cowboy."

"Let me get this right, Jen: You're *not* dumping him?" Alison bent over their hotel bed and stuck her face in her cousin's so that Jen could not avoid her. "I thought we had this all worked out last night. You came back here with your eyes red from crying, remember?"

"It was my fault, too. I told you that. I never made the boundaries clear. I thought maybe I could do it a little later. I know I was stupid," Jen rushed on. "I should've expected it, should've told him. He's eighteen, used to dating people like...Felicia."

"That's the whole point! How can you like someone who, until he met you, was dating her? Was dating who knows how many girls like her? You're going to be sorry."

Jen rolled over, scrunching her pillow in her arms. "You're probably right, Al. But I've liked him so long, waited so long for him to like me. How can I just walk away?"

Al punched her own pillow and reached to turn off the light. *Be fair,* she told herself. *And be honest. Is that what's really bothering you about Forrest? That he's had a wild past? Or is it that he likes Jen instead of you?*

"Besides," Jen said, "he won't do it again. He promised." She rolled farther over on her side of the bed. "Come on, Al. Let's let it go. I'm tired. And Daddy said we're leaving early tomorrow."

"That's why you were supposed to tell Forrest good-bye tonight. Good-bye, Jen. As in forever." Al tried to quit feeling like a hypocrite, but she couldn't. With every word, she knew herself better, and it seemed Alison Austin was not only a sore loser in racing, she was sore about anything her cousin got that she didn't.

Al shoved her feet to the very end of the bed, then drew them up close. *If only I'd seen him first.* But she should have known that Jen would be first. She'd always been. She had grown up with her parents' full support and help, while Al had practically sold herself into slavery just to ride in the NHSRA. *If I didn't have to fight Mom every inch of the way, I'd be a champion racer, too. And Forrest would be thinking about me right now, not Jen.*

"Al?" Jen's voice was grainy with sleep. "What are you thinking about?"

"Competing." Alison told herself that hiding her true feelings from her cousin and best friend wasn't dishonest, but she knew otherwise. Before she could say so, Jen spoke.

"I thought so. You did really good racing, Al. Especially since you don't get to compete much."

Thanks for rubbing it in, Al thought, but felt ashamed of herself.

Jen was sincerely trying to help. She was always trying to help.

"Al?"

"Yeah?"

"You ever wonder if we'll get to ride in the NFR?"

"You will."

Jen pulled the covers to her chin, and Al fought an impulse to snatch them away. *Get a grip on yourself! This is Jen you're mad at!*

"I hope so," Jen replied. "But you'll be graduating and leaving home in only two years. Then your mother can't stop you from doing what you want." Jen yawned. "I'm not sure if rodeo life is for you, but with your talent and try, if you want to ride in the NFR, you will. And in anything bigger, too."

"Bigger? Nothing's bigger than the NFR."

Jen yawned again. "Ever hear of the Exposition?"

"For years. 'The Olympics of the Rodeo World,' right?"

Jenny laughed softly. "That's right."

"But it's just a rumor. It'll never get off the ground."

"Maybe it will. And maybe someday, we'll ride in it."

"In your dreams," Alison retorted.

"No, Al," Jen said sleepily. "In *our* dreams. 'Night."

CHAPTER

7

WHAT ALISON HAD HOPED WAS JUST a rodeo romance proved more. Whenever Jen called, she was full of news about Forrest — what he and she had done on their latest date, how he was doing in the IPRA rodeos, at which rodeo she might see him next. As the weeks passed, Al clung to the belief that Forrest would eventually tire of Jen and drop her, but when Jen called one day in September to say that Forrest had invited her and her parents to visit him and his grandfather at their ranch in Colorado, Alison had to face facts.

"We're going next week, Al! We'll only be staying overnight, but can you imagine? Two full days with him! We haven't had that much time since the high school finals."

"No, I can't imagine," Alison answered, holding the phone from her ear while her cousin talked for nearly three minutes straight.

"...so it's all set, pretty much. What do you think?" Al heard Jen say when she listened again. "I know it's sooner than we planned, but that's the way it's working out. I'd like you to be part of it, if you still want to, Al."

What? Were they getting married or something already? Jen was way too young. What were her parents thinking? What was Forrest thinking? Was anyone thinking at all? "Don't see how I can, Jen," Al replied. "And this call must really be getting expensive for you. I'll just say congratulations and good-bye now, all right?"

"Oh." This clearly wasn't the answer Jen expected. "Why not? You don't want to? Or don't you think your mother will let you?"

"You think yours will?"

"Sure, with Daddy already announcing on the same circuit —"

Wait a minute! I've missed something. Al paid attention to Jen's next words and pieced together what her cousin had been saying. "You're doing the IPRA circuit next summer, Jen? Is that it? You're kidding."

"Not next summer. That's when I want you to come, too. I'm starting this year."

"With Forrest." Al's heart dropped to her boots.

"No, with Daddy and Mother. Instead of just watching Daddy's shows, I'll be riding in them."

Al leaned against a kitchen chair, fighting waves of jealousy. *At least it's not with Forrest.*

"You there? Al?"

"Yes." She didn't trust herself to say anything more.

"I wish you could start IPRA now, too, but I know how your mother is about school. She'd never let you miss, not even if my mother taught you along with me. I was thinking, though, that when summer comes, you can travel with us. You won't miss any school then. What can your mother say?"

"You don't want to know."

"It can't be that bad —"

"Jen, she practically divorced my dad when we first moved here! She's never said anything about it since, but I think she still hates the farm even now. And when I bring up rodeo, she blows completely."

"I know. So talk to your daddy."

"I can't. They're both gone."

"Gone? He said he'd test out your mother and tell you tonight. Daddy already told him about the whole plan yesterday. He says you've got your feet on the ground more than I do, and he figures two of us will get into less trouble than one." Jen hesitated. "Sometimes I don't think my folks trust me alone with Forrest."

"They're not the only ones."

"Al, I told you there's nothing to worry about."

"So far," Al said ominously.

"Anyway, Daddy says he'll talk to your mother, too, if she wants. But your daddy didn't think your mother was ready for that yet."

"I bet."

"'Cause first, you need a new horse."

Al lowered herself into her chair.

"Daddy's looking around. It's not the best time of year for buying, but even if it does take until winter, you'll still have at least five months to practice before you compete. We'll find a good horse, an experienced racer, so you won't have to worry about training him. He'll train you."

"What's wrong with Bobbin?" Al croaked.

"For starters, she's a mare. Too temperamental. You need a gelding. A quarter-horse gelding."

"Uh, Jen, not that everything you've already said isn't crazy, but don't you think a horse like you're talking about will be more than I can even think of affording? Besides, I love Bobbin. She was my first horse."

"But she's not good enough for IPRA. You are. You've got to get real."

"Me?" Al nearly screamed. "I didn't cook up this idea! Only you, Jen. You and my dad."

"And my daddy," Jen said calmly. "All we need is your mother's okay, and I think Daddy can handle that. He and Aunt Margaret say your mother's the most stubborn of the three of them, but Daddy says she still listens to her elder brother. What you need to do is start thinking about sponsors."

"Sponsors?"

"Yeah, partners who'll give you the financial backing to do this. You need to get a new horse, new equipment —"

"Now it's new equipment, too?"

"— flashier racing clothes —"

"I don't want to be flashy."

"— and money for traveling expenses: food for you and your horse, gas, entry fees —"

"It's impossible, Jen."

"Al." Jen took a long pause. "Do you want to do this or not?"

"I just don't think I'll be able to. There's so much to get, so many obstacles..."

Jen sighed. "I can't believe I ever said you had try."

Al jumped to her feet, nearly upsetting her chair. "I do!"

"Then quit saying no and get things moving!"

Rarely had Al ever heard Jen so impassioned, except when she was talking about... "Jen, do you want me for a traveling partner just so your parents will let you hang out with Forrest more?"

"Alison!"

"I wouldn't blame you," Al said quietly. "He's...terrific, Jen."

The line was silent for some time. "You think so?"

"You can't tell?" The confession felt good, and Al kept going before she had time to think. "I give you such a bad time about him mostly because if you hadn't got him first, I'd be after him myself."

"Oh."

"You're not mad, are you, Jen? I can't help how I feel. I've tried to not like him, but I can't. And…it's hard for me when you talk about him so much. So now that you know, I just want to know if the only reason you want me with you is to see him."

"No, Al. I…I wanted you because, well, we're best friends, and I know how much you love to race.…"

"You still want me? Now that you know how I feel about Forrest?"

"Well…" Jen considered. "You wouldn't try to take him away, would you?"

"Jen! He's your boyfriend. Besides, he never looked at me. It was always you."

"But if he did look?"

Now Al had to consider. "If he did, would you want him?"

It was a while before Jen answered. "No. I guess."

"Okay, then, no problem," Al said, fidgeting. "And I do want to race, Jen. More than anything."

"Okay." Jen sounded relieved. "Then get going on your sponsors and your mother. By the end of May, we'll be racing with the pros, Al. We'll find your horse soon. I'll call again after we get home from Forrest's. Bye."

"Bye, Jen. And thanks," Al said, but her cousin had already hung up.

The weekend weather was mild, as Forrest had hoped, and he and Jen spent hours on horseback, supposedly acquainting her with the Jackson Cattle Company's land, but really regaining the time lost by having to continue their relationship mainly by long distance.

It was their second and last day before he got around to asking what had been disturbing him most. He waited until after they finished their picnic lunch on a grassy knoll that overlooked miles of Jackson grazing land.

"Jen," he said, motioning her over to lean against him. "I know you get the letters I send."

"Yeah." Jen rested her head against his shoulder and took his hand in hers, examining it.

"So why don't you ever write back?"

She flipped his hand over as if it were a toy. "I don't write. Ask Al."

Forrest took back his hand and used it to turn her toward him. "Why don't you write?"

"I call." She adjusted her position so that she was looking at the vista before her, which meant she was facing the opposite direction again. Forrest wished now that he hadn't chosen such a good view.

"I know you call, Jen." he said, hoping she'd turn back to him. She didn't. "But don't you like getting my letters? Don't you like having something to keep when we're apart? To hold onto?"

When she made no reply, he said brusquely, "Or do you just throw them away?"

"For-rest." She smiled. "Course not. I keep them." Instantly, she was facing the view.

He put his arms around her, knowing he was getting nowhere. Unless he insisted, she wasn't going to write. He wanted it to be what she wanted to do, freely. All his other girlfriends and girl-friends-in-waiting had done it.

In a way, it pleased him that Jen was different from them, but it also made him feel less sure of her. She didn't live for him as others had; she made room for him in her own life. He didn't know if he should be satisfied with that.

"Forrest?"

71

He moved in and kissed her neck. "What?"

She wriggled, brushing him away. "I just wanted to know: What's it like, living in one place? Having so much around you? Always knowing that wherever you go, this is waiting for you?"

"I guess I never thought about that."

"Well, think." Jen squeezed his arm and snuggled closer to him.

"Honey, if you want me to think, you better not get too close."

Mock alarm made her eyes wide. She scooted away. "This better?"

"Worse." He leaned forward and scooped her up, taking several kisses before he let her go. "I don't know, Jen. I grew up here, always thought it was great. Tom and I'd go running around, playing cowboys and Indians, pretending to shoot each other off our horses and learning how to fall without getting hurt, not that we were concentrating on that. We played a million games out here." He looked around him and could see old remnants of forts they had built, territory they had "claimed," places that had been their secret meeting spots.

"That's right. Tom lives nearby, doesn't he?"

"Used to live at the place next door." Tom jerked his head south. "Since his mama died, he stays with us, works for Granddad, or did, before we started going down the road."

"Is Tom's place big?"

Forrest tickled her neck with his fingertips, and Jen laughed. "You keep talking like this, I'll think you only keep me hanging 'cause you're one of those gold-diggers. Yeah, it's a big place, but it's not his anymore. Even when it was, it wasn't a real ranch. Rundown. Worth zilch," he said with emphasis, "so forget about Rawlings."

"Well, all right." She sighed.

"You like the ranch, Jen? Our ranch?"

"Are you afraid I don't?"

Forrest didn't answer.

Jen reached for his hand. "I do like it, Forrest. Especially out here. The ranch house, though...it's too big. Doesn't seem...like a home."

Forrest shuddered, either from her words or from her fingernail, which she was trailing down his wrist.

"Must've hit a nerve," she commented.

"Yeah. You must have." He pulled her near and pillowed his face in her hair. "You trying to drive me loco, Jen?"

"How?" She turned to look at him, her red hair swishing behind her.

"You're leaving pretty soon, and you haven't said anything about us."

"I didn't know I had to."

"You haven't changed?" Forrest felt his throat tighten as he asked.

"I still like you." She put her hand on his arm.

"As much as you did?"

She moved to cup part of his chin with her small hand, and kissed him solemnly. "More."

"Then prove it." The words came out harsher than he had intended, and his breath came hard to him, but other emotions pushed at him, drove him on.

Jen looked unruffled, a soft smile on her lips. "I am proving it, Forrest." She slipped her arms around his middle, then drew back as far as he would allow. "I'm not handing you any lines, not making you any promises I won't keep."

He blinked, and suddenly noticed how tightly he was holding

her. He released her.

Her smile grew wide. She stood, picked up the remains of their lunch and reached for his hand. "Come on."

"We going somewhere?"

"No. I just want to kiss you." She walked to where their horses were standing and climbed onto her saddle, tucking the reins from Forrest's horse into her back pocket as she stowed the picnic trappings in her saddlebags.

"Can't you kiss me here?" Forrest put a hand on her horse's withers. "I'm likely to fall off if I'm on horseback."

"Not if you watch what you're doing," Jen said, handing him his reins. "Anyway, you told me you know how to fall without getting hurt." Her green eyes filled, and at last, Forrest could see the force of her feeling.

"You know how to fall without getting hurt," she repeated. "But remember this, Forrest...I don't."

CHAPTER

8

"GRANDMA, THIS IS IT! IT'S ALMOST TIME TO RODEO!"

Alison had been sitting on the pink floral couch in her grandmother Janette's apartment. Now she stood and gave the grayhaired lady a vigorous hug. "I still can't believe it! Dad and I are leaving tomorrow, and by Friday we'll be meeting the O'Neills for my first IPRA rodeo. It's happening. My dream's getting nearer. Someday you'll see me ride in the Professional Rodeo Cowboys Association's circuit."

"Not yet, thank the Lord." Grandma put her hands on either side of Al's face. "I'll keep praying until you're safely home."

"You're worried, too?" Alison sat beside her.

"I gave up worrying the day I let your father rodeo." Grandma shook her head. "You may think that shows the lack of a mother's love, letting her child do what she fears. But I learned that sometimes it does no good to deny one's child what has become his very life's dream."

"'Very life's dream.' That's it, Grandma," Al said, surprised a person so old could understand. "Riding's not just a hobby or something I like to do. When I'm on Ironside, it's like nothing else even exists. I think about racing all day in school." Al laughed. "Or I did."

75

She leaned into the couch's cushions. "This was the longest year of my life."

"At seventeen, I felt the same way. But now a year is hardly time enough for me to find my glasses." Grandma tucked a thick brownish-blond curl behind Al's ear, kissing the cheek she had just unveiled. "Thank you for spending the afternoon with me, dear, but now you must go home. Your mother is grieving for you."

"She's mad at me, Grandma, not sad."

The elderly woman gave Al a peculiar look. "Sometimes those emotions are one and the same." She chucked Al lightly under the chin with a wrinkled forefinger. "Do your best for her today, Alison. Let her know you love her, as she does you. Try not to argue. Remember, you won't see her again until you come home this fall."

"I won't see you. Mom could come to any of my rodeos. Dad said he'd take her, but Mom says if I'm leaving home, she's not coming after me. She's still upset that I won't be doing any more local rodeos. I thought she just went to them to check up on me. Dad always said she loved being there, but it sure didn't seem like it. He said once that going to any rodeo reminded her of when they met. I asked if that was good or bad. He didn't answer."

Al checked her watch. "It's still two hours before supper. Would you tell me how Mom and Dad met? I'd like to know how they fit into rodeo, now that I'm doing the same thing. Was Mom a racer? What did Dad do? I've asked them, but they always say we'll talk about it later. We never do."

"Well," Grandma began, "your interest is natural, particularly now. And your mother did give me permission to tell you the story when I saw fit." She arranged her reading glasses uselessly on her nose. "Your father keeps promising to get me a string for these," she commented, making sure the glasses wouldn't fall off.

"Grandma! The story!"

"Yes, yes. Well, your mother and father met at a rodeo in Madison. A girlfriend took her out supposedly to the movies, but she took her to the rodeo instead. Once your mother got past her annoyance, she tolerated the rodeo fairly well. Even enjoyed watching the barrel racing. But when the show ended, she wanted to go home. Her friend had other ideas. She had met a cowboy the previous year and hoped to see him again at the dance following the rodeo. She needed your mother to be with her." Grandma patted Al's hand. "You see, the girl's parents knew she'd get into no trouble with Eileen along."

"Sounds like Mom was a killjoy even when she was my age. Or was she my age?"

"Seventeen exactly."

"So she went to the dance and met Dad?"

"She met your father when she was looking for her friend. Apparently, the girl slipped away with the cowboy, and your mother got worried when they didn't return after eleven o'clock. That was her curfew. She'd never broken it before, but her friend had the car keys."

"So Dad took her home?"

"Perhaps I know why your parents have difficulty telling you stories, Alison. They're meant to be enjoyed, you know, not raced through."

"I am enjoying it. You're the one who said I should be getting home."

"So I did. Forgive me, dear. Yes, your father took your mother home, and when they got there, he stayed with her and her parents and her friend's parents until the police located the girl around three in the morning. The cowboy had left her intoxicated and disheveled, although he hadn't harmed her. Well, it didn't give your mother a very good image of cowboys or rodeos, but your father had made an impression, and whenever he was riding near Madison, he would drop by to see your mother. They fell in love, and were married when she was nineteen."

"That's why Mom hates rodeo? Because a cowboy got her friend drunk?"

"Alison. You haven't forgotten your father's accident?"

"He got it in rodeo? I thought it was from his work."

"It was from his work. He used to ride bulls."

"O-oh." Al couldn't take that tidbit in all at once. It explained so much about her father. And her mother. "Is that why neither of them talk about rodeo now?"

"Yes. The accident ended your father's riding career," Grandma continued. "They were already married at the time, and your mother had begged him to quit. She was pregnant with you, afraid she'd lose you both. She nearly did lose you when she saw him get gored."

"Gored?"

"The bull's horn nearly went right through your father's leg. If he hadn't moved, it would have caught him in the stomach area and probably killed him." Grandma paused. "They didn't wear riding vests like they do nowadays. He was blessed to get off with a broken back and leg. Recovery was an ordeal. He went from being a strong, athletic young man to one with an aching, unreliable body."

Al mulled that over. "I thought you said he got a horn in the leg, not that he broke it."

"Both occurred. It all happened, in a few seconds' time. Haven't you ever seen a man in a bad spot with a bull, Alison?"

"I never did hang around to watch. Not for a whole ride, anyway, especially if the rider had trouble. Mom says guys that ride bulls can't be trusted. For anything. That they live for themselves and don't care who it hurts." Al reflected. "When I was twelve, she made me swear I'd never even date a bull rider."

Grandma reached for her glasses. "That's the story; all I've been told of it. But before you go, I want you to remember another story that I read to you long ago."

"From the Bible, right?"

"Right, as you say." The old lady took a black tome from the end table and paged through it. "It's a short story the Lord Jesus tells of a man who found a treasure hidden in a field. Do you recall what the man did when he found the treasure?"

"Dug it up and was rich forever?"

"He hid it again and then sold all he had to buy that field." Grandma glanced up as Al stood. "The Bible says he did it 'for joy.' That's how the kingdom of heaven is — just like that treasure, worth all and more than anyone can ever own."

She reached for Al's hand. "Alison, as you go off on your own, remember this story about the kingdom of heaven, and the man who gave all he had for it. Don't exchange all you have for anything less."

The outdoor arena was small, but decorated and maintained in top rodeo style. Red and white numbered flags snapped proudly from the tops of each of the eight chutes, and patriotic banners flanked the entire arena. Behind the rails was the seating, enough for several thousand, Al estimated, and just about full. On one side was a shaded grandstand; on the other, a temporary awning covering the heads of several hundred people.

Ironside alternately lifted his front hooves, not stamping them, but working out the jitters. Al wished she could do the same. However, all contestants were to remain in queue until the drill team executed its opening exercises.

Music blasted from the loudspeakers, and Al waited obediently in line, looking at the drill team. Their American flags, red neckerchiefs, and long, loose hair danced with the wind and their horses' high-speed movements. Watching them, a smear of color and action, Al suddenly felt very young.

Beautiful women... A timeworn memory swam the deep waters of her mind, arcing suddenly and splashing into her consciousness. *A beautiful woman on a fast horse,* she remembered. *My first rodeo.*

She turned and signalled Jen, who backed up her mount.

"What, Al?" Jen whispered.

"Remember the first time my dad took me to a rodeo? The first one where I saw you ride?"

"Say what you've got to say fast. We have to be ready for the grand entry any minute."

Al rubbed Ironside's neck, and she felt him quiet in response. "That day I said we'd be world-champion barrel racers, Jen. We're one circuit closer to making that happen. Only one circuit away. I promised myself that one day I'd be — "

Ahead of her, the line began to move, and Jen reined her horse into it. "Al!"

"I'm coming!"

It was all Al could do not to wave her hat and whoop wildly as Ironside wheeled into the arena and sprayed gravelly dirt into the air with each pace. Music made the atmosphere vibrate, and Uncle Barney's voice over it told of the glories of rodeo.

Swirling colors surrounded Al: blurs of people's watching faces, banners and flags and freshly painted rails and bleachers, the green tops of a few wind-tossed trees around the arena. She heard whinnies and bellows from loaded rough stock, the pounding of a hundred cantering hooves, the clapping and shouting of a thousand hands. And through all the hubbub flowed her awareness of her own part in this ritual, this initiation.

She was no longer an amateur, but a professional, almost where she'd fought so hard to get. Al directed Ironside to follow the pattern the other riders laid ahead of them. The exhibition continued for several minutes, riders and horses flawlessly doing their part to delight the spectators and prime them for the drama to come.

Alison inhaled a self-satisfied gulp of dusty air and choked on it as she connected with a pair of eyes. Blue eyes, that rested on her briefly and continued their sweep. Eyes that seemed to look back into hers even when the cowboy who possessed them had followed the horseback parade out of the arena. Technicolor blue, she had finally decided months ago: the eyes of Forrest Jackson.

Ironside stopped automatically as the horse ahead of him slowed and the rider dismounted, leading the animal to where it would be left until needed. Al climbed from her own saddle as if she'd never ridden before. Her heel hung up in the stirrup, and as she hopped ridiculously and tried to pull it out, she felt a hand on her shoulder and saw another swiftly free her boot.

Not breathing, Alison turned, only to look into a pair of eyes that were not blue, but brown. Earthy brown. Brown like the hide of a bull.

It was Tom Rawlings.

Tom had hoped for a chance like this, but even in his dreams he hadn't been able to conceive it. Yet there she was: Alison Austin, standing more still than he'd ever seen her.

Tom knew it wouldn't last, and as he freed her boot from the stirrup, he regretted what he was doing.

Sure enough, once her foot hit the ground, Al pushed a hand against the hair that had fallen across her face. "Thanks, Tom," she said, and gave him a smile that was only payment for his efforts. Payment in full. Then she turned and led her horse away.

She remembered my name. But that's about it. Tom told himself his disappointment was senseless. Just because he had spent the year since the National High School Finals Rodeo thinking about her didn't mean she had thought about him a second during that time. And he hadn't expected her to. Had he?

Give it up, cowboy. You've got as much chance for success as a ninety-pound steer wrestler with the flu. But Tom couldn't give up, even if he knew with the same sinking certainty that during his ride the bull he had drawn would throw him and stomp him into jelly if he wasn't careful. Bull riding, like every pleasure, included a risk of pain. Where Alison Austin was concerned, that pain might be a lot more than even he was accustomed to.

Tom idly began wondering what his mother would advise. It remained a habit since her death because while she lived, it had been their way.

"Let's pray about it, Son," Tom could hear her saying, as she did about every decision from finding ways to help the hens lay better to figuring out how they would survive when the money ran out for the year. While Tom had been young, he'd quietly listened to his mother's prayers. But even before she died, he questioned to whom she was praying. Was it to the One who allowed his father to become so drunk he didn't care whether it was the table or his wife or son who received his blows? Was it to the One who allowed him to gamble away almost all his winnings so that he'd sold their land out from under them?

The Circle H... A small Circle of Heaven, his mother had called their pasturelands, with their leaning, weather-assaulted house and rotting sheds. She had loved the Circle H, and Tom had, too. He had cried aloud when they learned they had thirty days to move. His mother did all her crying inwardly, to her God, who never answered.

Tom swung into his saddle. If he was boneheaded enough to keep pursuing Al Austin, he knew one thing for certain: God would never hear his cry for help. If he won the gray-eyed barrel racer, it'd be all his own doing.

9

SOMEHOW, IT BECAME A TRADITION that after each rodeo, the four would separate to clean themselves up and meet afterwards to go eat. Sometimes that meant shedding their western wear and going formal, but more frequently it meant hot dogs and beans over the campfire. Jen would critique Al's performance and Forrest would pick apart his and Tom's team-roping run. Then, slowly, Forrest and Jen would lose touch with everything but each other. Tom and Al would take that as their cue to haul the couple over to the rodeo dance before they became insufferable.

Alison couldn't understand how her feelings for Forrest could withstand the daily onslaught of his devotion to Jen. She had enough opportunity to witness it. The four often rode together in Forrest's rusty white pickup on the way to various rodeos, chaperoned at a distance by Uncle Barney and Aunt Virginia, who pulled Al and Jenny's horses in the double trailer.

By riding along in Forrest's pickup, Al figured she'd realize that continuing to like him was as nutty as barrel racing without a horse. However, sharing each day's new adventures with him, if only on the outskirts, didn't erode her affection but forced it underground, where it dug deep channels into her heart.

Mountains, cliffs, and bridges pleased him, Al learned. He would stop the pickup and urge everyone to get out and labor up pinnacles just to see the staggering drop and the valleys and towns far below.

Alternatively, he hated tunnels and caves, would speed through the one and sit in the pickup sulking if anybody insisted on exploring the other. Al always stayed with him, claiming to hate the damp, enclosed spaces also. From these stolen times, she came to know that he loved lakes, rivers, oceans, and tolerated the desert only when it was in bloom. He carried large containers of water for horses and humans alike when traveling across what he called "stray beaches."

Alison didn't report any of these revelations in her weekly letters to her mother. Nor did she mention that one of the group of four she hung out with was a bull rider. Her mother would have forbidden her to travel in his company. In itself, this didn't bother Al, but the awful prospect of being driven even further from Forrest caused her to write her letters carefully and regularly.

She also made her aunt, uncle, and cousin promise not to mention Tom's name or his event to her parents. Jen smiled significantly at that, and Al realized her cousin thought she was interested in the pensive bull rider. Stifling her first reaction, Al decided to let Jen believe whatever she liked.

They had been on the circuit for two months before Jen voiced her suspicions. She and Alison were sitting at a concessions table, eating sno-cones and waiting for the two cowboys to haul them to their next destination, when Al made the mistake of saying that Tom had really roped his steer well that day.

"Set him right up for Forrest," Al commented, chipping away at her cone with the curved end of the straw. "You think they'll make the IPRA finals?"

"The regional finals? For sure," Jen said, smiling. "Or are you talking the International Finals?"

"International." Al crunched into her ice. "Why do they call it 'International' when they only call the PRCA Finals 'National'? When I was little, I used to think IPRA was the top circuit, not PRCA, just because of the names."

"I don't know. Doesn't seem to hurt either circuit, though. Everyone who's really into rodeo knows what's going on. You still think we'll ride in it someday?"

"If you're talking about the NFR, I'm planning on it." Al tipped the last of her cone into her mouth and crumpled the paper container. She aimed at the garbage can and let fly. "Bull's-eye!"

"I think they call that a basket, not a bull's-eye, Al." Jen laughed. "You really are getting into rodeo, aren't you?"

"Yes ma'am," Al replied.

Jen walked to the barrel with her own cup. While her back was turned, she asked, "And how about rodeo cowboys, Al? You feel any different about them?"

Al's shock had passed before Jen sat beside her. "Oh, you mean Tom." She giggled nervously.

Jen eyed her. "He's the only one I see you hanging around with. Or do you like someone else?"

"Come on, Jen," Al said weakly. "I'd be bonkers to spend so much time with Tom if I did, wouldn't I?"

"I think so."

While Alison tried to determine if Jen meant anything by her statement, her cousin continued. "So when does Tom get to know?"

Al raised her shoulders. "There's only a month left of the season for me. Think it's fair to start anything now?"

"I thought you already had started."

"Not really. Just the usual stuff. You know."

"Have you kissed him?"

"Jen!" Al glanced around her as if afraid they'd be overheard. "The guys will be coming back any minute. Think I want Tom to know we're talking about him? Besides, did I ask you any of this stuff about Forrest?"

"No. No, you never did. I used to wonder about that." Jen rested her chin on the heel of her palm and looked across the parking lot in front of them. "But then, you used to like Forrest yourself."

Used to. It sounded so safe to hear Jen put it that way. But it wasn't true.

Tell her, Al. Tell her you're still crazy about Forrest. Crazier. But Al resisted. Hadn't she already admitted that once? *Yes. And remember how good it felt? How you didn't have to deal with guilt?*

Rebellion surged up to answer. *I already told her once! If Jen wants to believe I'm over Forrest, let her.* Al sighed inaudibly. *I even wish it were true.*

Al knew Jen wanted her to find a boyfriend of her own so they could share each other's happiness. How could she hurt Jen by telling her the only boyfriend she wanted was Forrest?

Then a novel idea came to her: A month remained until she had to return home. What if...what if she gave Tom a little more attention than usual during that short time? It would make things easier for everyone, and maybe, given half a chance, Tom would turn out not to be such bad company. Maybe it was the solution she'd been searching for.

Or maybe it's the start of even bigger problems. Al heard the quiet voice in her head, but she ignored it, and was pleasantly surprised to find that the shrill vocal cords of her new plan easily outshouted their opposition.

"Jen, I think it is about time I give Tom a little encouragement." Alison's resolve slipped when she saw Forrest and Tom leaving a building and crossing the parking lot toward them. Even from that distance, Al could see that Forrest's grin was only for Jen, while Tom's shot straight at her.

So transparent, both of them. But Forrest had Jen's love, while Tom just hoped for hers. She'd been careful to be a friend to Tom and nothing more. Yes, she'd been blameless. So far.

Guilt grew in her with every step the two cowboys took. *But I won't lead Tom on. I won't even say I'll date him. I'll just be nicer to him. What's wrong with being nicer?*

It sounded good, but Al didn't convince herself. "Jen," she said, pulling her cousin near to speak into her ear. "I...think I'll wait a little longer to tell Tom anything, okay? I'm leaving so soon, and it wouldn't be fair."

Jen's green eyes flicked from Al to the strolling cowboys. "I think you're right," she said when the boys had almost reached them. "I don't think it'd be fair at all."

Tom's whole body ached, but it didn't quell the gladness in his heart. As he slung his bull rope over the arena rails and heaved himself up, he heard something behind him and instinctively dove the rest of the way over the fence.

"You're not making our job easy lately, Rawlings," clown-faced Suicide Sam growled, taking a hit in his side as the Brahma turned from his intended victim and took out his frustrations on the man with baggy pants. Suicide jumped and weaved, letting the bull chase him back to the catch pen.

Tom raised himself off the dirt, using his hat as a duster until he saw sour expressions from the fans that sat only a few feet away. "Sorry, folks," Tom said grandly. "But dust is just a fact of life for a bull rider."

One well-fleshed lady coughed delicately in response, but everyone else's attention was on the next rider, already shooting into the arena astride a mucus-flinging, horn-shaking hulk of bad-tempered bovine.

Tom didn't stay to watch the action. He had already enjoyed his, and Al and the others would be waiting for him by now. He would prefer losing his shot at the regional finals to missing a moment he could be with one of the IPRA's star rookie racers. This afternoon Al had ridden second only to her cousin. She'd be in an especially good mood. Maybe she'd even give him some time today. Some real attention. He couldn't be sure, but he'd sensed a softening in her, and he intended to take full advantage of it in the few days before she returned to Wisconsin.

Smiling to himself, Tom knew what Al would say about her performance: It was a lucky lick, the rest of the competitors were mainly local riders, it was the kind of arena Ironside loved and she'd just let him have his head. That was one thing about Al: She wasn't just pretending modesty, she *was* modest.

That was Al's problem, Tom decided as he walked and tried not to limp. Alison had big enough dreams, but she left them too much in the future. Yeah, someday she'd be good, but she wasn't yet, she'd often say. Someday she'd beat second-ranking Felicia Newcastle or maybe even top Jenny and take a victory lap herself, but that was a long way off. Tom knew that until Al claimed someday as today, she'd never do all she had the talent and skill to do. Her chance to discover that was about over for this summer. Tom felt that tragedy more sharply for his own sake than hers.

He reached Forrest's pickup and carefully checked his gear before putting it in the compartments he'd built into the two-horse trailer. Since Al and the others weren't around, he grabbed fresh clothes and some shampoo and headed for the nearby campground showers.

Tom always enjoyed a blast of cold water. He could wash a bad riding score or a slow roping time right down the drain, and when he emerged from the shower house, clad in a pair of twill dress chinos and a hunter-green linen shirt, he felt that tonight he'd make Al fall in love with him so deeply that she'd dream only of him during their long months apart.

The screen door slammed behind him, and Tom rounded the corner of the building, seeing nothing unusual about the man slumped against the wall. Drunks weren't an uncommon sight to rodeo, though maybe more so at four on a Sunday afternoon. But hangovers were nasty things to recover from. "'Bout as easy to shake as a pit bull with lockjaw," his father would say. Tom had never cared to discover for himself if it were true.

"Son, you don't look nothin' like a cowboy."

Son. Tom stopped dead as a sprinting calf that had hit the end of some roper's lariat.

"Got a buck for your old man?"

Tom mechanically fished in his back pocket. He fumbled with his wallet before extracting two twenty-dollar bills.

The man sitting in the dirt looked amused. "You gonna bring it over here? I ain't catchy, son. Won't hurt ya none to come closer. Don't care what your mama tol' ya."

His feet moved, but Tom's mind stayed distanced. He'd heard his father had been hanging around the IPRA circuit. Thankfully, Tom hadn't seen him before this. He'd hoped the hard luck Bob Rawlings had found since the death of his traveling partner had ended, but the man was in worse shape than ever. It was tough to believe this sodden, reeking, grubby cowboy had once been a PRCA world-champion bull rider. It was even harder to believe that he was Tom's own father. Harder, and far more painful.

"A couple twennies?" Bob Rawlings guffawed. "Heard you been doin' okay, kid. Got the regionals comin' up, don't ya? You can sure spare more than this."

Tom realized it would do little good to tell his old man that when expenses for gas, travel, food, equipment, and entry fees were taken out of his winnings, not much remained. What he had handed his daddy he'd carefully hoarded to treat Al. Now only a few bills lined his wallet. "Sorry. I can't give you any more —"

The older man waved his son's words away. "A miser, just like your mother. Selfish an' naggy, just like 'er." He staggered to a stand. "She didn't do me no favors by givin' me you, boy," he said, sliding his hand down the white shower house wall as he tottered away. "She didn't do me no favors at all."

Shame struck Tom more forcibly than his last two bulls had. He watched his father's haphazard progress and felt the impulse to head full-steam in the opposite direction and leave even bull riding behind. Was this Tom's destiny? To end up like his father? He was already following in Bob Rawlings's footsteps in too many respects. If he kept going, where would they lead?

"Tom?"

It was Jenny.

"Hi."

"You okay?"

He avoided her eyes by looking downward, only to notice that his shampoo bottle had fallen. He bent to retrieve it. "I'm fine." He raised his head tentatively and saw compassion on her face.

"That your daddy who just left here?"

Tom hooked his free thumb into his belt loop. "Yeah, that was my daddy. Makes a good rodeo spokesman, doesn't he? I'm hoping to grow up just like him."

Jenny cut to his real meaning. "Don't blame rodeo for your daddy's troubles, Tom. And don't think you'll end up like him just because you're in rodeo, too. There's a lot of fine folks that make up for the...for the —"

"The drunks? The has-beens?"

"— the ones who get hurt." Jenny's green eyes radiated sympathy. "Tom." She laid her hand on his arm. "I know you've got a lot of hurts inside you, just like Forrest does. I wish I could help you both. But I can't. We just...we just all have to do the best we can. We have to try to make it easier for each other."

"That's the answer?" Tom asked, his hope diminishing further.

"Only one I know of," Jenny replied, withdrawing her hand but not her attention. "You find something better, you let me know, okay?"

She took a step forward, then turned back. "No one else saw your daddy, Tom. Al and Forrest are still on the rodeo grounds, looking at her horse's leg. I came to tell you we're ready to go when you are." She scuffed the ground with the toe of her boot. "Are you ready, Tom?"

"Yeah," he said, and the word came out like a sigh. "Let's go."

CHAPTER

10

AUGUST CAME TO AN END and Al soon found herself not racing, but studying. This was a different type of competition, one she also savored. But no Forrest Jackson rewarded her efforts with his blue-eyed glance, and her hands had pen marks on them more often than sweat and horsehair.

She had ended the season honestly, for all the good that had done her. Tom still liked her, Forrest didn't. Tom had even asked to write to her, and Al told him no as kindly as she could. She then adopted a sisterly attitude, which he finally seemed to understand. His kindness and attention continued, but his smiles came less often, and a new sadness settled on him.

School gave Alison a focus away from rodeo, from Forrest, and she tried to concentrate on what preoccupied her senior classmates. She couldn't take Homecoming seriously, but she did attend meetings held by college representatives. She even brought home admissions requirements and brochures.

Her relationship with her mother improved as a result. Now they had something neutral to talk about: campuses and courses and degrees. The idea of college appealed to Al, but she couldn't forget rodeo. While she studied hard, she also kept Ironside and herself in shape. Her dreams of a university diploma mingled with those of a world-champion barrel-racing buckle. And a cowboy with unforgettable eyes.

Eileen Austin would have gaped at her daughter if not for years of etiquette training. "Alison, I thought last summer you just wanted to *try* professional rodeo before starting college. Or was I mistaken?"

Her daughter sat at the kitchen table, fiddling with what had started the ruckus: a letter from Jennifer O'Neill.

"I did say that," Alison admitted. "And I feel the same way." Her voice speeded up. "You can't tell how a whole circuit is in just three months. Besides, Ironside and I performed pretty well. I can use that money for college."

"What money? Your sponsors didn't cover everything. I hope Barney and Virginia didn't shoulder your traveling expenses. How many times must I remind you? Always pay your own way, Alison. Don't depend on others to do what is your responsibility." *Though I can hardly expect you to, with an example like your father.*

"I did pay for myself, Mother. And you're right. There wasn't a lot of money left after that, but it was the first year I raced Ironside. We were just getting to know each other. If I raced him this year —"

"You wouldn't even get your application papers in on time, let alone have anything to pay for tuition. No, Alison. I am putting my foot down this year. I don't care what your father says. I won't see you losing your chance to be educated. Don't you realize your whole future will depend on it?" Even as she talked, Eileen realized her daughter wasn't hearing. And she also felt sure that Alison would find a way to race come May.

It was a genetic defect, this madness for rodeo. Eileen knew her husband still adored the sport. Even her mother-in-law was blind where bulls and broncos were concerned. The reason for Janette's poor judgment escaped Eileen. Usually the elderly woman displayed a fair amount of wisdom, but in regard to rodeo, she was nearly as brainless as the rest of the Austins.

When Eileen had finished her remarks, Alison stormed off to her horse and Eileen to her station wagon. As she hit the rise of the hill and briefly felt nothing but air under her tires, Eileen lifted her foot a bit from the gas pedal. No doubt she was behaving as badly as her daughter: burning off her anger through speed.

Snow-lined cracks split the blacktop outside Senior Manor, and Eileen slowed even further as she approached, until she eased into her usual parking spot. She sat behind the wheel, looking at the white-etched asphalt. A sudden picture flashed before her: skittering fall leaves on a perfect black surface. As she left the car and stepped over a fissure, she dismissed the memory. In the years since then, many things had become worn and broken.

Though Janette wasn't expecting her, Eileen felt sure the older woman would be at home. She buzzed Janette's room; the security door unlocked but stuck. Eileen rattled the metal handle until the door came free. Her hand prickled with cold by the time she stepped inside the building.

On Eileen's last visit, Janette's door bore bright evidence of Valentine's Day that had been up for weeks. Eileen suspected her mother-in-law plunged into the holiday with such abandon because it gave her a chance to revel in even more pink than usual. But when she asked why Janette had not put away the decorations, Janette replied, "It's always a celebration of love where the Lord is concerned, Eileen. 'For God so loved the world —'"

"I'm familiar with that verse," Eileen said dryly. "Some fanatic waves it from the stands during every football game I've ever seen."

Janette had answered, "Then you must not view many games, dear. I've only seen it happen once or twice a season."

Eileen had dropped the subject of both the Valentine's door and the televised Bible verse, with no intention of taking either up on this visit or any other.

Janette's door was open and the Valentine's decorations removed, Eileen noted as she received her mother-in-law's embrace. However, an abundance of pink odds and ends still adorned the door.

"So good to see you, Eileen. But aren't the roads slippery, dear? What brings you here?"

"This." Eileen drew from her pocket a pink string with white rubber tips on either end. "An extremely belated Christmas gift."

"For my glasses." Janette handled the string as if it were a fragile piece of blown glass. "Harvey finally remembered."

Eileen made no reply, and Janette stopped attaching the tips to her glasses.

"Harvey didn't remember?"

"I'm afraid not."

"Well." Janette gave Eileen's hand a squeeze. "You are a faithful helpmate to him. Thank you for remembering. I didn't really need it at all, except —"

"Except that you haven't dared set your glasses down since you misplaced them at Christmas?"

The old woman chuckled. "I'm afraid I counted on getting my little string then and got careless too soon. I'm still ashamed at all the searching I put you through." She finished her adjustments and patted the hanging glasses. "I'll never lose them again."

"A shame they don't make strings like that for children," Eileen said, sitting on the couch.

Janette set a teapot to boil and came from the kitchenette with a plate of sugar cookies. "You're...having difficulties with Alison?"

"She wants to rodeo again this summer. She and Jennifer are plotting already. I don't understand why Barney and Virginia permit it. I'd hoped that once Alison got racing out of her system, that would be enough."

"Your family was never involved in rodeo," Janette remarked, sitting as Eileen took a cookie, "yet both your brother, Barney, and your sister, Margaret, are extremely active in it, isn't that right?"

Eileen felt as if she were confessing a crime. "My mother and father disapproved of rodeo entirely. But I don't know why —"

"And you yourself married a rodeo cowboy. Now isn't that strange."

"What are you getting at?"

Janette rose as the teapot began whistling. "I cherish the song of a teapot on a snowy day," she said, opening cupboard doors and drawers and finally reappearing with two filled teacups. "Makes me feel all cozy, drinking tea almost in defiance of the cold outside."

"You were discussing my family." Eileen took her cup and dipped a cookie into the warm liquid.

"Not really. I just was remarking that Alison has many people around her, whom she loves, who themselves love rodeo. Now don't you think it likely that she would be drawn to it also? After all, it is a very exciting sport, no matter what one thinks of it. A sport for the young, the dashing, the brave. Those with frontier spirits —"

"And holes in their empty heads."

Janette laughed. "Sometimes that does seem so. But rodeo has its draw, Eileen. And that draw generally passes. It is when the desire is denied that it becomes hard, unyielding, like a chunk of carbon compressed by pressure and time."

"Producing a diamond?" Eileen asked scornfully. "I hardly think so."

"You see the blooming plant over by the window? The cactus?"

Eileen stood and walked over to the pink blossoms. They were pointed, but spineless. She detected no fragrance.

"It's called a Christmas cactus because it blooms around Christmas every year. And only at Christmas."

"Then why is it blooming now?"

"I haven't the slightest idea. I bought it to bloom at Christmas, in celebration of Jesus' birth. But every so often it takes it into its head to bloom other times. And its flowers are just as pretty those times as when they bloom at Christmas."

"You're saying I shouldn't force Alison to 'bloom' when she isn't ready or try to suppress her when she is? I believe I know best about that, Janette. Alison's my child! I have no intention of allowing her to make her own decisions."

"She's almost eighteen. What will you do when she comes of legal age to do as she wishes?"

"Then I'll have no choice. But now I do."

"Yes, you have that right," Janette replied placidly. "And I think you're correct about Alison and rodeo. I don't think it's the place for her either."

"You don't?" Eileen felt her carefully planned argument disintegrating.

"I don't. I think eventually she'll realize that. She's much like you, Eileen." Janette gave her an affectionate pat. "She flourishes in stable, homelike environments. She creates those environments herself, doesn't she? For her animals?"

"I suppose she does," Eileen said, thinking of Alison's elaborate rabbit hutches and birdhouses and horse stalls. "It never occurred to me that that was what she was doing."

Janette offered her another cookie.

"Oh, I've let the first fall apart in my tea!"

"I'll get you a fresh cup, and we can start over, if you have time, dear." The older woman rose and made another trip to the kitchen.

"Do you really think Alison will be safe on the circuit?" Eileen asked anxiously.

"She's well chaperoned, and racing accidents are infrequent, thank the Lord. If she attempts to keep fulfilling her dream next year instead of this year, she'll likely be unchaperoned and highly rebellious against anything that suggests she isn't independent."

"So I should...let her go to keep her?"

"No. Go with her. Be part of her dream, Eileen. Alison would love to have you."

"Why on earth would she ever want me?" Eileen scoffed.

Janette left the kitchen and sat near her, laying an arm lightly across her shoulders. "My dear, if you don't know the answer to that, it's time to find out."

Al was conscious of her mother's hovering all evening, but she had little to say about it. If her mother was sorry, let her apologize. It wasn't right that she still treated Al like a child, and she was going to have to learn that one day soon.

Around nine o'clock, Eileen laid her sewing on the couch's arm and approached the faded brown vinyl recliner Alison was sitting in, her father's favorite chair.

"Do you have any mending for me, darling?"

Darling? Al looked up, knowing that was probably the closest to "sorry" she was going to get. It wasn't good enough, though. More than an apology, Al wanted to rodeo. *Just a few more months, she thought. Then I won't need anyone's permission about any —*

"Alison, I know you want to race, and I'm trying to understand why." Her mother stood, one hand resting on the recliner's arm. "We've...never really discussed it, at least, not thoroughly, not since you grew up."

Al squinted, hardly believing these words were coming from her mother. "You really want to know why I love racing?"

"Isn't that what I just —" Her mother stopped. "Yes. Please."

Al stared in front of her, past her mother, her eyes seeking an object for contemplation. At last she settled on the snowflakes falling under the yard light. Racing. Rodeo. A beautiful woman on a — but her mother would never understand that, and as the years had passed, Al's reasons for rodeoing had become more complex, more difficult to verbalize.

She felt the tingle of a well-timed turn, the rush of a faultless approach. The challenge and heightened awareness that came with competition, with performing in front of eyes that would detect any mistake. The acute sense of motion and balance. The dizzying feel of a good score. The companionship and teamwork with one's horse. The feeling of being young and free, sharing goals and dreams with Jen. The discovery of new arenas and landscapes. And of course, the thrill of an approving smile from Forrest.

A movement to her side brought Al back to the living room, and her eyes focused on the drifting snowflakes, then closer, on her mother's questioning face.

"I don't know, Mother." *Better stay on the safe side.* "I just...love it! All of it!"

"And you're...never lonesome? You never wish you were back at home with me and your father? You never miss us?"

Was this a trap? Of course she sometimes wished for a quiet night at home, with her mother sewing or baking and her father reading in his bedroom. A night like tonight, when no anger raised the voices of those she loved, and a sleepy peace drifted through the house like heat from the radiator. If only she could somehow bridge those two worlds, rodeo and home, instead of straddling them or jumping from one to the other. If only she didn't always have to choose.

Al began to speak, but an awful thought stopped her. *She's testing me, seeing if I'm still a little girl who needs her mommy. And if I say I do...* The outcome was terribly obvious: no more rodeo. Not this summer, anyway.

"No, Mother," Al answered quickly. "You know I love being home with you and Dad, but when warm weather comes, there's nothing I like more than being on Ironside. And he loves racing, too." She smiled enigmatically. "Uncle Barney and Aunt Virginia treat me like their second daughter. Jen's practically a sister. Rodeo's home for me, just like this farm is."

"You're at home...there," her mother said slowly. "And there's nothing...no one...you need?"

"Nope." Al jumped up and turned on the television. "Hey, I think you're missing 'Global Gourmet.'" She flipped through the satellite guide and found the program on the screen.

Her mother had moved to the couch, holding her sewing in her hand absently. Al took it and placed it on the scuffed-up coffee table. "Just relax. Watch your show. I'm going out to the barn to check on Ironside."

She kissed her mother's flushed cheek. *I wish I could tell you, Mother,* Al thought as she left, *I wish you could be there with me, be part of what I love so much.* But she left silently, knowing that some dreams could never come true.

CHAPTER

11

LAKESIDE, CALIFORNIA, OPENED the fast-paced outdoor rodeo season. Before long, Alison Austin reappeared, but the intervening months had changed her. She was gaining the dualistic personality of a serious competitor, at times almost predatory, except where Jenny was concerned. The two young women's friendship strengthened with their mutual determination to reach the International Finals, the IPRA's field of honor.

Tom felt even more drawn to Al, for he was undergoing the same galvanizing. He also wanted to be a champion, to restore the Rawlings name to its earlier association with fine bull riding, not fine spirits. He hoped success would earn him the Circle H, Al's respect...and perhaps his own as well.

Jenny, too, raced with new intensity. Her recently purchased barrel-racing horse, Cloverleaf, boosted her performance even as Jenny's relationship with Forrest felt the first pitfalls of fame. The latest cover of Rodeo News introduced his grin to thousands, and while Forrest rose in rodeo's ranks, he was also sinking. Though he spoke of marrying Jenny "sometime," he never spoke of loving her. Battling his advances became routine, like his apologies. Just as he relished the West Coast's beaches, daring the waves then dashing away before his boots got wet, he seemed to enjoy pushing Jenny past her limits, never thinking the backwash of this play might extend far beyond soaking leather.

Al remained oblivious to her cousin's troubles, taken by growing talk of another rodeo circuit. She often rode with Uncle Barney and Aunt Virginia just to hear them discuss it.

"Four, five years from now, I'm saying. No more. I'm hearing talk of sponsors signing already, of rodeo committees elbowing each other to get a show in their arena," claimed Uncle "Blarney." Like many other announcers, he was known for exaggeration, but he wasn't the only one spouting this tale. Al had heard many names for the coming phenomenon: the Olympic circuit, the Universal Pro Rodeo circuit, and most often, the Professional Rodeo Exposition. Though the names varied, everyone agreed that the circuit, when it materialized, would be the biggest, finest, richest string of national shows ever conceived, occurring only once every decade.

This fueled Al's competitive spark. Maybe she'd never win Forrest, but she could win beyond her imagination if the legendary circuit became reality. And she knew it would.

Al's break came at a night rodeo in Montana. Generally she and Ironside didn't perform as well under the bright arena lights, but something about the night made her sure, even before the race, that she would be taking her first victory lap.

She'd been so close in the past few weeks: coming in sixth, then staying in the fives, finally scoring an odd third-place. But the night of the Hustler's Annual July Roundup, Al knew she wouldn't be satisfied with third.

Jen had schooled her in the basics and from there, Al had formulated her own racing method. The system was intuitive, and used Ironside's strengths to their advantage. He could cut a barrel clean and fast, but he depended on Al to tell him when, just as he relied on her to signal when to make the burst at the end of the pattern. Alison still made errors, causing him to knock down a barrel or cut too widely, but she was improving every day they raced.

She trotted Ironside an hour before the rodeo began, then kept him limber with periodic walking. His black mane and tail gleamed from her grooming, and this once, she braided the first hank of hair by his withers. She didn't want him to look like Felicia Newcastle's mounts: primped and trimmed to artificial perfection, but she wanted to do something to mark the night, to mark this ride.

The air curling through the outdoor arena roiled her blood, awakening her as if from a long winter. She drank deeply of the elixir, every molecule of her body vibrating with life.

"Are you going for the feather-boa look now?"

Al turned to find Tom scrutinizing Ironside's braid.

"You again? I thought I told you to quit distracting me before performances." Al swatted his hand from her horse's mane.

"The day I distract you is the day I give up rodeo," Tom bantered, pointing at the braid. "Do you think a gimmick is going to give you speed?"

"Something is."

"Oh? Are you taking first tonight?"

Al didn't answer.

"You could, you know." He looked at her, obviously anticipating the argument they always had.

"I know." She heard applause and the announcer's voice. "Tom, I've got to go." She glanced at him, expecting his surprise at her answer but also seeing on his face what he hadn't shown in a long time: admiration, affection, even a strange pride.

As if he could take credit for anything I do, Al caught herself thinking, knowing she had to quit taking him for granted. He was an up-and-coming competitor. Whispers began predicting gold buckles in his future, and rodeo veterans began recalling his father's lost skill. Good old Tom was someone a girl could be proud to catch — only Al wasn't that girl.

"Got a surprise for you after you take your victory lap," he said as she mounted.

"Tom, I'm —"

"I found an Italian place in town."

"You didn't!" Apart from racing, Italian food was Al's second passion.

"And if you take first, I'll pick up the tab."

Al grinned. "It's your fault if I win tonight, then."

"I surely do hope so," he replied, and she nudged Ironside toward the starting line.

At the Italian restaurant they took a table not for two but for four after the rodeo that night, and Tom didn't pick up the check, either. Al did — out of her first-place winnings. It was the only reference to her victory she made, though Jenny and Forrest both commented on it.

After the meal, Tom sat back and slipped into his favorite pastime: watching Al and wishing he had a clue as to what went on underneath that abundance of long, dark-blond hair. If only he could tap her brain and hear the answers he'd waited two years to know.

Did he have a chance with her? The question still overshadowed his world. He was more certain of winning a championship buckle and owning the Circle H than he was of ever obtaining her love.

The first two things he had some control over. Hard work and perseverance could make them his. But Al Austin? What all would it take to win her?

Blue eyes? Blond hair? Tom wondered as he observed her demeanor toward Forrest. Almost from the get-go, Tom felt she secretly loved the bronc rider. So much pointed to it, but nothing had ever resulted, and her behavior, especially this summer, reassured Tom. If Al had been dazzled by the Jackson mystique, maybe it was finally wearing off. Maybe now she'd find a little room in her life for a bull rider with no attachments and a lot of heart. He wished fervently he had more to offer her.

Occasionally, Tom did date other girls, but only casually and never during the summers. He didn't want anything that might pose an obstacle for Al in case she suddenly became interested in him. He wanted a clear path for her, a clean run, so that she wouldn't change her mind halfway. When she came to him, he wanted it to be for the final go-round.

Tom had to admit that so far his dedication had brought him nothing but too much time alone, time he filled by riding and roping. It was probably to his professional benefit that Al thought of him only as a friend, but it was also to his personal loss.

So why don't you tell her?

Such a simple thought, so...frightening. Tell her? He could barely ask her anything. Any direct question he'd ever posed had resulted in 'no.' She wouldn't even let him write her!

Still, he sensed her need. Maybe Al wasn't as alone in the world as he was, but he knew she was at least as lonely. He had glimpsed her with her horse, when she thought she was alone. He saw the smiles fade and a wistful look replace her forced vivacity. She curried Ironside, sometimes for hours, until Jenny would come and get her, or an official would call her to race. Then she'd pick up her mask and go.

She wore it now, sitting across the table from him. She'd worn it all summer. Tom lived for the day when she'd let it slip, just an inch, so he could see and talk with the real Al Austin, and he could show her the real Tom Rawlings: son of a drunk, but bearer of a love so insistent that not even she could quench it. Someday, when he had the trophies and treasure to prove that he was worthy of her love, he would ask for it. Soon, he and Forrest would make their move into the PRCA circuit and real fame. Until then, he would bide his time.

At least once a summer, the O'Neills ranged out of their stomping grounds to visit Uncle Barney's sister, Margaret Iver, and her husband, Willy, on their Oklahoma spread. Generally the trip would occur around the time of the Sallisaw Lions Club Rodeo Inc., a top-paying IPRA show which featured more than forty thousand dollars in prize money. Barney would preside as announcer over the rodeo, and the young riders would try to grab some of the purse before moving on.

Unusually wet weather had made the summer even more humid. While Al basked in the relative novelty of travel and competition, her companions grew high-strung and irritable — except for Tom, of course. But Jen had her days, and it was on one of these that Al met a racer who seemed untouched by the heat or the miles.

Nona Ellsen had been on the IPRA circuit three years, she told Al, who had heard of the lean black-haired woman's skill and sportsmanship. "But I didn't always feel so good about racing or life," Nona confided, when they met in the horse barn. "It gets to you. I traveled with a pickup-load of other girls, and by this time every year, we were ready to throw each other out the window just to get some time alone, or relieve the boredom, or the tension."

Al listened as she brushed Ironside, hearing a full-time racer's view of the circuit and beginning to understand why nearly everyone around her was getting testy.

"Yeah," Al said as Nona stopped to give her horse a treat of Hor-C Vita-Bites. "I guess it would be different doing it all the time."

"Especially when you're depending on what you earn to keep you and Ol' Betsy in hay." Nona laughed. "Sometimes I just felt so...desperate. Seems silly now."

"What changed your attitude?"

"You really want to know?"

"Why not? I might be doing the circuit one of these years, as soon as I hear the Exposition is going for sure." Al put away her curry comb and weaved a single braid in Ironside's mane. "I think I could use some survival tactics, maybe just to survive my partners. They're getting kind of edgy."

"Happens to the best. All right, Al, I tell you what, how'd you like to come to a potluck supper with me tonight? It's hosted by the Glory Seekers. Free food, lots of singing, and a story or two. I think you'll get all your questions answered."

"Free food? I'm tempted to ask Jen along, but she'd probably bite my head off. She made it clear she wanted to BE ALONE PLEASE until the performance. I've never seen Jen shout, but that came pretty close. She'll feel bad about it as soon as she finishes her run."

"You know her pretty well."

"Very well," Al said, measuring out oats for Ironside.

Nona leaned over the stall, her arms folded. "Jenny's a great racer. And going to be greater."

Al felt a pang of jealousy. "I know."

"Does it bother you?" Nona asked, walking beside Al as they left the barn.

"It probably shouldn't. If I was racing fulltime, who knows what I could do?"

"Thinking of the mythical Exposition again?"

"You think it's a myth?"

Nona stooped to fish a piece of hay from inside her boot. "I hope not."

"You want to race in it, too."

"Doesn't everybody? Listen, Al, I'll meet you back here in about an hour. Be hungry and ready for fun, okay?" Nona surprised Al with a hug when she agreed. "And if you change your mind about asking Jenny or anybody else to come along, no problem. I ran into Sarah Bower just before I met you. She's coming, and I told her the same thing. Everyone's welcome."

"Okay." Al stood looking after Nona, then headed to the parking lot to find the O'Neill pickup and get into some dressy clothes for once, maybe her black flounce chemise or lacy floral chiffon. She had the pickup in sight before she realized she hadn't even asked if she was going to someone's house or some kind of party. "Guess it doesn't matter. Free food tonight and Aunt Marg's feasts all day tomorrow." Suddenly, Al felt a great sense of well-being. "Rodeo's not so tough."

Tom had nearly talked Al into scouring the town for Italian with him before Nona and Sarah arrived.

"You're going to be sorry," he said, grinning.

"That's what you keep saying. So what is Glory Seekers? A cult?"

"Yeah, started by the son of a Jewish carpenter a couple thousand years ago. They're Christians, Al. It's a religious meeting." Tom hooked his thumbs in his belt loops. He was trying not to adore her too openly, but the gauzy lines of her dress annihilated his defenses.

"What about the free food, and the singing?"

"Bait," said Tom, sticking out his elbows in a very western pose.

"You're saying Nona's tricking me into coming?"

Tom leaned against the horse barn, parking one foot against the wall behind him. "She probably thinks she's doing you a favor. She's a fanatic, you know."

"No, I didn't know. All I've ever heard is that she's a super racer and a nice person."

"She is. But she's a fanatic, too."

Al sighed. "All right."

"You're coming with me?" Tom asked, not believing his luck.

"No, cowboy," Al said, pointing to where Nona and Sarah were approaching. "I'd feel stupid bowing out now, and anyway, I'm hungry. You guys should have warned me about her and you didn't. So you're coming along as punishment."

"I'm coming," Tom repeated. He seized Al's wrist and whispered, "If we're drugged, kidnapped, and end up waving Bibles at our old friends, I'm holding you responsible."

"Just think 'free food,'" Al replied as Nona greeted them.

After a short walk to an enclosed pavilion, the four entered a room with fifty or so people singing to the music coming from a guitar and portable organ. They were shown to their seats and handed songbooks. Tom, sitting next to Al and an empty seat, and purposely away from Nona, nudged his partner. "They're smart. Singing first, eating later."

Al gave him an apologetic look.

"I can smell the food, though," Tom said, scanning the room.

"Can't be too long until we get it." He hummed the song the others were singing, then stopped.

"What's wrong? You look sick."

Tom shook his head. "Nothing."

Al went back to singing, but Tom couldn't, though he knew the words by heart. The song was his mother's favorite, "Jesus Paid It All." He hadn't heard it since it was played at her funeral.

How long the song continued, Tom couldn't guess. He was back at the Circle H, with his mother, in the world of love she created for him. He saw her at work in her garden, pulling up weeds to save for the chickens. He saw her making cookies, telling stories, kissing the bruises he'd gotten from falling off whatever he'd managed to mount.

Tom hadn't realized the singing had stopped until a man's voice punctured his reverie. A grizzled cowboy was in the midst of a sermon, rodeo style, and old, forgotten words like "grace" and "sin" mingled with "y'all" and "ya hear?"

Though clearly winding down, the man spoke animatedly about love, about forgiveness, about how everyone is worthy of God's wrath and eternal judgment. "The Bible says, 'for all have sinned and fall short of the glory of God.' That's all, ya'll. We're all in the same circuit, all got the same draw.

"In the end, it's not how ya rope or ride, it's what ya do with the One who died for ya," he continued, ruffling the sparse sprigs of hair on his head. "Do ya know God's Son, Jesus, who don't care a straw whether ya got a buckle or won a purse or not? All he asks is that ya come to him, knowin' that ya done a lot of bad. He's the only One can wipe that sin-score completely away. If ya ask his forgiveness an' give him the reins of your life, he'll give ya freedom like ya never knowed: a heart full of his love an' peace an' joy. An' eternal life. That means forever, ya'll."

111

The cowboy bent his head and prayed for his listeners, then asked those who were willing to come to the front to entrust their lives to Jesus as their Redeemer and Ruler.

Tom had heard altar calls before, but never had he wanted to go up to the altar himself and say the words the preacher was saying: "God, have mercy on me, a sinner. Jesus, save me by the blood you shed for me." That prayer had always been for little boys who tortured frogs, for wrinkled old women who lived alone. Now, for some reason, it seemed meant for him, too.

"Al, I..." he stopped, amazed. Alison's seat was empty. And there, walking slowly down the aisle, accompanied by Sarah Bower, was Al Austin. The two young women knelt at the altar, and Tom rose. He stepped past a weeping Nona, out into the aisle, felt encouraging hands urging him forward, heard prayers of thanksgiving — and then Tom turned and fled.

CHAPTER

12

"I'M NOT GOING HOME, JEN."

The redhead reined Cloverleaf so sharply that his black hooves skidded in the soft orange earth. "Al?"

Jenny's cousin was sitting in her saddle, looking at the Oklahoma hills. "I'm not going to college. I'm going to rodeo this year."

Whatever had gone on at the Glory Seekers' meeting had affected both Tom and Al deeply. Neither mentioned it, not even to each other, as far as Jenny knew. The two had performed well in the Sallislaw rodeo, but afterwards around the campfire and a late supper of hot dogs and beans, they had hardly eaten, hardly spoken. And Jenny didn't think the food was entirely to blame.

"Mom's already got me admitted, with a pre-veterinary medicine major. I've always liked the idea, Jen, but I guess I never thought it would actually happen. For the last two years, we've been talking about my going to college, becoming a vet, but this morning Aunt Marg had me sign some papers from Mom for financial aid, and after I signed, I felt...wrong."

"Too many debts?"

"Not as bad as I thought, actually. My tuition's covered, with scholarships and loans and grants. I've got a dorm room, a meal plan. Classes start the first week in September." Al paused. "All I have to do is show up."

"But you're not going to."

"No."

Jenny moved Clover so close to Ironside that the two horses nearly bumped shoulders. "Al, you're nuts."

"Yep. That's why I'm in rodeo." She smiled for the first time since leaving Sallislaw.

"I'm not kidding. I think you're making a big mistake."

Al's gray eyes contracted, as if flinching from a blow. "You don't think I'll ever be good enough. When the Exposition —"

"Al!" Jenny reached over and shook her cousin. "When? You don't even know it's ever going to happen. It was fun to dream about when we were younger, but you've got to get real. What's with you? You just keep letting my daddy fill your head. He doesn't know!"

"Even if it doesn't happen..." Al faltered. "...I still want to ride PRCA. I want to be a champion, Jen. Maybe it won't make a lot of difference to me in another ten years, but right now it does. I'm not going home. I can go to college later. I hate disappointing Mom, but I've been thinking about it ever since I signed those papers, and I've made up my mind."

Jen blocked out the view of her cousin with the brim of her chocolate-colored Stetson. "Al, I'm only going to say this once: I think you're giving up too much. If I was you —"

"If you were me? I'm all for it. Let's switch, Jen," Al retorted. "I'll be you, you can be me. You go off to college and leave me to race. Give me all your racing skill, your experience, your training. Then I'd also get your chances for a world championship, right? I'd get your mom and dad, who'll take you to any rodeo you want. I'd get your hair and your face. And while we're at it, I'd get Forrest." Al dug her heels into Ironside and within seconds had left the Iver's training arena and was on her way to the hills.

Jenny watched the horse and rider make the gradual climb and then reach the crest. When they disappeared down the other side, she turned Cloverleaf toward the house.

As Jenny hoped, Aunt Margaret was alone in the kitchen. Jenny carefully removed her boots and dusted her leggings before entering the room. She thought she came in quietly, but her aunt heard her.

"Jenny! I thought you and Alison would be practicing your runs until lunch."

"I did, too." Jenny took a chair by the kitchen table and straddled it, sitting the wrong way so that her chin rested on the curved chair back. "Al took off." She pushed up the sleeves of her tawny-colored tunic and looked at the hill over which Al and Ironside had vanished.

"Did you two have a fight?" Aunt Margaret wiped her hands on her apron, set a bowl in the fridge, then sat in the chair next to her niece.

"I don't know what to call it. Al's always been my best friend, besides Forrest, but sometimes I don't feel like I know her at all."

"Maybe you don't."

Jenny scuffed her socks on the floor. "Maybe."

"It's not such a bad thing, or so unheard-of, Jenny. You girls are facing choices that will affect you in ways no one could even guess, here in the present. It's a difficult age, a time of making up your mind about so many things. When I was eighteen, I made up my mind every other day, and changed it just as often."

115

"You did? You're the most stable person I know, besides my mother."

"I am now. Before that..." Aunt Margaret whistled. "I was pretty hot-tempered, trying to fight my way through my own doubts."

"And you...sometimes said things you didn't mean? Did things that weren't like you?"

"Yes, I'm ashamed to say. I had no anchor then, only a big ambition to be a famous racer. My parents despised rodeo, so of course that made me love it more, even though I loved them deeply as well. There was a war within me, Jenny, and it made me do a lot of strange things until I figured out what I really wanted."

"Good," Jenny said.

Her aunt appeared taken aback. "Yes, it was good. The best thing in my life. For I met Jesus."

Jenny's eyes glazed over, and as her aunt continued to speak, Jen retreated inside herself. *Al's fighting a battle, too. She didn't mean what she said — about Forrest or anything. Maybe she'll miss the first week or so of classes, but when she finds out what it's like to hang around the circuit while everyone else goes home or off to college, she'll wish she was going, too.* Jenny let her thoughts loiter there. *Home. No trailer or hotel or campground. Just a place...a place where everyone stays...*

Aunt Margaret was looking at her expectantly, and Jenny realized she must have asked something.

"I'm sorry, Aunt, I didn't hear what you said. I was just wondering when Mother and Daddy are coming back."

"In time for supper, they told me," Aunt Margaret replied, her smile fading. "You're worried about them?"

"No more than usual." Jen summoned a smile in return, and when she looked around the kitchen, the smile became genuine. Whatever her aunt was baking in the oven smelled so — homey.

Meal preparations sat half-begun on the white tiled counter, but even they fit into the orderly domestic scene. The whole kitchen was decorated in checkered red-and-white gingham with shiny gold-colored antiques perched on shelves and hanging on walls. Big windows with ruffled curtains let in the sunshine and the cool outside smells of the recent rain.

Ever since she was little, Jenny had loved the Ivers' house. It was a sanctuary where she and her mother had found refuge from life on the road. The pleasure of staying put, of being surrounded by funny, familiar knickknacks, and of sleeping in a bed that was neither in a tent nor in a hotel room were only some of the luxuries Jenny enjoyed about Aunt Margaret's and Uncle Willy's. Sometimes her mother would leave her several days on end. Then Aunt Margaret gave Jenny her full attention, splurging wonderful amounts of time teaching her racing tricks or taking care of the animals or making frosted cakes.

For Jenny, the little homestead was the one place where she had felt like a child, a normal child, who could play with dolls, or make a fort with the living room couch cushions, or take walks. During the short visits, she sampled how it would be to have a stay-at-home mother and daddy, a stay-at-home *home.*

She was always ready to leave when her own mother came and picked her up or said it was time to go. But Jenny had a war within, too. Sometimes, miles from Oklahoma, she found herself thinking about the little gingham kitchen and her aunt's relaxed, odd ways. Sometimes, Jenny still wished for a big fence to keep everyone home.

At the sound of the pickup door opening, Forrest snapped his belt buckle, hiding from view the laminated pictures of his daddy and granddad underneath. "Hey, Jen," he said, leaning across the seat to give her a hand in. "Where you been?"

"Just walking around."

Forrest didn't attempt to decode her statement. He didn't have to understand everything Jen did and felt, just as he didn't demand her understanding. Certain things, like pictures on the undersides of belt buckles, couldn't be explained or discussed without discomfort. Such things were personal. From the beginning, Jen had made it clear that she had her own life. If she wanted him to know what was going on, she'd tell him.

Still, she had been moping for days, roughly since they had left Oklahoma. Forrest hoped it was nothing more than the fight with Al, although that seemed to be over. Maybe it was time to see if there was anything he could do. "You want to talk about what's bothering you, Jen?"

"No."

Okay, he had tried. Best not to trespass on private pain, even the pain of those he loved the most. He'd learned that much from his granddad's upbringing. The old man had always been rigid, and though he had unbent a trifle after the death of his son, seeking comfort and love from Sterling Sr. was a little like warming up to a slightly melted ice cube. Forrest had developed the habit of not barging in where he wasn't invited. He expected the same courtesy from others.

"Forr, are you and Tom still planning to ride at Ellensburg?"

Jen's look of concern made Forrest smile. He kissed her, relieved that her worries were so minor. "Yeah, we are. All set, but it took a little working from Granddad to come out right. You afraid I'll forget you now that we're hitting the big-time?"

Jen moved closer to him. "Maybe I'll hit it, too."

"What about your folks?"

"As long as I travel with them, I think it'll be okay. Daddy's already doing a few PRCA shows now." Jen snuggled nearer, and Forrest could feel his attention shifting. "There don't seem to be a lot of options for me. Racing's what I've been trained to do, nothing else. I'm happy doing it, I like winning. I think I should just decide that's what I'm going to do. Besides, everyone I care about's in rodeo."

"Now that's good to hear. I was hoping you could do the PRCA circuit when we did, but I didn't know if it'd work out. I think it's going to be great, for both of us."

"Yeah," Jen answered, but Forrest could tell she wasn't completely convinced.

"Honey, it's going to be great," he repeated. "You'll see." He touched her face, her lovely red hair, and kissed her, not intending to stop until every doubt left her mind.

Eileen threw the crumpled letter to the scarred linoleum floor. Not coming home? Instead of starting college, Alison would become a professional barrel racer?

Grabbing a rain slicker from the entryway closet, Eileen stomped off to find her husband. Even if he wasn't an active part of this travesty, surely Harvey was behind it. Maybe if she took care of him, she could get Alison back as well. Action, at any rate, was better than the resigned despair in which she had so often accepted her adversities since coming to the farm.

She shoved open the barn door, passing through the milk house and standing at the edge of the stanchions. "Harvey! Harvey!" The way before her needed mucking out. "Harvey!"

He didn't come or answer. *Hiding out,* Eileen thought, disdaining to set one sole in the slimy mess before her. Shaking her head, Eileen retreated to the house. She would take her stand in the kitchen, her only stronghold on the farm.

Shedding her coat and shoes before she stepped into the entry-way, Eileen first headed to the bedroom to strip off her clothes. The medicinal smell of the barn clung to them, and changing to a clean outfit gave her the feeling of at least something remedied. She debated taking a shower, then marched to the kitchen to bake bread until her husband appeared.

As she measured out the ingredients, Eileen looked forward to pounding the dough into submission. She stirred the mixture and thought of trying to sell what she baked. They could use the extra money, heaven knew, and it might help change her daughter's mind into the bargain. Was Alison worried about finances? Had seeing those financial aid forms triggered her decision?

Farm debts had hung over the Austins' heads from the time Alison was a child. Farming had not turned out as Harvey promised, even with the generous but limited monetary boosts from Janette. Raising beef cattle, then calves, then sheep for profit had failed, each in its turn, though the current high-producing Holsteins and above-normal milk rates combined to bring Elder Valley Farm the closest ever to breaking even.

But Harvey hated milking, and more often than not, the evening or morning milking was performed by hired help, who took better care of the cows than their lazy owner.

Eileen had tried. She had pushed Harvey into milking, and at first helped with all the unexpected work milk cows involved. She had even learned to run a combine and haybine, of all things, and soon was cutting hay, feeding grain and silage to the stock, nursing sick calves — everything but birthing the dirty creatures — until she noticed the harder she worked, the more chores fell on her thin shoulders.

Too much was enough. Eileen reclaimed her own territory and turned back to cooking, cleaning, and attempting to restore the tumbledown farmhouse with scraps of money she pilfered from her husband's pockets. What happened to the cows, happened. Perhaps they'd lose the farm altogether and be forced back to Madison for employment. That prospect didn't trouble her as much as the threat of farm life forever. Or the horrible loss of her brilliant daughter to a life of barrel racing.

Eileen pounded the dough and reviewed her old decision to stay. Harvey had finagled the farm and sunk his daughter's affections into it so quickly, so deeply that Eileen knew Alison couldn't be transplanted without damage. Buying old Bobbin had been Harvey's masterstroke. Once Eileen saw the nag and her daughter mounted on it, she knew that if she left, she'd have to leave alone. And that was impossible.

Alison! The name rose like a cry from Eileen's heart, like a silent, shrill whistle audible to only the keenest ears. *I stayed here. I stayed here to keep you! And I lost you anyway.*

Eileen's fists forsook their will to strike. Knowing she was losing control, Eileen stumbled to her bedroom, and behind the closed door, she gave full voice to her helplessness until her body, too, became helpless, able only to shudder and weep.

No living soul was aware of her tears, except for the orange barn cat that took advantage of the lull in the rain to pass near the dining area's patio doors. The cat trod the grass carpeting of Eileen's promised sunroom and found its milk dish filled only with rain water. It padded away, curling its tail.

121

CHAPTER

13

ELLENSBURG. The name sounded like a dirge to Jenny's ears, and as she dressed in her family's hotel room, she couldn't shake a feeling of doom. She purposely wore her new racing outfit from Aunt Margaret: a satin rose-hued blouse and short set with cream trim. But not even this helped shake Jenny's blues. She hoped inclement weather would cancel the rodeo.

Sunshine poured down on the spectators' heads the afternoon of the first performance, and the bright, mostly white outside arena was anything but foreboding. As she took her place by Al in the grandstands, Jenny told herself to buck up. She hadn't lost Forrest so far, to either a treacherous woman or a bronc. But the uneasiness she'd felt since leaving Oklahoma persisted. What was it? Home-sickness? *Funny disease for someone like me,* Jenny thought, and tried to take interest in the arena antics below her.

"Look at that drill team," Al said, elbowing Jenny.

Even without their flags, practiced flair, and matching bay mounts, the women themselves would have been mesmerizing. Wearing sparkling red outfits and spotless white boots, each rider had long blond hair that drifted and wheeled with her horse's actions.

"All that blond hair reminds me of Felicia," Al remarked.

"Should," Jen said bleakly. "She's riding today."

"Which one is she?" Al craned her neck.

"She's racing. She's been making her move into PRCA this summer, too." Jenny didn't add that this was probably a likely source of her anxiety. Felicia had been gunning for Forrest ever since they'd broken up. When Jenny found herself competing in the same rodeo with the blond, she did her best to lay low. Still, unpleasant exchanges often occurred, and when they did, Jenny didn't curb her tongue.

Felicia was a threat. Instinctively, Jenny knew Felicia appealed to something in most cowboys. Al labeled it "bimbo appeal," but Jenny was afraid it went deeper and further than either of them could understand.

"Listen to that announcer, Jen. He did the NFR last year. You can almost taste it in the air, can't you?"

"What?"

"The National Finals. Yes, I think I like this circuit."

PRCA rodeo was more polished, Jenny had to admit. The announcer sounded like her father on an especially good day. His effortless, conversational flow established an immediate bond with the crowd while taking them in hand. He pumped the crowd, worked it, used his voice to inject excitement into an already loaded atmosphere.

The opening ceremonies finished, Al pulled down her visor and began slathering sunscreen on her arms, splattering the lace edges of her sleeveless indigo romper.

"Forrest's riding after the bulldoggers, Al. He's stretching behind the chutes, there. See him? Tom's with him, too. Wish they were up right away, so we could leave sooner." Jenny caught the attention of a roving vendor and bought her cousin a can of soda. "Thanks for coming with me, Al. I know you don't like watching."

"It's okay. Think your mom's feeling better yet?"

"If Daddy leaves her alone, she's probably fine by now. He should've come with me, then I wouldn't have had to drag you along."

"That's all right. I do want to see the racers, find out what I'll be up against next year."

Al didn't sound as enthusiastic as usual, and Jenny wondered if her cousin was already regretting her decision to postpone going home. Jenny knew Al's mother hadn't cancelled either Al's classes or dorm accommodations in the hopes that she would reconsider. Aunt Eileen didn't give up easily, but neither did Al. Jenny wondered who would win the battle of wills.

"Tell you what, Jen," Al said, turning away from the first bare-back-bronc rider, who tossed like a rag doll on his horse. "You announce this rodeo for me, and I'll be just as happy not to watch anyone ride. Except Felicia and the other racers. I want to see that. Oh, and the team roping. Think Tom and Forrest have a chance?"

"They're good," Jenny replied. She took a few seconds to get into the mood, then started announcing in a low voice, to Al's quiet laughter. Jenny kept up a steady, hilarious patter until the steer wrestling ended and the saddle-bronc riding began.

Looking down to the chutes, Jenny saw Forrest climbing in as another cowboy burst into the arena and was thrown before his mount's second jump. As Forrest made his final adjustments, the rodeo announcer cited Forrest's home town and told the fans that he was the son of that great bull rider, Sterling Jackson Jr., who had taken six world championships in bull riding during his career. The announcer didn't mention how that career ended, and Jenny thought she saw Forrest's shoulders shake as he hunched over his bronc. She hoped she was wrong.

"Forrest's up?" Al asked, shading her eyes before averting them. "Do your stuff, Jen."

Jen resumed the old game, but when the gate opened, her mouth closed. The white bruiser Forrest rode dwarfed him. The horse hadn't looked so big in the chute, but now Jenny wondered how the thing had fit in.

The bronc's heavy, powerful legs thrashed incredibly fast for his bulk, but Forrest held onto his buck rein, defying the horse's ducks and dives, displaying balance, strength, even spurring. It reminded Jen of that beautiful ride he'd made so long ago on Cloudburst at the National High School Finals Rodeo, but this ride showed the skill he'd gained since then. Forrest Jackson was a professional. He belonged in the Professional Rodeo Cowboys Association. Jenny knew it as surely as she knew she would lose him.

And then, Forrest was on the ground.

The white horse sailed over him, still bucking, but Forrest lay, unmoving. A crowd of cowboys hid him from view in an instant, and Jenny struggled to see past the shoulders of others also straining to see.

The cowboy huddle broke to admit a stretcher, and as the paramedics carried Forrest from the arena, Jenny saw him raise an arm, then push himself up to sit.

"He's all right," Al breathed, and suddenly Jenny was conscious of her cousin leaning hard against her. "Oh, Jen." Al used Jenny's arm as a rope to lower herself to the bench. "I'm so...so thankful."

"He's okay, folks," the announcer drawled. "Takes a lot more'n that to get a good cowboy down. Put your hands together and pay 'im off. Forrest Jackson's not taking home anything else today, unless he has better luck with his team roping later on."

"Want to come with me?" Jenny asked, trying to control her anger.

"Where? To see Forrest? Fine, but the announcer said —"

"Don't you know anything yet? That's what they always say, unless someone dies on the spot. Come on, Al." Jenny hastily led her cousin down the grandstand aisle.

Forrest's injuries weren't as bad as Jenny had feared. They consisted of a banged-up left cheek, a skinned elbow, and a slightly pulled leg muscle, but he and Tom did their roping run — well enough to hope for a placing if their time held during the rest of the go-round.

Jenny hadn't tried to talk Forrest out of roping. She knew cowboys, especially her cowboy, too well for that. But his bullheadedness irked her. After the rodeo, she left him with sketchy plans to meet at his and Tom's hotel room. First, she meant to return to her hotel and spend some time trying to ease her mother's aches, since Forrest allowed no one to ease his.

"Let's go down and see if Jen's here yet," Forrest told Tom, who looked at him over an issue of *Pro Rodeo Sports News*. "I'm feeling more uptight than a steer with a bulldogger breathing down its neck."

Tom set the magazine on the table between his and Forrest's beds, covering his lariat. "Jenny said she'd call." He sat up and rubbed his side.

"Maybe she can't. The phone's off the hook now. Her mama's headache must be even worse. Jen was pretty upset that last time I called." Forrest grabbed his second-best hat, a plain white Resistol that lacked the class of his black, gold-studded arena hat. He stuffed it on his head. "Maybe she had to sneak out to meet us."

Tom forged past him and ahead, while Forrest left the door open behind them. "If she's not down there, we probably won't be able to do anything tonight. And Jen's folks are leaving early in the morning," Forrest said glumly.

"We're not," Tom pointed out, making his way down the long hall to the windowless stairway at the end. "I want to do some celebrating, Forr. Some eating, at least. Staying in a hotel is great, but I'm starving."

"Me, too," Forrest answered, feeling more than seeing his way down the dim passage. "You'd think the PRCA'd pick a better hotel than this chintzy place." He ran his hands over the deep purple, red, and gold paisley wallpaper, seeing no richness in the royal colors. "Maybe there'll be something else we can grab to eat in the lobby. You check while I look for Jen."

Light and activity greeted their entrance. Forrest hadn't even wandered to the lobby window before Felicia Newcastle and a group of seven or eight cowboys and cowgirls breezed past him. He looked out the window, hoping Jen's pickup was in the parking lot or pulling up the driveway.

"Forrest?"

Felicia's voice, a mix of Southern sultriness and sophistication, hadn't affected him in years, but for some reason, both her voice and her manicured hand on his wrist heightened his agitation.

"You waiting for someone, Forrest? Me, maybe?"

"Jen," Forrest answered firmly, but he turned from the window. "You seen her?"

"Not since she hustled out of here after the rodeo. You all aren't still waiting for her, surely?" Felicia asked, moving her hand to his forearm. "You boys must be perishing from hunger. Why don't you come with us? It'll be my treat. You can't rope and ride like you all did today without craving a thick steak and a drink or two afterwards to pay yourselves off."

"Tom had the ride, not me." Forrest glanced out the window, but Felicia's words hit home. Cokes and chips from the vending machine near their room had been his and Tom's only reward for their stellar team-roping time and Tom's seventy-eight point bull ride. "We are kind of hungry, but we're waiting for Jen. Her mama's sick, and —"

"Oh, is that it?" Felicia turned to her crowd, which milled restlessly. "Val, aren't the O'Neills staying at your hotel? Didn't you say they were just leaving when you came over here?"

Val grunted, occupied with the black-haired, miniskirted buckle bunny at his side. "Think they were headin' to the Steak Shack." He took a swig from the can in his hand. "Which is where we'd be by now if you'd stop yakkin'. You comin', Forrest? Tom?"

Just to be recognized by the veteran cowboy was an honor. Forrest hated to reject his first invitation to join the PRCA elite. "What do you think, Tom?"

"If Jenny's there, we'll find her. If not, we can come right back, after we sink our teeth into a steak and baked potato. Right now, I could even eat a bull."

"I don't know —"

"Make up your mind, Jackson," Val said, leading his girlfriend by the hand. "I'll get the Suburban an' drive up front. If you're not ready by the time —"

"They will be, sugar." Felicia smiled him away and pulled out a small notebook from her sequined purse. For the first time, Forrest noticed that the purse matched her short silvery evening dress, and that both were complemented by the blond beauty above and below the hem and neckline. "Here, Forrest. You go on ahead and write a note to your girlfriend. Tell her where you'll be. That way she can come too, and poor ol' Tom won't expire from hunger. Go on." She held a pen out to him.

Forrest jotted down some words, then asked for another sheet of paper. "For the door, in case Jen goes there first," he explained.

When he finished and began walking to the lobby desk, Felicia snatched the notes from him. "If you all aren't out there when Val pulls up, he'll leave you. He won't leave me. I'll take care of these."

Forrest grinned and shook his head. "I don't think so, 'Licia. I'll just take care of 'em myself."

"Suit yourself," Felicia answered, but retained one of the two identical notes. "You do the desk, I'll run up to your room. Come on, sugar; it'll take far too long for you to do both. Quick, what number?"

"One-oh-four," Forrest answered, "And be sure to close the door."

Felicia was gone in a flurry of long legs and high heels.

Forrest walked to the desk clerk and asked that his note be given to Jenny O'Neill. He hadn't turned from the desk when a gray Suburban drew up, honking its horn.

"We'd better go," Tom said.

Forrest followed his partner. Once safely in the Suburban, he accepted the glass handed him by a ravishing brunette who begged him to tell her how he could take a fall like he had today and still come back to top the go-round in roping. Forrest guzzled his liquid tongue-loosener and felt its effect immediately, launching into the story and spicing it up to the whole carload's delight. He hardly lost a beat in his tale when Felicia stuck her head in the vehicle and called the brunette away momentarily. Only the brunette, and not Felicia, returned.

"Felicia says to go ahead, Val," the brunette said, worming her way back to Forrest. "She met some guy in the lobby."

Forrest relaxed and slurped his second vodka, continuing the yarn as Val gunned the motor. The Suburban lunged, fitting so well into Forrest's narrative that the passengers shrieked and laughed all the way to the first stoplight.

Jenny felt the hands of her cousin, but their comfort couldn't penetrate the deep place into which she had withdrawn.

"Gone?" Jenny asked again. "But she wasn't even sick. A headache. Just a headache. She got them all the time. I get them. People don't die from headaches!"

Aneurysm, Jenny heard her father saying. *A broken blood vessel in the brain, daughter, they're telling me. And nothing we could have done to stop it, even if we had known. I'll not have you thinking your mother...passed on...because of anything you or any of us did. There was no helping it, my girl. My girl...*

Was his voice just part of the day's nightmare? Her father had slipped away to the lounge, she and Al had gone for ice to replenish the melted cubes in her mother's washcloth. Virginia O'Neill wasn't dying then! She wasn't dead now. But they had taken her away, hours ago, and Jenny could understand none of it.

"Jen?"

Al's voice this time. Jenny raised herself from the bed where she lay: her mother's bed, where her mother had last lain.

"The desk just got a message for you. From Forrest."

Forrest. The name roused Jenny, and she turned to the bed table.

130

"But the phone's back on the hook. Mother doesn't have a headache now.... Why didn't he call?"

"I guess he did call, only not here. This isn't his writing. They must've copied down what he said. Want me to read it to you?"

Jenny nodded and lay down.

Al sat beside her, touching her hand. "Forrest says Tom's gone out to eat, but he'll wait for you at his room and to please come as soon as you can. He says if he's catching some sleep, come on in and wake him up because he's more hungry than he is tired. You want to go see him, Jen? Maybe it'd be good if we all ate. Your dad went to get something at the lounge. Jen?"

"I'm not hungry." She didn't open her eyes.

"But you haven't eaten since —"

"Neither has Forrest." Jenny sluggishly looked around the room, still hoping to see her mother. "He doesn't even know about...any of this, does he?" she asked in a monotone.

"I don't imagine so."

"I think..." she pushed herself to a standing position, letting Al's hand drop to the bed, "I think I'd like to go see him."

"I'll drive you."

"I can drive," Jen said in the same flat voice.

"Not tonight," Al said gently. "I'll drive you over. I won't intrude on you two. I'll just wait in the lobby until you're ready to come back or decide what you want to do next."

Next? Jenny wanted only to die too. Mutely, she followed her cousin downstairs, outside, to the pickup, seeing nothing. She hadn't even realized Al had stopped the vehicle at Forrest's hotel until Al announced it.

"You go ahead, Jen. Remember Forrest's room number?"

"Second floor," Jenny answered vaguely.

"Room one-oh-four. Want me to come with?"

"No." Jenny stepped out of the pickup. "If I'm up there more than a half hour, Forrest'll bring me back to the hotel, so don't wait long for me." Jenny slammed the door, then opened it. "Al?"

Her cousin's gray eyes still held tears, and Jenny wondered without interest if she looked as worn from crying as Al did.

"Yes, Jen?"

"Thanks." Jenny pushed the door closed and plodded to the hotel.

No message awaited her at the front desk, and Jenny wished she hadn't stopped to check. The man had stared at her. Apparently she did look a wreck. She climbed the stairs to Forrest's floor, thankful for the dimness and somber colors.

Room 104. Jenny halted before it, wishing now that Al was with her. Al had been her strength throughout the ordeal, holding her while she wailed hysterically at finding her mother dead, tracking down her father, calling the police or whoever had come over to take…the body. Now Jen felt so alone. Even to Forrest, could she relate what had happened? Could she stand to say the words and make it all real?

The door was open a crack, and Jenny pushed hesitantly, expecting darkness. She was only half wrong. A candle burned at the end of the room, shedding weak, flickering light.

A candle? Jenny stepped forward, into the room, leaving the door open behind her. The hall light was better than the candlelight, but only encroached on the blackness partway into the room, ending at a pair of…feminine feet?

Jenny saw the rest of the picture as a series of rapid-fire snapshots: high heels, the backs of long, curved legs, a short, pale dress above them that glimmered in the candlelight. A woman, whose hair flowed down her back and rippled with the embraces of the man standing beyond her, holding her, his hands buried in her tresses. A cowboy, with dark chaps that stuck out on either side of the woman's slender legs. A cowboy, wearing a black, gold-studded Resistol hat that pushed against the woman's bleached-blond hair, tilting her head backwards. Forrest.

And Felicia.

Jenny's screams echoed down the hallway, stairway, lobby, parking lot, subsiding only as she collapsed into the pickup and repeated one word over and over: "Home! Home! Home. Home..." Her tears overtook her voice, but Al got the message and brought her back to the hotel.

Once there, Al took over: finding Jenny's father, getting her dinner, doing all their packing, staying up with Jenny through the night. Al saw them off the next morning, but Jenny didn't fully realize she and her cousin had split ways until she crossed the Washington state line. Her father prodded her with talk, which Jenny answered in mumbles. Only the radio comforted her. The familiar country-western tunes brought her back to a time of happiness, and she submerged into them as far as she could, surfacing partially to attend her mother's funeral and accept condolences from what seemed like everyone in Gillette.

Jenny and her father stayed with friends until after the funeral. Then they made a last stop at their trailer house and climbed into the pickup again, heading westward, to a little house in rural Oklahoma.

14

FORREST'S MORNING HANGOVER quickly became habitual. After the hazy night with Val Nolan and unidentified company first at the Steak Shack, and then, inexplicably, at the Ellensburg circuit of private parties, Forrest awakened with a sense of guilt sharper than the noises assailing his head. Jen, however, couldn't be found to hear his confession. From dread at displeasing her, Forrest passed rapidly into fear. Where on earth had she gone?

Tom had been little help, preoccupied with his own night's consequences. But they had finally tracked Jen down, only to learn that she would neither see Forrest nor accept any phone call or note. Traveling to Oklahoma had only gained them entrance into the Ivers' country blue living room, where Margaret had regretfully relayed the news: Jen was recuperating from her mother's death and would not compete for at least the rest of the season. Al, too, was out. She'd returned to Wisconsin to grieve with her family, then stayed on to pursue an eight-year veterinary degree.

The two young men wandered for weeks afterward, showing up at arenas like lost calves who didn't know what to do with themselves — until the rodeo began. Then they rode with abandon, each on his bronc or bull, caring nothing for the danger: spurring madly, angering their mounts, riding the edge between control and disaster. Their efforts propelled them upward in the PRCA's Crown Royal world standings. In roping, however, their timing was off, their throws wild, their catches sloppy. After each rodeo, they drank, to celebrate...and forget.

One night in October, after competing well in riding, miserably in roping at the Industry Hills Charity Pro Rodeo, Forrest and Tom took their positions at the nearest thing they could find to a cowboy bar in City of Industry, California.

"You gonna try callin' Jen again?" Tom slurred, spilling half his schnapps on the table, then studying the design soaking into the splintery wood.

"Naw," Forrest answered. "Looks like a bull, don't it?"

"What?" Tom asked blankly.

"That spot you made on the table. Reminds me of a bull..." Forrest's mind began replaying an old childhood reel, a feature film set in San Francisco, starring Sterling Jackson Jr. Forrest stopped the movie before its climax and gestured over Tom's head for the barmaid to bring refills.

As she approached, he noticed a derelict rise from where he'd been drinking and dozing at the bar. The drunk followed the barmaid, banging into the tables she carefully avoided as she carried her tray over her head.

"Tom," Forrest said hoarsely. "Think we got a show comin' up. Some ol' boy..." His words dwindled as the man and maid came closer. "Tom. Your daddy." Tom turned and Forrest took his drink, observing the familiar scene.

Tom and his father traded little chitchat during the exchange. Money was their only bond, and once that was transferred, the interview ended. Bob Rawlings did lay a hand on his son's back before leaving, a touching sight, Forrest thought. He watched the broken-down champion leave the bar and felt almost glad his own father had died. Sterling Jackson Jr. had died with respect, at least.

"You gonna let him do that your whole life?" Forrest slammed his drink down his throat before recalling that they only had a few dollars earmarked for the night's festivities. Now, thanks to Bob Rawlings, they had a fistful fewer.

"What?"

"Don't sit there askin' 'what' all night. You gonna let your daddy take our drinkin' money all the time?"

"Wasn't drinkin' money," Tom mumbled. "Was entry money."

"For the rodeo tomorrow? What're you thinkin', Tom?"

His friend managed a wobbly grin and scratched his brown head of hair. "Thinkin', Forr?" He laughed. "Haven't done that since —"

"I know. Since Al left. Why didn't you ever tell her you were loco about her? I didn't even know. Thought that ended with high school."

"She knew," said Tom. "I know she did. Didn't matter —"

"Like me an' Jen," Forrest slipped into Tom's mournful tone. "Didn't matter."

"Sorry, sorry," Tom babbled, flopping his hand on Forrest's arm.

"Yeah," Forrest said. "So, what do we do now?" He explored his pockets and disgorged a few dollars. "Too late to hock anything or wire Granddad. Have to do that before the rodeo. Now we better get some sleep an' hope we win tomorrow. Or is it today?"

Tom flung his wrist on the table and narrowed his eyes at his watch. "Today, I think. Better get to the pickup. I get the passenger side. Where'd we park, anyway? Forr," he said, grabbing his friend's unbuttoned sleeve in drunken earnestness. "Where'd we leave the horses?"

Forrest stood, staggered, then straightened himself, helping Tom upright. "We got the horses bedded down hours ago. They'll sleep good, anyway," he said, thinking of his pillow for the night, the steering wheel.

They left the bar, arguing about where they might've parked the pickup.

Margaret Iver spread the open book on the kitchen table, pausing in her reading to look through the window at her niece riding the crest of the hill. Sunrise made both horse and rider blazing images, black silhouettes against the fiery oranges of morning.

Margaret turned to the words before her:

As the deer pants for streams of water,
so my soul pants for you, O God.
My soul thirsts for God, for the living God.
When can I go and meet with God?
My tears have been my food day and night...

"What're you reading, my red-haired beauty?" Willy asked, pouring himself a cup of coffee and offering her one in the unspoken language of those long, and happily, married.

She shook her head at the coffee. "I'm in Psalm Forty-two."

"Still?" He sat down beside her and smoothed a wrinkle in the checkered tablecloth, then covered his wife's hand with his, resting his finger on her wedding band.

She smiled dully. "I can't seem to move out of it since Virginia's funeral." She raised her eyes to the hills, but the sun flooded over them. No sign of horse or rider marked the horizon. "How do you think Jenny's doing, Willy?"

"San frantastic, considering." He sipped his coffee.

"Considering?"

"That she's a sweet, lovely girl — lost and in misery, unable to be comforted."

"Yes." Margaret quickly reread her verse. "This is my comfort, Willy. Our comfort. I know Virginia loved the Lord and is with him now. I know he's strengthening me despite my sorrow at losing her. I can read his Word, pray to him, speak with him, with you. But ...but who does Jenny talk to?"

They both looked out the window, where their niece passed each day, riding, riding, riding aimlessly. She was yet nowhere to be seen.

Margaret stood and leaned over the counter, pressing closer to the window. "There she is, Willy." Relief colored her voice. "She's doing the course. She's racing again."

Willy did not look up. "A peculiar but endearing lot, racers. Never have understood you people. Why do it if she's not going to compete?"

"Security. The security of routine." Margaret reseated herself. "I wish I could reach her."

"Maybe you can," Willy said eagerly. He'd obviously been waiting for this moment. "And maybe only you. Work with her, Margaret. Ride with her, teach her. You still have your old racing books?"

"And some new ones, but —"

"Then join her, meet her on her own turf. Break out Prince and show her the stuff that made you two winners."

"I couldn't. What Prince and I do anymore hardly qualifies as racing."

"You know that's not what matters." Willy brought his cup to the sink, rinsed it, and set it in the dishwasher. "Teach Jenny about racing, then teach her about the Lord, through your love for her. You two used to fritter away hours together over the most addle-pated nonsense. You both loved it. And she's always listened to you."

"But she was a little girl then," Margaret protested.

"She's a little girl now. Give it your best. I have the utmost faith in you, and in the Lord. Don't be afraid to share her pain. Maybe she can share your joy."

"My joy? What joy have I felt lately?"

"It's buried, but it's there." Willy laid his fingertip on a verse further along in the psalm. "'Why are you downcast, O my soul? Why so disturbed within me? Put your hope in God, for I will yet praise him.'" He kissed his wife's cheek. "I've been praying about this since Jenny came to us. She came to *us*, Margaret. Don't you think that means something?"

"Yes, of course. And I've tried to talk with her, but she never seems to hear me."

"Don't talk," Willy said, kissing her again. "Live. And love."

Al sat cross-legged on her study desk, leaning forward until her face touched the cool window. City lights reflected in the lake below her dormitory, and past the lake. The city itself shimmered, stealing glory from the stars above it.

The dorm register kicked in, and Al let it blow on her bare legs until the vent grew hot. She slid ceramic bricks over the openings and stood in front of the plate-glass window, her plaid cotton night-shirt hanging just below her kneecaps. The dorm room's lights were all off, so that she was invisible to the world she looked down on.

The scene often compelled her to put her books away and gaze on it. Here she had seen the leaves turn color, then fall, leaving sharp-elbowed tree limbs that became black with night, gray with day as they stood sentry along the lake's edge.

The lights in the water reminded Al of arena lights. Even though she had found friends and unexpected pleasure in her classes and in campus life, rodeo was something she couldn't completely forget.

She still was half-surprised to be at college, half-shocked at the circumstances that had snatched her from the arena and plopped her at academia. Once she fled Forrest's hotel, Jen had sunk into herself, and Al couldn't reach her. Al knew she couldn't race on her own, and more than that, she felt a poignant longing for her own mother, a desperate desire to fly home and see that death had not robbed her as well.

After a weekend of home-cooked meals and homespun conversation, Al found herself at college. The strange surroundings had disoriented her, but frequent calls and visits from her mother and grandmother, and less frequent calls from Jen, made Al's transition easier. Four years, her mother reminded her, and then she could start veterinary school. Another four after that, and she could come home and work with the animals she had always loved. Forever.

"Dr. Alison Austin," her mother had begun calling her, and it sounded good to Al, felt good to finally have her mother's approval. Not so good was the sound of Jen's voice, spiritless and impassive, yet a reminder of something...best forgotten. For now.

Alison went home for weekends and breaks whenever she could, reveling in the new peace between her mother and father. Grandma often came to visit, and they would play cards or tell stories, or even sing. Somehow Grandma always made the evening end with Bible reading, and Al enjoyed the whole fabric of these nights, filled with the thick weave of family.

She spent long hours outdoors as well, helping her father with chores or making sure Ironside hadn't forgotten her. Though the weather made horseback rides chilly, both she and the gelding loved racing through the woods, tramping over the crunchy leaves, seeing an occasional flake of snow. Winter. It would soon be here. Soon midquarters, then finals. Christmas break...and spring. She and Ironside could race at the local rodeos come summer. He had to keep sharp; they both did, in case...

Al hopped from the desk and flipped on a lamp near her biology textbook. She opened it, studying a table of taxonomic classifications that had to be memorized before morning. She pushed her curls back from her face and took a rubber band from the desk drawer, binding her hair into a thick ponytail, never noticing the picture that tipped out of the drawer and fell noiselessly to the tiled floor. It was a picture of two cowgirls and two cowboys standing in front of a beat-up white pickup, draping their arms around each other and grinning crazily. One of the group stood apart, throwing his black, gold-studded hat in the air.

Although he wasn't looking at the camera, Al could still see his Technicolor eyes.

CHAPTER

15

THROUGH THE NEXT YEAR, OUTWARD SIGNS of Jenny's malaise disappeared while the inner gall grew. She rejected all contact with circuit racing but threw herself into the race itself, absorbing all her aunt taught her, devoting whole days to working the pattern, mentally and physically. Cloverleaf grew stronger, swifter, and despite her aunt and uncle's best efforts, Jenny hardened.

While competition had always been important to her, it now became paramount. Day by week by month, she itched to make her comeback, to grind smug Felicia Newcastle and her mount into the dirt at last, to wear a PRCA world championship buckle. To have a single focus that would give her shattered life purpose again. But always thoughts of Forrest stopped her. And thoughts of her mother.

It'll never be like it was, Jenny thought, drifting into the soliloquies that had come to drown out all spoken voices in her life. *It'll never —*

"Jenny? Jenny?" Aunt Margaret's call finally broke through.

Jenny looked toward the house and saw her aunt flapping her apron, a sign that meant some urgent reason for summons. Walking Cloverleaf, Jenny rehearsed the new nonverbal racing signals she had learned. These indeed might be the clinchers to fame.

"Jenny, your father's on the phone." Aunt Margaret reached for Clover's reins. "I'll cool your horse down. You go on inside."

Jenny slid to the ground and kicked the soil from her boots at the door. She took her boots off altogether before crossing the blue shag of the living room. Picking up the phone and putting it to her ear, Jenny slumped onto the couch. "Daddy?"

"My girl, my girl. Jenny. And how good it is to be hearing your voice!"

Her lips felt the faintest touch of a smile. *Daddy's laying the Irish on even thicker since he moved to PRCA.* "It's good to hear you too, Daddy. What's going on?"

"And can't I be calling my girl for no reason at all, if I'm wanting?" he asked, sounding comically offended.

"An' sure I am that you're not doing just that," Jenny said in her worst brogue. She reverted to her normal Wyoming accent. "What is it, Daddy?"

"That's my girl, always cutting to the finish. It's this: I'm thinking it's time for you to be joining me."

Her father evidently took her silence as an indication that she was considering his statement. "I've got the trailer in travel shape, and I've a new green pickup ready to haul you and Clover to whatever rodeo I'm going to."

"Green?"

He chuckled. "Irish, Irish, my girl. It's what makes me stand out, my ticket to the top shows. Though I'll not have you thinking I'm doing anything but first-rate performances even now," he rushed on, listing a dozen or so names of places Jenny had been contemplating.

"You've got all those shows lined up?"

"And more." When he spoke again, his Irish, along with his

voice, had softened. "But I'm needing you with me, my girl. Won't you give your old dad a chance? You can go back to Margaret's and Willy's if you decide to. But I'm feeling..." He cleared his throat. "I think it would be pleasing to your mother, looking down at us, to see that we're still together, still a family."

No other words could have affected Jenny as much. *Family. Home...on the road?*

A jangle of thoughts assaulted her. *Back where you started? You won't find your mother there. You won't find Al. It won't be the same.*

No, it won't. Jenny made herself understand this. If she were to go back, it wouldn't be with any blinders on.

Forrest will be there. Forrest. And Felicia.

A candlelit scene flashed through her mind, but Jenny extinguished it. "When...do you want me, Daddy?"

"That's my girl! I'll be coming through next week."

Seven days? Hardly time to say good-bye, time to think what her decision would mean. *No,* she corrected herself. *I'm closing the door on the past. And on the future. No more regrets, no more dreams. From now on, it's racing. Just racing. Now.*

She listened to her father's happy exclamations and plans for them, all the while weighing what she would bring with her, what she would leave. *The books Aunt Margaret gave me, the racing outfits she's made, Clover's new tack.* All these things would go. The love and consolation her aunt and uncle had given her would stay, along with everything she associated with her mother or Forrest — though she had already disposed of most things connected with Forrest.

I can do it. Alone.

Jenny repeated this until she heard a long break in her father's voice. "What, Daddy?"

"Are you agreeing with me or not? Or are you wanting to get

started before the Friday night performance?"

"Friday. Friday's fine." Jenny listened to his farewells, then dropped the receiver in the cradle. "Friday." She took a deep breath, and when she released it, she released her history as well. "From now on, we ride."

She left the house and found her aunt walking Cloverleaf outside the practice arena. Jenny reached for her horse's head, waiting as her aunt climbed down. "I think I'll do some more practicing before we eat. Daddy's picking Clover and me up Friday, and we need to be ready."

Jenny saw the disappointment and questions in her aunt's eyes, and before she mounted, she kissed the middle-aged woman. "I wouldn't have been ready for the circuit without you. Thanks, Aunt Margaret. It's one thing I won't forget." She swept into the saddle and kicked Cloverleaf into a gallop.

While they'd each ridden at the PRCA's circuit finals, the NFR had been beyond the grasp of both Forrest and Tom. But a new season brought new chances, and as they strategized and practiced and entered all the big-money rodeos they could before hitting the PRCA's 125 rodeo per year ceiling, the two cowboys found little time for self-pity — except after a show.

In some ways, Tom had it easier than his traveling partner. Al did not make occasional appearances as Jenny did. Each time Forrest saw her and couldn't get near her, he drank harder than he had before. When Jenny made it clear, again and again, that she had no desire to reconcile, Forrest took to calling himself "Forrest Fire" and began establishing his own harem...one night at a time.

Tom soon began adopting his partner's ways, and found the

same emptiness that drove Forrest to greater depths each passing weekend. They made it a rule not to drink when it would interfere with their performances, but once they did that last run, they made up for their abstinence.

But they were strong young men. Alcohol didn't affect them, much. When it did, they cut back a little, practiced a lot, thought less about life and more about rodeo. And so it was that by the end of the year, they rode the bubble into the NFR.

That is, Forrest did.

Tom only made it for team roping, and as he pondered his friend's greater success, he was pretty sure why Forrest had made the Finals and he hadn't. Tom loved riding as much as Forrest did, but Forrest had experienced broken dreams as a child, losing his mother to rejection and his father to death. He'd learned to live with loss, to go on despite it, or maybe *to* spite it. But Tom felt each new loss mounting on the last. When he didn't make the cut in bull riding, he spent many nights alone, thinking.

Even in the hardest days of going down the road, when the pickup or the tent was his and Forrest's only option for housing, and a hot dog their only option for nourishment, Tom had felt better about himself. He had something valuable then that he knew he was losing. Self-respect. *Or maybe,* he thought, *it was just self-righteousness.* His father still came for handouts, but he'd stick around to drink, swap glory-day stories, and listen to Tom's and Forrest's latest conquests in and out of the arena. Yes, Bob Rawlings was beginning to fit right in with his son. Or was his son beginning to fit in with him?

"For all have sinned and fall short of the glory of God." The words of an old cowboy from Sallislaw rang in Tom's ears sometimes, and not even the world championship buckle that he and Forrest won for

roping muffled them. The words spurred Tom on, but so did the drinks, so did the women, so did the riding and roping — in the opposite direction. Tom felt he couldn't keep up with the speed of his lifestyle much longer, but a new season began, and the pace grew even more frenzied.

Traveling was easier now, with the money and prestige they had won. But drinking became more expensive, drinking buddies more numerous. And parties. And women. And still the demand to perform, to win.

"For all have sinned and fall short of the glory of God."

Now Tom knew sin, and he had the distinct feeling that one of these days, he would fall short, like a poorly thrown lasso. When sober, he feared he already had. When drunk, he could make the idea float away. When practicing or performing, he could block out any thought of it. When he slept, his dreams tortured him.

His only satisfaction was inside the arena, but even that space seemed to be closing in. He tried to ignore it and made it through another season. Made it, and made it big, wowing capacity crowds at Fort Worth, Cheyenne, Salinas, Pendleton. The year passed, a collage of icepacks, adhesive tape, and "medicinal" alcohol administered liberally by a string of assorted buckle bunnies.

After performing at the Cow Palace, Tom nearly collapsed. When Forrest woke from his own excesses, he pummeled his friend into shape for the NFR a month later. And after ten days of competition at the Thomas and Mack arena in Las Vegas, he and Tom walked off with a second world champion team-roping buckle. And Forrest won the world for saddle-bronc riding.

Celebrating began, instead of ending, at the NFR's year-end awards banquet in Caesar's Palace, where both cowboys were too soused to stand without help. They did the town that night, and

Tom never could remember all that happened. He did recall a barroom fight with his father, and then another with someone who tried to fight his father. He remembered the startling flash of a blade, and cutting pain in the hand he stretched to ward off the interloper. He remembered his father shuffling toward the exit as he lay on the floor, looking with detached interest at his own blood. He remembered waking in a hotel room and the phone ringing him to his senses. He looked up to see multi-images of Forrest answering it and setting down the receiver after only a few words.

"Tom?"

"Yeah."

Forrest sat on the corner of the bed, holding his head. "How's your hand?"

Tom lifted it and saw a neat, white wrapping. "I don't know. What happened?"

"Got a little help for you last night. You're patched up okay, but you probably won't rope or ride for a while." Forrest lifted his hat from the phone table and set it gingerly on his head. "You...were drinking pretty hard."

"Yeah." Tom's stomach knew the full truth of it, and Tom crawled off the bed, intending to make another pilgrimage to the bathroom.

"Tom."

"Yeah, Forrest, what? I've gotta —"

"Your daddy was drinking, too. He died last night. Car crash. Hit a train."

Tom staggered into the bathroom and retched, purging himself of what he could. Forrest was gone when he emerged. By early evening, Tom had bought himself a Silverado and a single-horse trailer, thrown his gear in the back, loaded his mount, and left Las

Vegas. He had one plan: to return to the Circle H and see his father buried at the Mancos Woodland Cemetery, next to his mother. As for rodeo, the awful, dead feeling in his stomach remained. He drove away with his one good hand, hearing a Bible verse that replayed over and over, like the clatter of hail on the windshield.

PART III

Dream Riders

16

"SPORTS SECTION!" Al yanked the door closed behind her and surged up the entryway steps, pushing off the third and fifth to miss the loose board of the fourth step. Still wearing her winter coat, although she had paused long enough in the garage to kick off her barn boots, Al sprinted toward the newspaper in her father's hands. "Dad, I've got to have the sports section. I want to know if —"

Al saw the headline and read. The tension in the newspaper ceased as she released it and did a two-step around the kitchen table, adding a move she hadn't done since high school. Her socks slid across the worn gold-print linoleum. "Fran-tastic!"

"Thought you'd know about it by now, Al. Didn't they announce it on the radio?"

"The radio's still broken. That hanger you put on to replace the antenna doesn't make it. When I went to do chores, the paper hadn't come yet, and I knew I'd wake you and Mom if I turned on the set." Al kissed her father's prickly face, her lips brushing his sixties-style salt-and-pepper sideburns as she straightened. "Have they been talking about it on TV?"

"How should I know? I'm not the one who watches that thing, and your mother's gone to town. Left before I was even awake. Can't understand why Rhoda puts up with her visits. Sun's barely up." He shook out his newspaper and paged to the variety section as Al headed into the living room.

She found the remote hidden under the magazine rack and channel-surfed until she saw a likely-looking newscaster. The black box at the bottom of the screen identified the station as ESPN. Al settled into her father's brown vinyl recliner.

The announcer was reciting hockey scores, but ESPN handled big-league rodeo news, and according to the article in the newspaper, ESPN would be the main station to transmit the Professional Rodeo Exposition, billed as the world's first hundred-million-dollar rodeo series. ESPN would surely take every opportunity to parade their baby before the world, but Al could hardly stand wading through the hockey scores to see it.

She glanced through the bay window at the snowbanks along the curved driveway and traced a crack in the recliner's arm, making the tear worse.

Maybe the newspaper has another article somewhere about the Ex. Al kicked the footrest back into the recliner just as the Professional Rodeo Cowboys Association's logo flashed on-screen behind the announcer. Al thumbed up the sound.

"...and the PRCA officially announced early this morning that the Professional Rodeo Exposition, in partnership with the top associations and sponsors of professional rodeo, will start after next year's season. Hopeful contestants will be looking past the National Finals Rodeo this year to the biggest year-long event in rodeo history: the Pro Rodeo Ex."

Alison listened to the fifteen-minute report, memorizing the information and watching clips of the hottest names in rodeo air their feelings about the Ex's impending opening. The reigning Miss

Rodeo USA said the news made this Thanksgiving the most thankful ever, and that she was going to cross her fingers the entire time so that her sister, Felicia, would get a chance to barrel race for a million. Al grimaced, but the interview quickly passed on to others.

"Greatest thing to hit rodeo since the horse," said one cowboy, his blue eyes bursting with Technicolor. Al leaned forward.

"And will you be riding in the Ex?" The reporter shoved the mike near the cowboy's face.

The cowboy swiped his smooth chin with the back of his hand as if wiping off his brilliant smile. "Hope to."

"In which event? Team roping or saddle bronc?" the reporter pressed.

The cowboy appeared neither hurried nor bothered. He looked into the camera as if he could see millions of fans and wanted each to share rodeo's finest hour with him. "I hope to ride in both events. Wouldn't miss it for anything. Not a second of it — not even eight seconds."

The reporter gave a perfunctory laugh and turned to the camera as the cowboy nodded and ambled away. Al watched him disappear down the dusty length of some indoor arena.

"And that was Forrest Jackson," the reporter drawled, stepping forward to block out Forrest's lank, retreating form. "Forrest is a two-time former world champion in team roping and the current top contender. He'll also qualify at next month's NFR for saddle-bronc riding, rodeo's classic eight-second event in which he is a three-time world champion. Forrest comes from a line of champions — his daddy, Sterling Jr., took six world championships in bull riding before the sport did him in. I'm sure Forrest'll keep up his daddy's good name at the Pro Rodeo Ex. All the stars of professional rodeo will be out for the Ex, and I bet even those cowboys whose chaps have turned to dust'll be watching from that roundup in the sky."

The scene cut back to the studio announcer. "We'll be waiting to see who the Ex chooses for this invitational rodeo series. Scouts worldwide will be monitoring next year's big bucks rodeos, selecting the top ten world contenders and top rookie in each of the seven events. But young riders shouldn't despair if they don't make the cut. Wild-card contestants can register for a chance to ride in each of the fifty Pro Rodeo Ex season rodeos. And everyone — veterans and rookies alike — will have to qualify at each rodeo to compete in the titan of all professional rodeo series, the Pro Rodeo Exposition. In other news, the baseball strike continues —"

Al switched off the set and stared at the opaque screen, seeing in her mind's eye an image of a blue-eyed cowboy with a smile responsible for scores of country-western heartbreak songs. She still had a verse or two of her own she could have added to them.

"Going to try for the Ex, Al?" Her father leaned against the recliner and touched her lightly on the shoulder in a great show of affection, for him.

"I'd love to." Al smiled but knew it was a smile made by her lips only, not like Forrest's now-famous smile.

"But?"

"You know how Mom would react. I hear the same pep talk after every quarter: 'Well done, darling; you made the dean's list. But don't look back — keep going, and after you're done with your degree, then...' She's said it three times a year for almost four years. The problem is, Dad, the Ex won't wait. I'd have to compete this coming season just to have a hope of qualifying."

Father and daughter looked up as a battered cream-colored station wagon turned down the driveway, spewing snow and skidding up to the garage. A woman with a tightly curled strawberry-blond hairdo pointed a garage-door opener ahead of her like a gun, repeatedly pressing the button, her hand moving up and down with the motion.

"Al, I haven't showed your mother I've got much sense, and she'll probably be furious with me, but I think you should try for the Ex. Promise is looking strong. The neighbor girl's been working him daily in the old shed, all winter long. You've kept yourself in good shape. You're rusty, but if you start training right now, you could be ready to race when the season starts over. I've saved some money, and you could travel with Jenny and Uncle Barney, hit the southern shows —"

He halted as a distant slamming of doors came from the garage. "This is your chance, Al. If you want to take it, take it. I'll help." He folded his newspaper under his arm and walked into the kitchen. Al followed.

The door opened and Eileen Austin entered, carrying two brown paper bags. She kicked at the loose entryway step before coming into the kitchen and setting her parcels on the counter. "Hello, hello. Shut the door for me, will you, Alison? I couldn't manage it with these bags." She rummaged through the groceries as Al obeyed. "I picked up a few more things for tonight's feast — nearly had to bang the doors to pieces to do it. They kept me freezing outside, saying it was too early to shop. Can you imagine?"

She talked on as she put away her purchases. "I bought some fruit for the Christmas Julekage. We'll have to bake that one of these days, Alison, or your grandmother will make our names mud at Senior Manor and all over town, too. That's the problem with living in a small town — one of the problems, I should say."

Al took the plastic container of translucent green, red, and yellow fruit and put it in its traditional place in the top of the pantry.

Her mother pushed past her, putting a pack of Velveeta on the bottom shelf and slamming the pantry doors. Then she surveyed her daughter, hands on her hips.

"Alison, you're a positive mess. You still haven't changed from your barn clothes, and anyone could drop by this morning." She moved nearer to tuck a dark-blond lock into Al's ponytail. "What's worse, you reek. It's bad enough you insist on laying off the hired man and taking over the milking whenever you're home on break, but don't you even think to wash up afterwards?"

"She was excited, Eileen." With his big farmer's hands, Harvey signaled Al to speak.

Al faced her mother. "That's right. They're going ahead with it. The Professional Rodeo Exposition will begin —"

"Yes, yes. Now rodeo's trying to preempt Thanksgiving, too. I heard all about it at the store." Eileen opened the fridge to put the produce away. "Pro Rodeo schmo. So what? You've moved beyond rodeo, Alison. In a few more years, you'll be the best little vet on this side of —"

"How would you feel about Al being the best little barrel racer before she's the best little vet? There's plenty of time for her to finish up her degree afterwards, Eileen. Right, Al?"

Al's competitive drive stopped short of her mother. In a contest with Eileen Austin, Al felt she wouldn't even make it out of the chute. She lowered her eyes as her mother swung around.

"Is that true, Alison? You are quitting school for...for rodeo?" Eileen stood by the sink, where she had started to wash a head of lettuce.

"I wouldn't be quitting, just taking a breather...if I did decide to try for the Exposition. I want to think on it. I just heard about it a few minutes ago." As she felt her mother's eyes slide away from her,

Al shot a look at her father. "But I just might want to see if I can ride in it," she added.

Harvey smiled and sat down, opening his paper like a shield as his wife wheeled to face Al. "You have one quarter of undergraduate work before you go on to veterinary school. One quarter! I've never heard such complete and utter —"

"If I make it in the Ex, you get a mansion instead of this old farmhouse, okay? And we'll get the equipment Dad needs for the farm. And I'll finish school without any loans." Al laid her arm around her mother's shoulders. "There's not much chance I'll qualify, even if I join the Women's Professional Rodeo Association and try for the Ex as a rookie."

Eileen stepped away from her embrace. "I'm not a fool, Alison. Whenever, wherever you compete, you succeed, even if you're just doing summer shows. I thought after Ironside died you'd given up for good, but as soon as your father managed to rustle Promise over here, I knew: It was starting again."

"Rodeo helped Al get through last year's school bills, Eileen. It's helped her get through every year's bills. She belongs in rodeo. The whole town knows that, all except for you. Why else would they chip in for Promise?" Harvey ventured.

"I'm not sure that they did." Eileen looked at him suspiciously. "Who in this town has enough money to buy a good barrel horse?"

Harvey's head sank beneath his paper. "Promise was given to Al in the town council's name. That means the whole town bought him." He hazarded a glance at his wife before gripping his shield more firmly. "They're proud of her, Eileen, like you should be. Al's put Gilman on the map."

"I know, I know." Eileen turned to stare at Al. "You win, but you risk everything, every time. For what? To what end? I thought I'd pulled you out of that...that expressway to nowhere. I thought you were on your way to safety, security. A comfortable, sane life. But I was wrong. You're going right back." Her face registered fear, not anger, a much more difficult emotion for Al to confront.

Al steeled herself. *I'm not giving in. I tried it her way, and I still think about rodeo as much as I did when I left. Maybe I need to go back. Maybe I have to. I love...well, there's something about rodeo that won't let me go yet...* Al didn't allow her thoughts to stray further. "Mother, to make the Ex, I'd be competing against the best in the nation, the best in the world. I've never ridden in the PRCA circuit, and I've never even tried Promise in competition. Anything could happen. Least of all that I'll be chosen."

Her mother's mouth was a bitter line. "I suppose I'd have more of a say in this if we'd helped put you through college, which I wanted to do, if we could have...if your father hadn't gone and played cowboy and got himself...oh, Alison, think about this, think about your future! If you fall in with some shiftless bull rider who'll maim himself and you too —"

"I promise you that will never happen," Al said, unable to curb a glance at her father.

Eileen charged on. "— or if you get hurt out there, ruin your chances...I won't forgive myself." She leveled her gray eyes at Al's. "I won't forgive you either, Alison. I couldn't. Or you." She looked at her husband, who was watching the debate over his paper.

"It's her choice, Eileen." Harvey dodged behind his newspaper.

"It is my choice, Mother. Mine. I don't want this to become a conflict between you and Dad."

"Well, it is, my dear." Eileen spun, slamming the lettuce into the sink as she retreated to her bedroom.

Harvey set down his paper. "Kudos, Al, you won the first go-round. Maybe you should've been a bronc buster instead of a barrel rider." He winked. "Keep it up and you'll be wowing them at the Ex, too. And your mother'll be there to cheer you on, if I know anything about her."

Al slowly walked to the sink and turned off the running water. "I hope you're right, Dad," she said, picking up the head of lettuce her mother had dropped and shrugging off the sudden chill that was only partly due to its wet, icy leaves.

Eileen wept into a pillow that was by now soggy. Not that anyone cared. She hadn't expected Harvey to come after her, although she had hoped that perhaps her own daughter hadn't come to disregard her the way her husband of twenty-four years had. But there was no penitent knock on the bedroom door.

When the last teardrop dried on her cheek, Eileen tried to wring out another. It would never do to let them think they hadn't hurt her. They had, badly, and they had to know. She wished they would know.

Eileen knelt on the double bed, feeling the worn knot pattern in the yellow spread sink into her flesh. Though her background boasted a solid Irish heritage, somehow the strong Catholic faith of her grandmother had not come down to her mother or herself. Had Eileen believed in penance, the tiny knots on the bedspread might have been useful tools for subduing her flesh and overcoming sin. But Eileen did not believe in sin, only stupidity. That, in her experience, was what caused life's disasters.

Alison, Alison. I swear to God that if you — Eileen corrected herself. *I swear you won't make my mistakes.* She took little comfort from her vow, knowing the small measure of her own power.

At such times, atheism seemed about as comforting as a cold shower; nevertheless, Eileen had learned to employ both heavily in the past decade. Despite everything she could think of to battle her desperation, however, it grew more unmanageable every year.

Alison was the only good that had come out of her marriage, her life. And now the only good was leaving. God knew when she'd come back. If she'd come back. There didn't seem to be a reason for Eileen to ever leave her bedroom.

17

BARNEY "BLARNEY" O'NEILL GREETED the security guard and approached the arena fencing. He lifted one green, gold-studded cowboy boot and leaned it on the white railing closest to the dirt floor, looking through the bars to watch his daughter working her quarter horse.

Though the Tex Williams Memorial Rodeo was long over, Jenny didn't seem to notice. Fans and contestants alike had given generously to aid the bull rider's family, then gone to the dance in the next building, where Barney himself had officially welcomed everyone. Because of the alternating darkness and strobe lights of the dance hall, almost an hour had passed before Barney realized his daughter wasn't there.

The dance's driving bass thrummed through the arena walls, and the sleek black gelding seemed to keep time with it, galloping hard, turning an imaginary barrel and sprinting to the opposite side, making another hairpin turn and bolting to the far end of the arena. Horse and rider completed their last circle only a few feet from where Barney leaned against the fencing.

Churned-up dirt landed at the stunted man's feet. He made no move, waiting and watching as the horse dashed to the unmarked finish line and stopped abruptly at the chutes, spraying more dirt. Then Barney cupped his hands and hollered, "And a very nice run that was, Jenny my girl!"

The young woman atop the black horse turned. Barney couldn't see her face, but her trademark chocolate-brown Stetson swiveled, and its silver-buckled band caught the arena's lights.

"Come down here, will you, daughter?"

Jenny posted toward him, dismounting and tying Cloverleaf's reins to the bars in a quick motion. "Yes, Daddy?"

"How is it that you're not at the dance, and everyone else is having such a good time?"

Jenny scuffed the dirt with her boots, getting soil and bits of debris in their western etching, a lighter shade of brown than the leather. "Because Cloverleaf and I didn't have a very good time tonight, Daddy." She ran her hand down the horse's black, sweaty neck.

"And didn't I announce to thousands of people less than two hours ago that you had the best run of the night? And they clapping and cheering for you and Clover both? You were one of the main publicity draws, Jenny. You disappointed no one except yourself. Tex's wife and children will be having plenty of money to see them through. Be happy and proud of that. Now give your horse and yourself a bit of rest. Come join the others."

Jenny stroked Cloverleaf as she untied him, letting the reins dangle in one hand while the other worked like a curry comb on his thick neck. "I'll have to give Clover a good rubdown first, and by then I probably won't feel like dancing. I want to think about what went wrong, so it won't happen again."

"You and Cloverleaf can't be in the sixteens or below every night, my girl. Now give your old father a chance to dance. No other woman there will be seen with me, not even for charity."

"Are you sure it's them?"

Barney heard the teasing in Jenny's voice. He reached his hand toward her, seeing a trace of the babe Virginia had prayed for for so long. He could never look at Jenny without thinking how proud Virginia had been of this daughter of theirs, the girl who had her mother's knack of cutting through the blarney, in horses and in people. "And you may be right," he admitted, wishing she would answer his smile with her own. "My sitting out might not be the ladies' fault at that. But I'd trade my mustache for one dance with you, my girl. Will you have me? Just one dance, to show that the world's best barrel racer still loves her old dad?"

"One dance, then. If you don't mind being seen with me."

"Jenny, if you are feeling so bad about your time, and you coming in first, how must the other girls be feeling? To be beaten by such a ragged pair as you and poor Clover?"

Jenny touched her father's arm, dusted with reddish freckles like her own. "All right." Her voice seemed to smile, even though her face refused the action. "I guess I am making too much of it. But with the NFR coming up and now the Exposition —"

"Sure things, both of them. You and Clover will be stealing the show. Now come and escort your old dad to the dance. Do a two-step in honor of Tex's memory. I'll be waiting for you by the gate."

Jenny gave a short nod and swung into her saddle, walking Clover around the arena for several more minutes until she disappeared out the gate at the other end.

When she returned, she was freshly showered and dazzling in a racing outfit he hadn't remembered seeing before: a satin shirt and short set with cream trim. The rosy brown fabric matched her hair and complexion.

"And you look like an angel, Jenny. A heavenly angel."

Jenny slipped her hand in her pocket and walked beside her father down the concrete walkway that stretched the length of the arena.

Barney repeated snippets of circuit gossip before breaking his news. "Oh, and I had a call tonight just before the rodeo. From your Uncle Harvey."

"Nothing's wrong?"

"Not a bit. Alison's decided to throw her hat in. She's trying for the Exposition at rookie status, applying for membership in the Women's Professional Rodeo Association. I'm thinking you and the other WPRA'ers will be glad to have her when you all take the Ex by storm, won't you, my girl?"

"If she makes it."

"And don't you think your cousin will be making it?"

"Has she even competed lately?"

"She's been busy with her schooling, but Harvey did say Alison rides in an IPRA rodeo now and then, though she's never tried the PRCA circuit. But last summer she won enough to pay all her college bills and bring some home to the farm besides. Harvey was saying she made Top Hand for July and would have made it for August, too, if she hadn't stopped competing when her horse went down."

"Ironside? He got hurt?" Concern softened the edge to Jenny's voice.

"They put him down. Had to, Harvey said, and I didn't feel right asking why. Before that, Alison and Ironside were taking the purse whenever they raced." Barney paused. "They had found their stride."

"Poor Al." Jenny glanced toward the back of the arena, where she had left Cloverleaf. "Losing Iron —"

"Ah, but you must be looking on the good side." Barney patted

Jenny's back. "She took Top Hand before he left, beating every full-timers' monthly winnings by three hundred dollars. Surprised them all with that, I wager, not being a rodeo regular." Barney's tone took on the shimmer of nostalgia. "But then she and you were always ones for surprising. I'll never forget the saddle and scholarships you bagged at the National High School Finals Rodeo. But you upset girls three years older than you more by getting Forrest Jackson to notice you than by all your winnings."

Barney stole a look at Jenny, watching for a flicker of emotion in her green eyes. "Then what happened, Jenny? You, Alison, Forrest, and his roping partner were closer than five bulldoggers in one pickup those next two summers, until Mother left us and you went away to Oklahoma. After that, I never saw you four together again. Even tonight, when Forrest won the saddle-bronc competition, you didn't even look his way. He looked yours, but you weren't looking at him. And you never do." *And you never smile anymore, either.*

Jenny was slow to reply. "Things change, Daddy. Didn't Mother's death change you?"

Barney swallowed his surprise. His daughter rarely mentioned her mother's death, and never so directly. Barney thought Jenny had buried her mother's memory and love as she had Forrest's. The sudden interment was both hopeful and painful.

"Yes," Barney replied, his voice uneven. "Your mother's death changed me, my girl. And only you are knowing how much. I pity Tex's wife, having to raise those five little ones all by herself. At least the children didn't see their daddy's bull wreck, and that's a mercy. It was difficult enough for me when your mother left us. I know it was hard for you."

Barney quickened his steps, putting distance between himself and the pain. "I didn't quit my work, though," he said, squeezing the tears from his voice only thanks to long elocutionary practice. "I kept announcing straight through, a hundred rodeos that season. And I didn't quit my friends, either, my girl." He put his arm around his daughter. "Jenny, don't you think it's time to find your friends?"

Did he read anger in Jenny's eyes? Sadness? Barney wasn't sure. He waited for her to speak, watching her so hard that he nearly bumped into one of the pillars in the arena's lobby. He held the glass door open, and as Jenny moved past him into the night air, she replied. "A lot of things changed after that summer, Daddy, for almost everyone I knew. Mother died, I went away, Al had to go to college, Forrest and Tom went on to glory, Tom eventually disappeared." She let the words trail behind her like a lasso that had missed its mark.

Her father caught up to her as they approached the noise and lights of the dance hall. "Old times can come back, Jenny. Harvey asked if Alison could travel with us after the NFR. I told him yes. Now don't be arguing with me, please, my girl; I think it will be good for you. You're needing your friends."

He raised beseeching palms, but Jenny was looking past him, down the hall, where a cowboy wearing a gold-studded black hat and blue chaps leaned against the shadowy entrance to the dance.

"Hey, Jen. Good win tonight."

Jenny had passed him safely the first time and hoped to give her father his dance and leave safely as well, but some of the fans had recognized her and asked for autographs. She'd been stupid to wear such obvious rodeo clothing, especially this outfit. And now Forrest had made his way through the crowd. Jenny had no escape — unless she made one.

She raised her voice to cut through the music. "Good win your-self, *Forrest!*"

"Forrest Jackson?" In one body, the crowd turned and surrounded him. Jenny slipped away, the darkness helping her to leave the dance hall unnoticed.

She went to Clover, but even the quiet of the horse barn and the repetition of currying him didn't stop her shaking. She'd avoided being close to Forrest ever since he and that bimbo —

"Hey, Jen."

He'd guessed well in figuring where she would go, but then Forrest always was a good guesser. How had she been so dense as to be caught with him twice in one night? Fans meant everything to Forrest, and now, for some reason, he had ducked them to find her.

Jenny tried to keep the curry comb steady, watching sidelong as Forrest walked toward her, past stalls filled with horses, talking to those he recognized, halting to lay a hand on the hides of animals he'd known for years. Since the NFR was so close, few riders were taking chances with their mounts. The barn was unusually full, as the dance had been, with the backbone of rodeo, the riders and mounts who drew the crowds. They would probably be on the road again tomorrow, but tonight the horses would rest and their riders would unwind.

All except for Jenny. *How can Forrest be so relaxed?* She fought a flame of resentment. *Why shouldn't he? Why should anything bother him?*

Jenny tried to calm herself, knowing her anger was unfair. She had decided to end their relationship, not he, but she had endured many agonizing nights wondering if she'd decided right.

The way he was looking at her now made her feel even more

unsure. Four years had passed, but those blue eyes still seemed to look at her as if she were the only girl in the world.

Was I wrong about him? Should I have given him another chance? The thought flickered timidly, then burned, fueling her anger. *No, he was wrong, not me. Ellensburg —*

"Clover's looking good, Jen."

He had reached them. Jenny faced her horse's black hide, pushing the curry comb over it. "Yeah, he looked really good tonight. Great score, wasn't it?"

"Not your best, but *the* best, Jen. Good enough to beat Felicia. Even I can be happy with being the night's best, if I did all I could. You used to feel the same way."

Jenny dropped her comb in a bag hanging on the side of the stall. She ducked her face behind the wall to check Clover's feed and escape Forrest's eyes.

Talk to him, a voice said inside her, but Jenny turned to go. "Good night, Forrest."

"It could be." He moved forward to touch her, his hand a shade below her shoulder blade.

"Let me go. Now."

"Don't get your Irish up. I just want to talk to you. Been a long time since I did."

"Never bothered you before."

"I didn't think it bothered you. You're the one who left me, remember?"

I remember my mother dying, Jenny thought. *And I remember you and Felicia Newcastle —*

"I was stupid, Jen. I've told you that, or tried to. I never stopped needing you, but even when you came back, you weren't there. Not for me, no matter what I tried. All you had, everything in you, was for rodeo." He was still holding her arm. He moved closer. "I came to this benefit for one reason: to see you, talk to you. Find out what went wrong. Meant to do it years ago —"

"But riding got in the way? Or was it roping?" Jenny couldn't help herself. "Or was it a certain barrel rider?"

"Matter of fact, it was a barrel rider. You." Forrest's grip loosened, but his hand stayed where it was. His voice dropped low. "Felt good to see you at a dance again, even though you weren't with me. When you were dancing with your daddy, I thought about how we used to dance together, every dance we could. What happened, Jen? Will you tell me, finally? Or don't I ever get to know? You going to keep me guessing forever?"

"Let me go, Forrest. You're drunk."

"I don't mind competition, long as it's human. But how's a cowboy to compete against rodeo? Tell me, Jen, and I'll let you go. I've been wanting to know for a long, long time, and when I saw you tonight, all in your rosy red, the outfit you wore when I last saw you in Ellensburg —"

"I should have burned these clothes." Jenny's look was a slap.

Forrest appeared stunned. "Maybe you should have," he said at length.

His hand fell from her arm, but Jenny could feel it, could feel his eyes on her as she walked away, could see his face in front of her, even after she left the arena and went inside her hotel room.

Jenny turned the television to a satellite country music station and strode to the bathroom, shedding clothes and turning up the heat on the way. She rubbed a soapy washcloth around and around her face, removing makeup and nervous perspiration. When she finished, her skin was clean and pink, and her face looked like a little girl's.

171

She stared at herself, fighting a rush of loneliness. In her reflection she saw the face of who she'd been before her mother died. She saw the face of the girl who laughed with Al Austin and Tom Rawlings, the girl who had her whole life planned when she was thirteen years old. That girl had stupidly fallen in love with Forrest Jackson. What made it worse was that nothing had changed.

18

TOM STOOD AT HIS WINDOW, DRINKING COFFEE. The trees were snow-laden, the rocks and grasses of Colorado's high country coated in fresh white. Tom set down his mug to button his fleece-lined jacket. It was going to be a cold morning with the cattle today. Cold, and maybe even more lonesome than usual.

The phone stopped Tom's exit. He reached for it, setting his rope in front of the toaster. A smile spread across his face as he put the receiver to his ear and heard the familiar voice. "Forrest! You cow-hand, what're you doing up so early?"

"You're the cowhand, Tom. And I'm not up early. Haven't gone to bed yet. You been watching me lately?"

"No. I've been hearing about you, though. Are you going to take the championship in roping or riding? Your grandfather's been pre-dicting you'll do both since August. I think he's right."

"Thanks, but Granddad gives me a different story when I call him. Listen, Tom. You heard about Carl?"

"What?"

"Carl Shorn, the guy who replaced you as my header, buckshot, when you ran away to the Mancos Monastery."

"Yeah, yeah, quit rubbing it in. What about Carl?"

"His throwing arm's been bothering him bad. Doctors say he's torn some ligaments...maybe in two. But Carl won't let them do anything 'til after the NFR. He's superstitious about stuff like that. It's hurting him. Me, too. Could wreck things for the NFR, and this is my first shot at roping since you quit. You know how I love to rope at Vegas, Tom."

"I remember, Forr. Sorry to hear about all this."

"Don't have to be sorry. That's why I called. Been thinking maybe you'd take Carl's place."

"At the NFR? No way."

"No riskier than Carl throwing with a bad shoulder. He's doing worse every day."

"What does he say about all this?"

"Says he can do it. Says he'll be fine. I don't think so...I think you can."

"Forr, I've been out of PRCA roping almost as long as I was in it."

"But you rope every day on the ranch, right? Just to keep your hand in if nothing else, I bet. Right?"

"Yeah, but it's —"

"No different. Still got your horse?"

"Yeah, but —"

"He in good condition?"

"The best, but Forrest, I —"

"You're used to the crowds. You're used to me. We work well together, Tom. Wish you'd think about it."

"Forrest, I'm sorry you're in a bind, but right now, I can't help you. Maybe you're right. Maybe it'd work. But I've got my own work up here. My uncle's got a choke hold on my daddy's ranch, and I've got to show him that I can be his brand of dependable. As soon as I do, he'll let me buy the Circle H."

"You got enough cash for that? A cowhand?"

"I didn't blow it all when we were competing. And your grand-dad pays me well. If I keep saving for another —"

"Ten, fifteen years, you might just make it. Come on, Tom; money's what'll impress your uncle, not punching cattle. Come with me, have a blast, win big, maybe stick around for a shot at the Ex, make history, then go back home with your pockets full and buy your ranch. We'll all be happy."

"Carl included? He's got a wife and kid to support now, doesn't he?"

"Listen, Tom —"

"Sorry, Forr. I can't cut Carl out. Not until he says I can. But that's not it anyway. My uncle's given me his terms: I have to show him I'm not the wild man I was a few years ago. He has to see that I'm done with the boozing and the partying —"

"And the bull riding?"

Tom smiled. "He didn't mention that. I don't think it's rodeo he's against. He just wants to know that when I take over the Circle H, I'll run it right. Another year or two of working for your granddad, and I'll be able to, Lord willing. We'll be real ranching neighbors again, Forr. Maybe then I'll do some roping for you, if Carl's still out. But right now, I can't risk it. I'm sorry."

"Tom, when you went straight, you went all the way. And then some."

"I've tried to explain that. I've been saved, Forr, I'm a new crea-ture —"

"You're a fool. But it's your life. You're the best partner I ever had, best I ever will have, probably. And you're wasting yourself on a dream that's got about the same chance as fog on a sunny day in Utah desert country."

"I don't think so, Forr, but even if you're right, it's still my dream…what I've got to do."

The silence told Tom his friend was rattled. Forrest wasn't known for talking, but he wasn't known for being quiet, either, not when he'd been drinking or had something on his mind. And when it was anything involving rodeo, Forrest was single-minded as a milch cow's calf. He had the same kind of intensity good bull riders did: a burning, instinctive focus that made him take whatever was thrown at him for eight seconds — and climb right back on the next time.

Bull riding. If I rope for Forrest, maybe I can do some bull riding on the side. Tom considered the temptation, then rejected it. That was over, along with everything else. Along with everyone else.

"Listen, Tom." Forrest's measured voice came on the line again. "Carl's out for next season, even if he can throw in the NFR. He knows it; he's just not owning up to it yet. I'm getting a new partner. That's decided, by me and Carl's wife. She doesn't want him trying to compete and maybe doing worse damage, maybe blowing his whole career. He needs a break. I need a partner. Think about it, Tom. I'll be calling again."

The line went dead.

Tom stared at the receiver in his hand before hanging it up. It had been hard enough walking away from rodeo, and now here was another chance he had to pass up. There wouldn't be many more.

But it was impossible with the Circle H hanging in the balance. Al wouldn't be riding the same circuit anyway, though it probably didn't matter. She had never even answered the one letter he'd dared write her. When Forrest called again, Tom knew he'd have to tell him no.

Part of him deeply, almost desperately, regretted turning Forrest down, the part he had kept in check for two years. Up here in ranch country it was fairly easy. Tom loved the land, the peace. He rarely felt the urge to chase after rodeo or even seek whatever excitement town life might offer.

As for female companionship, he desired the company of only one woman who was thousands of miles and obstacles away, a woman who had never been able to see him even when he was right in front of her. So instead of dating anyone, Tom threw himself into his work. At the day's end, any wildness left in him felt tamed and tired.

Still, it sometimes surged. When he had to tangle with a herd bull, when he sensed the animal's power, a whiff of rodeo wafted his way. Or if he caught a second of bull riding on television or heard some old wrangler talk about his days with the bulls, Tom could smell rodeo fever hovering nearby. Then all he could recall was the ride: the wild, glorious, ride. Memories of too many stale beers, too many miles, and too many faceless females faded, and he had to fight to remember why he'd ever quit.

It'd been so long since Tom had had an eight-second fix, but his body remembered the euphoria: hair-trigger nerves; adrenaline pouring through his veins like springtime river water; pounding music and clapping that sped up his heartbeat; stomping hooves and a bull's bellow, then riding raw power wherever it took him.

That was the problem. It had taken Tom places he never thought of going. Roping, riding bull was one thing, but how did you separate that from the rest of a typical rodeo cowboy's life? Would it be possible to live clean and still compete? Was he that strong yet? And did he even want to return to what brought back so many memories of Al? Wouldn't it be better to keep trying to forget her as she had forgotten him?

Tom grabbed his rope from the counter, then froze. *Should I go, Lord? Can I?* Even to him, it sounded too much like begging. He left without waiting to hear the answer.

"Come on in, Rawlings."

Tom stepped into the spacious wood-furnished dining room, taking the chair near the old man who had spoken to him. The servant who had ushered him in melted away in the shadows of the vaulted room.

Only two place settings lay on the mahogany table in front of Tom, but half of its considerable surface, the half nearest Sterling Jackson Sr., was filled with bottles, dishes, and a rustic centerpiece of curved, weathered wood resembling horns and garnished with dried Colorado wildflowers.

"Thanks for asking me to dinner, Mr. Jackson," Tom said as he was seated.

"Meant to have you over for Thanksgiving but never got around to it." The old man made an impatient wave, then fiddled with the jade bolo at his throat. "You heard from my grandson today?"

"Yes, sir. This morning."

Sterling watched as the servants filled Tom's glass, then his plate, heaping it with a succulent slab of prime beef from the ranch's own herd, a monstrous baked potato, a crisp Caesar salad, and other assorted entrees, including some fancy spinach concoction that proved Sterling's longtime cook hadn't given up trying to civilize him.

Sterling gestured for the head servant. "Tell Annie I want simple food, not these confounded messes." He took a bite, then stabbed the spinach with his knife as if murdering it. He fixed his eyes on

Tom, who had bent his head before eating. "What did Forrest want? Does he think he'll take the titles for roping and broncs?"

"You probably know about that better than I do."

"You're right, son." A wily smile cracked open the old man's lips. "Forrest called me right after he called you. I've mulled it over, Tom, and I'm ready to make you an offer."

Tom nodded, but continued working on his prime beef.

"I'm talking to you, son. Look at me."

Tom set down his knife and touched the outside of his lip with his napkin, laying the folded linen beside his plate. "Mr. Jackson, I don't think I want any offer. I'm happy working here with you; you've always said you're pleased with my work. If we can't leave it at that —"

"Don't get excited. I'm not trying to hogtie you, son. If you don't like what I've got to say, you don't have to take me up on it. Despite my reputation —" Sterling Sr. said, interrupting himself with a satisfied chuckle, "— I don't push everyone around. I think I've treated you fair these two years."

"Yes, sir. And I think I've given you fair work in exchange."

Sterling looked him over, and Tom felt edgy. The old man waved at him. "Go on; go on eating. I forget you've put in a hard day today. Most I did was argue with fancy-pants lawyers. Cows are much more reasonable, Tom. And horses are way smarter. Go on, eat. Didn't invite you to supper to see it turn cold."

Tom resumed eating but kept his eyes on Sterling.

"Forrest says you won't rope with him. Now, I understand why not, with your uncle hanging your daddy's ranch over your head like a big ol' carrot, but I can solve the problem for us all."

"I'd be interested in knowing how."

"You rope with Forrest, and I'll talk to your uncle, see if we can come to an understanding about the Circle H. I'll wrangle out a reasonable mortgage and stand for the down payment myself. All I ask is that you keep it under your hat until you square your account with me. My reputation'd go down the hole if folks found out I was getting soft-noggined in my old age, lending credit. What do you say?"

Tom shook his head. "No, thank you."

Sterling stopped himself from pounding the table, knocking over the crystal saltshaker instead. He batted at the servant who tried to retrieve it, then held up a crooked, accusing digit. "Rawlings, I can count the number of 'no thank yous' I've heard on one finger."

Tom took up his fork and ate in silence.

The old man looked past the table to the end of the hall where flames blackened the stones of a wall-sized fireplace. His hand curled around his collar. "Forrest needs you, Tom." Sterling's voice lost its stridence. "He's got a chance at matching his daddy's fame if he keeps doing well, but his mind won't be on his ride if he doesn't have a roping partner he's sure of. He's got a shot at two world championships this year. I'd be mighty proud if he won 'em."

"I'm rooting for Forrest too, Mr. Jackson. I hope he does you and his daddy's memory proud, but I can't cut out another cowboy just because Forrest or you want me to. I don't know if I could help Forr anyway, and I doubt my uncle would let go of the Circle H if you stepped in. I've got to earn my daddy's ranch."

"Accept a loan from me and arrange to take over the ranch yourself." The old man's voice raced. "Keep your mouth shut and your uncle'll never know the difference. Then rope for my grandson. You can earn the ranch when you come back."

"I'd still be cutting out Carl." Tom shook his head resolutely.

"Can't do it. I'd love a chance to be in the NFR again. There's more rodeo left in my blood than I thought. But right now, I can't. Forrest must have told you I said that. I want you to know he was and is the best buddy I ever had. Best partner, too. But we're going separate ways right now."

"This have anything to do with your new religion? That religion tell you to let a man down when he needs you?"

"I guess it does have to do with what I believe. Everything does. If I could really help Forrest, I'd go. But not with another man in the way, one who also needs something. If Carl stepped out, maybe I'd take up the slack, but there are lots of guys Forr could have head for him. I'm a risk. I don't know if I'm ready to go back to rodeo. Don't know if I'll ever be. Do you think a man has any business rodeoing when his heart's not in it?"

"No." Sterling took a long draught from his glass, nearly emptying it before he set it down. "No, I don't. Not if a man's heart isn't there. But yours is. No argument, young 'un. Yes, your heart's with ranching, but it's also with rodeo. Tell me you've got bull riding out of your system, and I'll tell you you're a liar. Maybe you don't have a heart for roping anymore; if that's so, Forrest is better off without you. But you've still got bulls in your blood, just like my son. Just like your daddy, for that matter. If he was alive, he'd tell you the same. In his time, Bob Rawlings was one of the best. Before my son died, Bob never gave up, just like my son never did, just like Forrest never does. That's why our families have been friends for three generations. But I can see that friendship fading just like the sunset."

Sterling downed the rest of his drink. "Yessir, Bob Rawlings was a world champ. Don't think he would've believed his son was a quitter. Glad that train spared him the shame of seeing this day."

Tom rose. "Thanks for supper, Mr. Jackson. Thanks for the offer.

181

If there comes a time I can take you up on it, I will. But I doubt that time will ever come." He picked up his hat from the side of the table as he walked away, quietly closing the front door behind him.

CHAPTER

19

Al urged the brown gelding with her knees as they started the pattern. Promise pulled to the right, but Al jerked the reins and got him back on course. Even so, they rounded the first barrel far too widely. Al dug in her heels; the quarter horse picked up speed, scattering sand with his hooves as he made a much tighter circle around the second barrel.

Promise raced up the straightaway and approached the final turn of the pattern, then slowed, fought the bit, and rubbed the barrel with his flank as Al forced him around. The horse came alive at the sprint to the finish, his breath and Al's flying behind them in white vapors.

Patting Promise's neck more out of habit than praise, Al directed him toward the girl standing on the shed's sandy floor. She pulled her scarf over her mouth for warmth as she waited for the girl to speak.

"Time's nineteen point twenty-two," Stacy said, holding out the stopwatch.

"No, I don't want to see it." Al groaned. "Prom, what's wrong? He's still fighting me, Stace. Almost a straight week of this, and he's still competing with me."

"The time's better."

"When nineteen is better, it's time to hang up your hat." Al moved Promise into a walk around the course. Even walking, Promise still resisted. Al slapped the horse's neck, her leather chopper making a flat sound on Promise's thick hide. "What's the problem? Don't you like sharing your practice arena with chickens?"

Al edged Promise near the poultry corner where one chicken of what was probably a small flock emerged from a round hole and strutted around its fenced yard, pecking at the sand Promise had sprayed inside its domain.

Stacy said. "Sometimes all those chickens come out, if we practice long enough and the shed's warmer. There must be a couple dozen, but I don't think they bother him."

"Then I'm out of ideas, Stacy. Promise is pitiful, or else it's me. Has he given you any clues? He's in great shape, but he's just not performing. He was much better even when I started working with him this fall before I left."

Stacy sat down on a hay bale. "I'm sorry, Al. I've got to tell you. It's my fault. I ruined him. But I didn't know. Promise just always wanted to start with the right, and I let him. I didn't know you always went left, and your mom —"

"You did what?"

"I wanted to tell you, but your mom said not to."

Al pulled Promise up short and looked at the neighbor girl over her shoulder. "What did my mother tell you? Out with it, Stacy."

The girl kicked at some hay near her boots and crossed her arms, tucking them underneath her down jacket's armpits. "I was exercising Promise one day after you left for college, and your mom came out to watch; she even clocked me. Prom and I did a seventeen-seven. I thought it was great, but then your mom said seventeen was really something, 'cause Promise had always been left-sided."

Alison had moved Promise into a walk as Stacy spoke. He continued plodding the pattern while Al stuck out her lower jaw and blew her breath upwards, attempting to thaw her nose *and* keep her cool. Whatever had happened, it wasn't Stacy's fault. That much Al knew. "So Promise has been running from the right for...how long?"

"About three months."

Al let Promise fight her around the second barrel, then broke pattern to move toward Stacy. "And he likes it? He wants to go right?"

"I guess."

"It's okay, Stace. I'm not mad at you. I just wish you'd told me this a week ago. I've been thinking Promise was going sour, and here he just wanted to show me his new trick."

Al rubbed the spot where she'd slapped her horse, though Promise had suffered less from the slap itself than from the indignity. "Don't pout on me, Promise. So you've turned into a righty, huh?" She removed her chopper and scratched Promise's neck just the way he liked it, massaging his tough hide with her thumbnail. "Sorry, Prom. I should have known it was my fault, not the chickens'. And not yours either, Stacy, although I do want to talk to my mother about this. She didn't tell you to correct the pattern?"

"She said if Promise liked it, we should keep running it, and not to tell you. I didn't know what to do. I tried to make Promise go back to the left, and had —"

"About as much luck as I'm having, I'll bet."

"Worse. He fought me hard. Danced like my grandma's pet poodle."

Al laughed. "Well, at least he didn't try that with me." She laid her hand on the horse's chest, then donned her glove. "He's not too warm. Let's try another run, Stace. This time Promise's way."

Al wheeled to the far end of the shed and started the run. Promise began well, and when Al turned his head toward the right, the horse found his stride. Al hardly had to guide him around the barrel. Promise made a tight, quick circle and shot to the other side of the course, executing another good loop and heading for the final barrel. He seemed to slide around it, and Al didn't even need to urge him down the straightaway. She leaned forward, enjoying the old rush of air and speed. It was almost like riding Ironside.

Stacy was screaming before they slowed and came back around. "Seventeen, Al, seventeen!"

"Flat?"

Stacy stopped twirling the watch on its string and checked. "Point one-two."

Al pushed back her hat. "That'll do."

"No kidding!"

"For today, Stacy. Tomorrow and next week, seventeen-twelve will be a failure. You're sure you clocked it right?"

"I think so."

"Well, next week the timers will be fixed and we can really see how he's doing. But it felt like a seventeen. Faster, actually. Let's quit for now. I shouldn't have done that last run after working Prom so long already, but I wanted to see if that really was his trouble."

"I'm glad it was. I'm so sorry, Al."

"It's all right. Maybe Prom's always been a righty at heart. Or maybe he just wanted a break." Al began the horse's cooldown.

"Seventeen-one." Stacy shook her head. "I didn't think Promise could go that fast."

"He really likes running to the right, and I think he'll soon be

giving me speed he didn't know he had. We need to get into the sixteens, or we can forget the Ex. And we won't forget the Ex, will we,
Promise?" Alison asked, taking the pattern at a trot — this time from
the right.

Eileen slid the slab of wood back over the hole in the metal-sided
shed and walked quickly toward the house, skirting the winter-
deadened sumac and raspberry bushes and passing behind the slat-
ted screen of the rusty satellite dish. She felt like a sneak spying on
her daughter, but it was the only way to learn things in this strange
knot of people called a family.

Eileen threw her coat into the closet without hanging it up, then
forced herself to bend down and retrieve it. *Try to be a good example,*
she thought out of habit more than resolve, which had been dulled
by time. *Try to offset Harvey's influence.*

As false proof of her occupation for the last half hour, Eileen
hurried to shape some biscuits and get them into the oven before
Alison returned, but the dough refused to stick together. Eileen
ended up having to knead it so much after she got enough milk into
it that she finally threw the whole mess into the garbage.

She turned off the oven and rested her flour-powdered hands on
the cupboard, continuing to berate herself. *It didn't work. That horse
is running even faster.* Funny to think that what she had hoped
would ruin Promise was turning out to make him a more efficient
racer. *Promise, the righty, was swifter than Promise, the lefty. Ha.*

The irony made Eileen wonder, as she often did in times of
despair, if perhaps there wasn't a God after all. Some divine being
must be twisting her life's course into such tortured curves and
eddies. She felt ashamed of having tried to sabotage her own

daughter, ashamed to be driven to such acts to protect Alison. It was necessary, but despicable.

Eileen ran her hands and arms under the stream of the faucet, feeling good, cold water that was ablution for a semi-atheist. Then she went to the closet, grabbed her coat, and headed to the car without bothering to leave a note explaining her absence. She doubted anyone would miss her anyway.

"I know you've done all you can with the shed, Dad." Al hung her coat in the closet. "The sand's a great idea, but that hard ground underneath is still dangerous. And heating that thing! I can't believe Mom lets you. It must be breaking the farm."

"That's the farmers union's generosity. No way your mother would've let me heat up that old electricity guzzler otherwise, even with the chickens in the corner. I was thinking of using gas, but the guys insisted."

"I wouldn't have been able to ride at all if you'd used gas. Ever tried to compete in those old arenas in the winter when they're gas heated?"

"Yep. Turned in some of my best scores, too."

Al patted his shoulder. "Guess I'm not as tough as you. Gas — or diesel, or whatever they use — it's hard on the eyes. Sometimes I felt I wasn't seeing the course clearly. Ironside hated it, too."

"Ironside was a good horse, but picky. Promise giving you problems in the shed?"

"No, but I'm not pushing him like I want. If I tried pulling too much speed out of him, he might slip. I can risk a lot of things, but not an injury."

"How you coming on whittling down your time?"

"Well, we're still going by the stopwatch, but according to Stacy, we hit sixteen eighty-five early this morning. She was struck dumb."

"Sixteen. Not bad."

"Not good. We could do better, but like I said, I'm afraid to push him." Al pulled out a chair and sat by her father at the kitchen table. "Heard from Aunt Marg or Uncle Willy yet?"

"Got a Christmas card the other day. Said Marg's busy with day care and Willy's busy finding somewhere else to hang out after chores."

"I know. I already read it." Al reached for the cereal box and poured herself a bowl of bran.

Harvey pushed the milk and honey toward her. "Something bothering you, Al?"

She waited until she swallowed. "No."

"You keep asking about Marg and Willy. You got something cooking with them?"

"I've always got something cooking. Like you, Dad." Al grinned. "Where's Mom?"

"She and Rhoda went shopping, I think."

"Wasn't she just at Rhoda's yesterday?"

"Yep." He shrugged. "You know her moods."

"I know." Al stood to look out the living room window but didn't see her mother's car in the driveway.

"You going to tell me what you're up to, Al, or do I have to trick it out of you like your mother does?"

"She just thinks she tricks it out of me." Al stepped back into the kitchen. "I was going to tell you anyway. I called Aunt Marg the other day and asked if I could stay with her and Uncle Willy until the season begins. I know she's got her hands full with day care, but I figured I could help her part of the time and work Promise the other part. They've got the perfect setup for racing, still in great shape. I asked all about it. They don't even have to heat their shed much, the winters are so mild. We could work the course outside, too."

"Sounds good."

"But I'd miss Christmas with you."

"I don't mind."

"Mom would."

"Al, I told you a long time ago that you've got to decide what's more important: your racing or your mother. You can't be worrying about her if you're planning to be the best. You need focus. She'll understand. I was the same way when I was riding bulls."

"Dad, I don't think you realize how much being together at Christmas means to Mom. I don't want to hurt her if I can think of any other way of doing what I have to do."

"Great, sweetie. But don't worry about Mom. She's tough. She loves you. And she wants you to do well, even at racing. She just likes to kick up her heels every once in a while. Keeps her feeling like a young filly."

"I still think Christmas means more to Mom than you guess. But if Aunt Marg says yes, I'm going. I have to. I checked the trailer and truck already. They should make it to Oklahoma."

"Should. And by the time you're ready to come back, you can buy a new one with your winnings. 'Til then, you can haul Promise with Jenny and Uncle Barney, once the season starts."

"They said it was okay?"

"Yes ma'am." Harvey grunted as she flew out of her chair and hugged him hard.

"All I need is another okay from Aunt Marg, and I'll be on my way! Got my application for WPRA in, got Promise's papers. Even packed my things already. I keep them in the shed."

"Then they should smell real good when you're ready to go."

"I don't care. I just…Wait a minute. Why did Uncle Barney and Jen take so long to say it was all right?"

"I think Barney was upset about Tex Williams's bull wreck. Barn sounded pretty down when I called, but he perked right up when I told him about you. Said yes right away, I forgot to tell you. Then he called up later that night and left a message, said he had to check on a few things. Good thing your mother didn't hear it."

"But everything's okay now?"

"Everything's okay. I'll have your mother talk sense into Aunt Marg…wait a minute. I'll talk to Marg myself. Your mother's still not speaking to you after the spat you two had about Promise's pattern. I'll call Marg and let you know her answer tonight."

"No, Dad. I want to talk to her. I only want to be there if she and Uncle Willy want me. I felt the same with Uncle Barney and Jen. I wish you would have waited and let me call. It's been a long time since I heard from her. I wanted to make sure it was all right with her, too…not just Uncle Barney. I don't want any problems with Jen."

"Jenny? Having a problem with you two traveling together? Maybe you're getting forgetful in your old age, but I remember how you two were. Like a matched team, only giggly beyond bearing. Barney probably wanted to make her promise to keep quiet before he let you come along. You almost drove him crazy the summers you rodeoed together."

"We drove a lot of other people crazy, but not him. He loved it as much as we did."

Al poured her soggy cereal down the sink and grabbed an orange from the festive basket on the counter, an early Christmas gift. It was too late to be eating breakfast. Al hoped it wasn't too late for other things. "We sure did have a lot of fun. Me, and Jen, and Forrest...and Tom. There'll never be another time like it."

"Your mother thought she'd lost you for sure. You were doing so great in the IPRA summer shows, I was all for you going full-time. But your mother used your aunt Virginia's death to get you into college. I always regretted that. Maybe you would've been a world champ by now. Who knows?"

Who knows? Al echoed silently. *Forrest and Jen didn't work out. Maybe Forrest and I...forget it,* she told herself. *Promise and I might make the Ex. Nobody gets all they dream about. The Ex would be enough,* she told herself, but knew it wouldn't. Not by half.

20

ROWDY WITH EUPHORIA ON THE FIRST DAY of the NFR's ten-round competition, more than seventeen thousand noisy fans occupied the University of Las Vegas's Thomas and Mack Center. Almost three million dollars was at stake, and everyone wondered who would win it. Attractive women in coordinated western wear prowled the bleachers, selling beverages to thirsty spectators. Sales were high but would get even higher when the bucking and yelling began.

Most of the crowd had found their seats when the lights began flickering. The announcer had started cuing the audience long before, reminding them about the concessions and souvenirs, commenting on the upcoming show, slowly whipping up emotions and expectations.

Soon all fans were asked to take their seats and keep them. Opening ceremonies would start with a blackout.

Music which had been playing for an hour emerged from the background as the crowd quieted. The lights dimmed, then died.

From his seat in the arena, Barney O'Neill leaned forward, joining thousands of others who strained to see in the blackness. The crowd waited, hardly breathing the warm air with its scents of popcorn and nachos, man and beast and dirt. Food and drink were forgotten in the anticipation. Hardly anyone moved.

Not so in the chutes. There sounded the clang of hoof against metal, snorts, pawing. The loaded broncs tested the strength of their confines as they would soon test the mettle of their riders. Like Barney, like the entire crowd, the broncos waited, feeling the banked energy charging the arena.

Spotlights from four corners pierced the air, and in poured four lines of sequined riders wearing red, white, and blue. Each rider carried a streaming flag and rode a pale Palomino. The horses cantered in formation, meeting in the arena's center around a stationary white horse whose rider held an oversized American flag. The spotlights focused on the flag as the white horse reared and turned a circle with thrusts of its well-defined hindquarters, a toned mass of lines and bulges.

A voice reverberated throughout the arena, reciting the names and feats of cowboys and cowgirls long gone, paying tribute to rodeo clowns — funnymen who kept the crowd in stitches and bullfighters who kept bulls from giving cowboys stitches. Music that had started low at the beginning of the Palomino parade swelled as the voice was joined by other voices adding names, dates, and accomplishments of rodeo legends.

Each voice rose above the last, a mixture of male and female voices proclaiming male and female heroes of the modern West. The Palominos pushed into a gallop around the arena, in and out of the spotlights, a moving circle of horses rotating from its pivot: a white horse whose rider bore the American flag.

The horses stopped and faced inward. The music halted. A spray of fireworks ascended from all sides of the arena in a shower above the flag. Gunpowder scented the air; colored flames arched downward. The white horse reared and came to earth, wheeling in a figure eight, its silken mane and tail flying. The flag rippled with each turn as the fireworks subsided in weak, scattered bursts.

When the white horse stilled, the Palominos closed in on their color guard. The house lights came up, and the national anthem began.

Rising to his full five feet six inches, his hat over his heart, Barney mouthed the song of the stars and stripes, and fought, as always, the patriotic lump choking his words. This was another reason he loved rodeo, and it exceeded even the contests and glitz and excitement. Nowhere else could he so fully express his love for his country. Nowhere else did thousands of voices rise in such agreement as during rodeo's opening ceremony.

Barney thought of the riders, racers, and ropers whose love for their country and their sport made rodeo what it was. Bareback-bronc riding usually opened the competition, and tonight fifteen riders would place their bodies at the mercy of animals who also loved what they did and whose aims were directly opposed to their riders'.

The three rough stock events — bareback-bronc riding, saddle-bronc riding, and bull riding — were aptly named. Death was there. And glory. At the NFR, the chances for both were greatly magnified.

The house lights returned to full strength following the ceremony, and Barney could almost hear the television cameras zooming in, could almost feel the tension in the first rider up.

The announcer gave the rider's hometown and season earnings. The crowd leaned, trying to get closer. Barney couldn't see the young cowboy's face, but he'd seen thousands like it at this moment before the chute opened and the horse exploded. Usually the face was a taut mixture of terror and determination.

Around Barney, the crowd awakened. They cheered or whistled

as the rider eased onto his mount. The bronc slammed its hooves into the side of the chute, eager to buck unfettered. Barney felt himself caught up in the thrill of rodeo, that uncertain second before the gate opened and anything could happen — and usually did. Rodeo. It was a great sport.

In the saddle-bronc dressing room, Forrest Jackson shouted and swapped vows along with the other cowboys. Tan Ferguson had scored a seventy-nine — a hard tally to beat. The ride was solid: good timing, action, position, lots of exposure. Forrest watched the television screen, knowing his turn would be up soon and also knowing he would have to ride with everything he had to top Tan's score.

"Think you can catch Tan, Forrest?" Surf Garret asked.

"He drew Hurricane. If he don't do it on Hurricane, he won't do it at all," answered Johnny Ogalla, his thumbs in his belt loops.

"Thanks, Johnny." Forrest grinned. "So it's all in the horse? Who'd you draw?"

Johnny snorted. "Skoal Thunder."

"He'll chew you up an' spit you out, Johnny." Surf whooped. "Ain't all in the horse." Surf turned to Forrest. "You got a chance on Hurricane. Me, I drew Huff 'n' Puff."

"Tough luck." Huff 'n' Puff, like Skoal Thunder, had moves not even the best could stick to...or score well on. Tan's position looked pretty safe from Johnny or Surf. With Hurricane though, a seventy-nine or eighty might just be possible, since half the score depended on the animal's performance. Judges liked a strong bucker, and Hurricane was certainly strong.

A solid roan, heavier than most of the broncs, Hurricane was known to break to the right and then kick like sixty, throwing power to his rider without throwing him a nasty curve. It was tough to stick to the saddle with all that forceful bucking, but Forrest was good at sticking.

Hurricane predictably gave an honest ride. Though he often sent off-balance cowboys sailing, he didn't fake and twist as did the more treacherous broncs who sometimes fell and pinned their riders. The only problem might arise at the gate, where Hurricane was infamous for bucking blindly, regardless of everything — chute bars, or gate, or gate men. He'd wounded more than one cowboy coming out of the chute.

Forrest planned his strategy as he watched the next rider, fingering the thick braid of rope that would serve as his only anchor to 1,500 pounds of thrashing bronco. He watched the rider buck off before the eight-second mark, then Forrest gathered his gear to take his own place in the chutes.

Before he went, Forrest slipped a note to an old friend, a retired cowboy who now wore NFR colors. Forrest asked the cowboy to see that the folded paper got to Jenny O'Neill. Then he approached the chutes.

Hurricane was loaded and waiting. Forrest and others fitted the bronc with his flank strap, bridle, and saddle, pausing to pat the horse and talk soothingly.

While adjusting the straps to Hurricane's muscular frame, Forrest anticipated the feel of sliding into the saddle. He flexed his legs and stretched, knowing he had to fit Hurricane better than anything else on the horse. Forrest had to fit and stay fitted for eight seconds of eternity.

Forrest lifted his heel and spun his blunt spurs. He tightened his chaps, rubbing a spot of dirt from the bright blue. Then he anchored his hat and eased onto his horse, seizing the buck rein where he figured he'd gain the best leverage for this particular mount. Not too short, so Hurricane wouldn't pitch him over the dashboard. Not too long, so he wouldn't go flying off the back end.

Hurricane skittered and Forrest held tight, hearing his name echo through the arena, hearing the chute boss ask if he was ready, hearing the announcer recite his season's winnings, feeling more than seeing the thousands of eyes watching him.

Forrest balanced a forearm on the top bar of the gate, then nodded to the gate men and forgot about everything except the horse underneath him leaping from the open chute.

Holding his heels on Hurricane's shoulders, Forrest marked out his mount, avoiding disqualification and giving his horse the best opportunity to buck him off on the first jump. Then Forrest slid into Hurricane's rhythm, synchronizing his spurring action with Hurricane's snappy bucks, absorbing them into his body, letting them pass through and out. Forrest moved with the bronc, matching him, ignoring the pain, making the ride appear smooth, rehearsed, like a display of power planned and choreographed by them both. The two exemplified the classic professional saddle-bronc ride: man and animal in wild, beautiful tandem.

Suddenly Hurricane thrust his head between his forelegs and bucked incredibly hard, adding an impossible twist. He followed with another jaw-breaking buck and twist in the opposite direction, his hide stretching with the contortions.

Forrest rode it out, trying to keep in time and balance, but the horse sunfished and Forrest's right foot slid out of the stirrup just as the whistle sounded.

Hurricane recovered, resuming his bone-bending bucks. The pickup men drew their horses alongside and one helped transfer

Forrest from the bronc to the arena floor. Hurricane pranced and took his payment in the form of the audience's clapping.

"What a ride!" The announcer's voice resounded throughout the arena. "Gives a whole new meaning to the word 'horsepower,' don't it? You knew Hurricane was a power packer, but who ever figured he could do the twist so good?"

The fans hooted and clapped as Forrest waited for his score. Had he made an eight-second ride or blown his stirrup a hair before the whistle? Depending on what the judges saw or thought they saw, he could be facing a great score or a score of zero.

"Eighty-four!" the announcer roared.

The scoreboard lit up. Forrest threw his hat in the air. The crowd rained applause on him.

"Guess the judges loved that fi-nesse, folks," the announcer crowed. "Forrest Jackson makes it look easy, don't he? And that's how to do it, boys. Take what you get and make it look like it ain't nothing at all. Good thing Forrest blew that stirrup after the whistle, though, or he would've been sitting with a no-score. Thank you, Forrest Jackson, and thank you, Hurricane!"

Forrest collected his hat and left the arena. Now he could watch the rest of the events in relative peace...until the team roping.

As he accepted congratulations and traded handshakes behind the chutes, he wondered if Jen had been watching his ride. He looked around the faces clustered near the fence, hoping to see her but knowing from the sensation in his gut that she had not shown — again. At last he walked toward the locker room to prepare for his next event, almost grateful for the absorption rodeo demanded. For while he was riding or preparing for a ride, nothing except the event itself could claim his attention or tear at his heart: not even the world's best barrel racer.

∞∞

At the opposite end of the rough-stock chutes, a horse and rider erupted from a narrow runway to the arena floor, turning around a barrel almost faster than anyone could imagine. The racers before Jenny had compressed some segments of the course and softened others, but Clover ran true, leaning into the barrels without tipping into them, his body and Jenny's a tilted, molded line.

They circled the second barrel, then shot to the far one, Clover cutting in a little too much and Jenny compensating so she wouldn't rub the edge with her leg. She slackened the reins, but Clover was done with the barrel and racing to the timers, black tail high and streaming, ears forward. It was a solid run. They both knew it.

"Fourteen point two-eight," the announcer drawled. "A good run, even in this small arena. It's what we've come to expect from Jenny O'Neill. That'll put her in the money. Yes, a mighty good run."

A good run. The thought repeated in Jenny's head later at the stalls. *A good run. But we have to do better. Next round, we have to get in the point-ones, or...well, maybe we'll lose the round.*

Strangely, the menace of losing didn't have its customary bite. Even Clover seemed inordinately pleased with his score. His tail had been sky high during the victory lap. Maybe Clover's enthusiasm was what was affecting Jenny, but she had an uneasy feeling the reason for her slack attitude went beyond her horse.

She reached into her pocket and retrieved a crinkled piece of paper. *What was Forrest thinking when he wrote this note? Does he really mean it?*

If he did, it hadn't stopped him from getting a bang-up score in the saddle bronc's first round, although he and Carl hadn't done so well in the team roping. When Jenny and Clover took their victory

200

lap, she knew Forrest and Canyon had ridden over the same path.

Their paths had always run close, even though Jenny fought hard to keep them separate. Now, more than ever, Forrest seemed set on stopping her.

Jenny knew her emotions about his recent show of interest should be more focused. She didn't need Forrest Jackson, champion saddle-bronc rider or team roper or ladies' man or whatever title he was competing for nowadays. What she needed was a friend, and oddly, his note said Forrest was applying.

For the first time in years, Jenny untethered old memories and let them run a few minutes before she tied them fast again.

Forrest...why did things have to change?

So many times she'd asked the question. Asked it of God, she supposed, though God never answered. She'd put herself to sleep asking "Why?" after the death of her mother. She'd filled hours of daylight asking "Why?" after Forrest's betrayal. The months she'd spent with her aunt and uncle in Oklahoma, safe from the world, were all filled with the question.

It was time to quit asking and go on. But on to what? For what? Jenny's dream had been to win the PRCA world championship in barrel racing. Last year she had won it, and was on her way to winning it again...and it didn't seem to matter so much anymore.

She wondered how Forrest would react if he knew she was satisfied with winning a round with a less-than-perfect score. He'd implied she'd changed, that she was driving herself too hard. Maybe he was right.

Tonight Jenny felt a strange quietness. After the NFR, Al would be riding with her again, and her father, "Blarney" O'Neill, would be bringing them from rodeo to rodeo. But there would be no white Ford ahead, driven by two young cowboys hauling a double-horse trailer and bound for glory. Tom was gone from the rodeo scene, and Forrest would be too busy worrying about scores and living out his stardom to rekindle the love he once had for her. Maybe her father thought old times could come back, and maybe they could, partly. But only partly.

Jenny felt the paper in her hand and looked at Forrest's tiny script. Then she tossed the note in the garbage can.

CHAPTER

———

21

———

"SO YOU'RE GOING. YOU WON'T EVEN STAY FOR CHRISTMAS."

Alison hung up the receiver and turned reluctantly. "I'm sorry, Mother, but if I have any chance at all, I've got to get good practice, and Aunt Marg —"

"I heard. She should have asked me before she volunteered anything." Venom spilled from Eileen's voice.

"She didn't volunteer," Al countered quietly. Bad enough that she should bear her mother's rage. She was determined no one else would. "I asked."

"So the shed your father set up for you wasn't good enough? Just what does it take to satisfy you, Alison?"

Alison choked back rising anger. "Maybe it does take a lot, but I have to try this. I won't be barrel racing my whole life, you know."

"No, I don't know." Her mother's gray eyes had the look of storm clouds laden with lightning. "Do you?"

"I love competing, but I don't intend to do it year-round."

"It seems when you and Jennifer were traveling together, I heard differently."

"Well, yes, but then Aunt Virginia died, and Jen didn't even finish the rest of that year. It felt good to come home, to have you and

Dad and the farm, to ride Ironside for fun, not for a prize. It was hard getting into college at first, but by the next spring, I knew I didn't want a rodeo life. I need stability, family ties."

"So do I, Alison. I need you here." Her mother was now pleading.

"I will be here, only not this year. It won't seem much different than when I'm away at college. You know how much I'm gone during the school year. Except for the past few years, I was away most of the summers, too. The only difference you'll notice is that I might not make it home for Thanksgiving."

"Or Christmas."

"Next year, I will."

Eileen pulled out a chair and flung herself into it. She set her elbows on the table, supporting her forehead with her fists. "I can't live for next year, Alison. Do you know how many times I've heard what's going to happen next year? How I've heard everything will be better then, everything will be different? 'Next year' and 'tomorrow' are everything your father pins his hopes to. He figures if there's no possible way to improve the present situation, why, next year there will be; tomorrow there will be. You're beginning to talk and act just like him. I can't stand it."

"I'm sorry I didn't tell you earlier about practicing at Aunt Marg's, but I didn't want to until I knew I could. I've got a chance at the Ex. Can't you be a little happy for me?" Al laid her hand on her mother's bowed back.

"Oh, I am happy. Now I get my television back." Eileen pushed away from the table. "Since the National Finals Rodeo began, you've spent more time with the television than with me. I know where I stand. Go ahead. Rodeo with Jennifer and Barney. Stay with Margaret for Christmas. The worst part of this is, my own family is helping to ruin you."

"I'm sorry, Mother, that you're so against rodeo. I'm sorry you blame it and Dad for everything that's wrong in your life. But this is my choice, my dream, my life. I'm choosing rodeo, and I'd do it no matter if Dad and Aunt Marg and Uncle Barney fought me as hard as you have, as much as you always will."

Al felt words dancing on her tongue like a match before it touched gunpowder, but she couldn't stop them from exploding. "Maybe I won't come back even if I don't make the Ex. Maybe I'll decide I want to rodeo. I'm tired of college. You chose it for me. You filled out the papers, arranged the scholarships, grants, work-study, housing…everything. You've controlled me more than Dad or anyone else ever thought of doing!"

Eileen's back was to her. She looked motionless.

Al took a step forward. "Mother, can't you understand —"

"No. I can't. I never will." Eileen turned. Her gray eyes seemed large, dead. "Go pack, Alison. You'll need to get an early start. Oklahoma is a long way off. You'll want to travel as far as you can tonight; there's supposed to be bad weather tomorrow all the way down through Iowa. Go on. I'll fix something for you to eat."

Al took another step, but her mother held up her hand. "Please just go, Alison."

Though Al regretted some of her words, she went, knowing an apology would be pointless now. Besides, there were preparations to get through before Promise could be loaded and all Al needed would be packed into the pickup.

Maybe this is the way I had to go, no strings attached. But I won't always be in rodeo. Mom must know it, just as I do.

Al took her coat from the entryway closet and descended the steps, nearly catching her boot on the fourth step. Her father hadn't fixed it right after Thanksgiving as he promised, just as he'd never called Aunt Marg as he'd promised, Al suddenly remembered, feeling slightly sick. He'd probably planned to do it...tomorrow.

Filling the cooler with food did nothing to ease the ache inside Eileen. Alison was leaving. Who knew when she'd be back? If she'd be back.

Eileen worked like an artist, folding wax paper neatly around each of the roast beef sandwiches she placed into the cooler. Neatly, like a present. The only gift she could give her daughter this Christmas, the first Christmas Alison wouldn't be home. Neatly, like a hug around each of the sandwiches.

She reached in to place a flask of freshly squeezed lemonade, checked that the potato chips wouldn't be crushed in transit, made sure the lid on the container holding carrot and celery sticks wouldn't leak. Touched packets of homemade cookies, a Tupperware container of ranch dip, and another holding several chicken sandwiches.

Last of all, she slipped in a note.

Closing the lid before she could take the note out, Eileen set the cooler near the doorway.

I should bring it to the pickup now. She looked at the cooler, thought of her words on the paper. They would probably appear hastily scribbled to her daughter, but those words had been etched in Eileen's daily existence ever since she had come to the farm.

Her daughter was leaving, and Eileen could see no reason to postpone the decision she'd been putting off for so long.

Why, then, did she step back to the cooler, lower her hand to raise the top, slide her fingers down until they met the stationery? Why did she close her hand and take the paper out?

206

Not now. Alison must never think her leaving is the cause.

It was no one's fault. Merely the logical result of an illogical union. Eileen tucked the note in her pocket. How did the saying go? Bad news can keep?

After...Christmas. After she's proven herself on the circuit, Eileen thought. *I can wait that much longer.*

She lowered the lid of the cooler, as if sealing a coffin. She could almost hear a priestly chant: "Into thy hands, O Lord, we commit the spirit of this, thy daughter...." The balm of burial, worded to console those who had lost a loved one and hoped they were sending that loved one to a better world, gave Eileen no reassurance as she grieved over her daughter. She was sending Alison to a purgatory worse than the nonexistence following death.

And there was nothing she could do about it.

Luck at least, Alison.

Eileen took her hands from the cooler. The lid fell shut.

Al hopped out of the pickup and slammed the door. Her dark boots contrasted starkly with the snow. She raised her eyes to look at her mother.

Eileen stood several feet away, wearing a bright red down-filled jacket that seemed to swallow her. Her hands didn't stick out of the sleeves, or if they did, they were hidden. Her arms crossed tightly in front of her, wrapped protectively around her body.

"Bye." Al hugged her mother, and Eileen kissed the side of Al's face. "I am sorry I have to miss Christmas, but next year, I —" Al could have bitten her tongue off. "I mean, it won't happen again."

Eileen pulled out one of her hands and touched Al's hair, smoothing it, tucking it behind her ear. "Good-bye, Alison."

Al hugged her again. Her mother's hand went around her back. When Al straightened, Eileen's eyes softened. Al turned away, afraid of the tears in her mother's eyes. "Bye, Dad."

"Bye, Al." Harvey hugged her quickly and gave her a little push toward the pickup. "Better go on, now. It's cold out here."

"Yes, Alison. Remember to watch the weather. Don't drive when you're too tired. Remember, you're hauling a trailer."

"I'll remember, Mother."

"And call as soon as you get to Margaret's."

"I will, Mother. Don't worry." Al climbed into the pickup cab and started the engine.

Harvey moved near his wife. "Go on, Al. Get going. Promise shouldn't have to be in that trailer unless you're moving. Be sure to give him a break when you can."

"I will, Dad. Bye."

"Good-bye," her mother answered. Her father said nothing.

Through the rearview mirror, Al watched her parents until she reached the curve in the driveway. Her father turned back to the house before then, but her mother stood, her bare hand lifted in a frozen wave.

Al stopped at a gas station just before crossing the Wisconsin state line. So far, the trip was going well, but she had to stop every few hours to stretch and water Promise and wasn't making good time. They had a long way yet, and snow was predicted all the next day.

She filled up the tank quickly and bought an atlas, her real reason for stopping. *Here I am, planning a trip to Oklahoma without a map. Glad Mom doesn't know.*

She sketched a tentative itinerary, checked on Promise, made sure all her mirrors and windows were clean, then drove on.

They were in Missouri before Al stopped for the night. Uncle Barney had sent a list of good lodging places, and Al used a pay phone at a small gas station to reserve a room. She checked on Promise again and drove the thirty miles to an informal bed-and-breakfast called the Grand River Ranch.

Promise had a good run, rubdown, and clean stall that night, and Al slept well in the small upstairs bedroom, dreaming quietly in a four-poster bed draped with a filmy white canopy.

The next day, they entered Oklahoma before stopping. Al had wanted to reach the end of their trip but forced herself to pause regularly for Promise. She had to be satisfied with another of Uncle Barney's lodging places — a small, plain farmhouse on a rolling brown landscape.

Underneath the withered grass, the earth had taken the orange-red tones Al always associated with Oklahoma. Seeing it made her feel close to Aunt Marg's and Uncle Willy's.

When Al walked into the farmhouse to claim her room, the television showed the NFR calf roping. She quickly registered and walked into the living room, letting the run finish before she asked the man who was lying on a couch how Forrest Jackson and Carl Shorn had done in team roping.

"They had a bad run, honey."

"What happened?"

"Can't tell ya much. Ol' Carl wound up for the throw, but there weren't hardly no direction to it. Wild and short. Then he held onto his shoulder like it hurt to beat all. Doctors are looking at him now. No report yet, but I don't think it'll be good."

"I'm sorry to hear that."

The man turned to her and scratched the underside of his fat knee. "Where you from, honey?"

"Wisconsin."

The man nodded. "You shore don't sound like you're from around here. You in rodeo?"

"Yes. I'm in rodeo." It felt good to say it.

"Barrel racer?"

"Yes."

"Well," The man swung his feet off the couch and thumbed at the space he'd created, "better take yourself a seat, then. Racing's coming up."

"Thanks. I'll watch it from my room."

"No TV up there. This's the only one in the house."

The woman who had helped Al get Promise settled in his stall entered the room. "This's my husband. Jim, meet Alison. Go ahead and watch the racing, honey. Your horse is fine for now. Nice looking animal. I'll leave the light on so you can find your way to him later on. You'll need to study the racing if you're fixing to do it yourself."

Al sat on the brown and yellow plaid couch, as close as she could to the end. The man next to her had the familiar aroma of a working farmer, what Al and Jen had nicknamed "Eau de Barnyard." Funny how the smells of home never changed. A farm was a farm in any state, and the people who worked them smelled the same.

Dad used to smell like that a lot. Now I do, or did. Al thought of her parents and wondered if she should call home. *Better wait until the trip's completely over, then Mom won't have anything to worry about. We should reach Aunt Marg's by mid-morning if we take that little road west of —*

"There she is. That's my girl," Jim said, waving his thick arms. "Go, Jenny! Flex around them barrels, Clover!"

Al watched her cousin execute the pattern. It seemed a slow run, but only because Jen and Clover were so smooth. Al wasn't surprised when the commentator exclaimed, "Thirteen-eighty!"

Jim acted awed. "Thirteen-eighty! Thirteen-eighty, and looked like they were barely moving. Every time I watch that girl and that there horse, I can hardly stand it, seems so slow. But they fly!" Jim whistled. "Just smack *float* that course."

Jim's wife, Ataline, agreed. "That's the one you want to study, honey," she said to Al. "She took the world championship last year, and looks like she'll do it this year, too. Name's Jenny O'Neill. The horse she rides's Cloverleaf. Don't figure you'll forget the names. You'll hear 'em time and again if you're doing the barrels. Nobody better, though that Felicia Newcastle and her Wellington are a close second. Best study her, too."

"I will," Al replied. She watched the second rider, Felicia Newcastle, make the pattern with a fourteen flat. Al stood. "Think I'll check on Promise, then get some sleep."

"Don't you want to watch the rest of the riders, honey?"

Jim turned to his wife. "Why should she? She just saw the queens of barrel racing. Swish! Them girls plumb float that pattern!" He looked at the television as he talked. "Go ahead, honey. Take care of your horse. I'll let you know if anything else worth watching happens."

"Thought there were fifteen riders," Ataline sniffed. "You act like there're only two."

Al heard the wife and husband debating as she headed to the door.

"What's that girl's name that's staying here?" Jim interjected. "Her full name?" Al heard him ask as she rested her hand on the doorknob. Without knowing why, she listened as she turned the knob and opened the door.

"Alison. Alison Austin."

"Got a good sound to it," Jim murmured. "Think maybe I'll start watching for her, too. Al Austin. Yes, that do have a ring: Al Austin on Promise."

Al smiled and softly closed the door.

22

THE OLD MAN STOOD WITH HIS BACK TO THE WALL, staring at Tom Rawlings, who hardly acknowledged him from his seat before the log cabin's window. Sterling Jackson Sr. touched his gray felt brim in a gesture Tom thought strangely uncertain.

"You're fired, Rawlings."

Tom settled his long legs in a more comfortable position on the windowsill, resuming his gaze toward the snow-capped trees. He had known that if Carl let Forrest down in the NFR, it would only be a matter of time before Tom himself, like the snow balancing on the boughs, would also fall. Sterling had a way of getting what he fondly called "even."

"So Forrest and Carl are out of the roping," Tom said in a detached voice. "Sorry to hear that. But how do you figure firing me is going to fix anything? The NFR Committee won't let me step in and rope in Carl's place."

"They won't let you rope now, but they would have before," Sterling growled. "If you'd gone and done what I asked you, when I asked you, then Forrest —"

"Would still be out a roping partner. It doesn't work that way, Mr. Jackson, not with me. Not with Carl refusing to step down. You earn your way to the NFR. You work at it, get a few breaks with good animals and good purses, then maybe you make it. Carl made it. He deserved to stay in as long as he could."

"Don't tell me about the NFR, son. Forrest and Forrest's daddy made the name Jackson an NFR name, a world champion name. Just like the name Rawlings could have been if you weren't so weak-kneed." The old man punctuated his words with his knobby finger.

"If I hadn't chosen a different life." Tom couldn't help letting a little of his anger lash his words. He had been so close. A few more years and he would have had the Circle H. Now he was fired, and his uncle would think he couldn't keep a job. He'd probably demand another seven years of servitude, just like Laban. "Forrest and his father did make Jackson a world champion name. *They* did, Mr. Sterling Jackson Sr., sir. They. Not you."

"Or you. Now pack up your bags and hit the trail."

Tom cocked his head and pushed back his hat. "Already packed. Forrest called me last night, just before he called you, probably. I figured what you'd do." Tom stood and ambled into his bedroom, reentering the open living room/dining area with a large khaki canvas bag.

"You going to rope for Forrest now?" Sterling sounded hopeful and a tad subdued.

"I'm going to move on to another ranch and keep working until I own the Circle H."

Sterling's flint returned. "You can't hurt me by hurting Forrest."

"I think you're wrong. But I'm not doing this to hurt either of you. Carl is out for the coming season. All right. Forrest can choose another partner from hundreds of hotshots out there: Bruce Storey, Al Conley, Winky Blackmont —"

"Tom Rawlings."

Tom hoisted the bag to his shoulder. "Good-bye, Mr. Jackson.

Next time you see me, I hope it'll be as your neighbor." Tom stepped past Sterling.

"Just wait a doggone minute! I'm trying to make this easy for you, son. Now nothing's holding you back. Go rope! Get back on your bulls! Don't let it slip away until all you've got left are your memories...broken dreams...broken like field chaff...." Sterling's age showed through his speech — unsteady, wavering. "You got it in you, the same stuff my son had; what Forrest has. Now don't be a fool and waste it." The old man said his last words in a breathy rush, then leaned on the table. "Forrest ask you to rope with him when he called?"

"Yes."

The skin around Sterling's eyes crinkled. "You won't?"

"I can't."

"Can't stay here, neither." The old man nervously touched his collar. "Get on, now."

As Sterling watched, Tom loaded his Silverado, filling the back end with some heavier equipment from the shed near the cabin. "I'll borrow a horse trailer and be back for Tamarisk when I'm settled."

"Where you heading?" Sterling muttered.

"Doug Vandor's place. They said they could use a hand."

"Not moving very far away."

"I'm staying as close to the Circle H as I can." Tom climbed into his vehicle. "Take care, Mr. Jackson. May God bless you."

"Send up a prayer for yourself if you're in a praying mood. I'm all right."

Tom rolled down the window and started the truck, backing it out of the driveway. Then he straightened his wheels, cut through the snow, and drove away from the large landholdings of the Jackson Cattle Co.

෴

"Margaret has all the red in her hair that Oklahoma has in its soil." Willy was saying, cracking his cobwebbed joke once more on the occasion of the Ivers' first supper with their niece from Wisconsin.

"And how is your mother, Alison? She rarely talks about herself, but I know she was sorry to lose you," Aunt Marg said.

"She's fine." Al took a spoonful of mashed potatoes as if to avoid elaborating.

Margaret waited to speak until Alison's mouth was almost empty. "How does your mother feel about your going away and quitting school? With only one quarter left, is that right?"

The left corner of Al's mouth twitched. "One quarter left of undergraduate work," she corrected. "Four years of graduate study after that."

"I see. What does your mother think about your leaving all that unfinished?"

"She's not too happy about it, but —"

"Not too happy?" Willy guffawed. "Never known Eileen to be 'not too' anything. Mediocre, that's one thing your sister is not, Margaret. Then, neither are you."

Margaret took her empty plate to the sink, also collecting her husband's. "No, don't get up, Alison. You haven't finished. I'll just clean up while you keep eating." Margaret nodded over her niece's head to dismiss her husband.

"Well, Al," Willy stood. "Ol' fire-breather wants a word with you, I surmise." He kissed his niece. "There. That's an asbestos kiss. I give them to all the day-care kids on Margaret's hit list. Protection for myself and those upon whom I bestow it." He skedaddled from the dining room as Margaret pretended to throw a plate at him.

"He never lets me get away with anything." Margaret sighed, smiling as she rinsed the dirty dishes, then took a seat beside her niece. "I suppose it's why I've made it this long. Your mother, your uncle Barney, and I were known as the three firebrands when we were growing up. I'll never live it down."

Margaret touched Al's hair, searching for red highlights within the brownish blond. "Your hair belies you. You're a firebrand, too, aren't you? You just don't show your temper often. Your mother did mention that you and she had a disagreement when you left, though. Don't you think you ought to call her? It's getting on to evening, and your mother's the early-to-bed, early-to-rise sort."

"Oh, I forgot. I did promise to call her as soon as I got here." Al stood and bused her dish. "But I've got to check on Prom first. Then I'll call Mom."

"Alison." Margaret's voice had a low, compelling quality, a rumbling tone, almost like a nicker: the legacy of her years around horses. "Call your mother now. She's waiting. I've been hoping you would do it on your own, but with the excitement and weariness of travel —"

"It's not that, Aunt Marg. I don't know what to say to her anymore. Not since I decided to rodeo." Al's fingertips slid along the wooden tabletop. "I feel...out of words with her."

"Or out of sorts? All she wants to hear is that you're safe, Alison. Perhaps that's all she wants to hear about rodeoing, too. It's a failing mothers have, always wanting their children safe, always wanting them happy."

Margaret reached for her niece's hand. "Please call her, Alison. Give her a good, long talk. Once you're on the road, there won't be time. I know that much from experience. And be sure you let me speak with her when you're done." Margaret stroked the back of Al's hand. "You need to work to remove the wedge between you and your mother, Alison. Come, you can use the phone in the living room and watch the last of the NFR as you talk. I'll keep the volume low."

Al followed her aunt into the next room, crossing the shag carpet to reach a couch upholstered in country blue.

"Sit here, Alison. I'll get the NFR on. Jenny's got the championship sewn up tonight if she and Clover come anywhere close to how they've been racing." Margaret adjusted the television while Al dialed the phone.

After a few minutes of silence and several brief exchanges, Al hung up the phone.

Margaret stared at her. "Alison, I wanted to talk with your mother as well."

"She wasn't there. And Dad was in a hurry."

Margaret watched the NFR competition until a commercial break. "Your mother's gone a lot lately, isn't she?" Her voice was soft.

"I don't know. We all are, I guess."

"Yes. You all are." Margaret said no more, not even during commercials.

Willy Iver found his wife and niece barely able to communicate when he came home — about anything other than the results of the NFR, that is. The riding had been over for at least a half hour, but the two women were still going strong.

No fans like sports fans, Willy thought. *And rodeo's got the worst slack-jawed couch competitors of them all.*

"Did you see her round that second barrel, Alison? Jenny was in top, absolute tip-top form. When she stayed with us, I thought she was good. Very good. Far better than I ever was. But now she's... she's simply —"

"San frantastic!" Willy supplied, surprising them both from their huddle. "So Jenny's a two-time champion. No shock to anyone, but Barney will never quit bragging now."

"And Clover!" Margaret continued, hurling her back against the couch and looking heavenward. "That horse pulled his own leg... did you see him? He actually repositioned his hoof to avoid brushing the barrel. Now that's a racer!"

Al nodded. "That's Promise...soon. He's got it in him. Tomorrow we really start training, and we're not letting up until the Ex."

"Until the Ex is over, you mean. How exciting the next two years will be for you!" Aunt Marg hugged her niece and launched into another boisterous conversation.

Feeling like he was watching a tennis match, Willy tried to stop the volleys between the two women. "How about some butter brickle ice cream to celebrate Jenny's triumph?"

"I don't even know how I'm going to describe that girl's performance," Margaret gushed, squeezing Al's hand. "Everyone will want to know. I'll have to do a write-up for the town paper. How can I say it? She and Clover simply fly over the course. They simply —"

"Plum *float* that pattern."

"Alison! Where in the world did you get that expression?" Margaret demanded. "It's terrible. I might use it, though. There's something fitting about it. Willy, did you hear —"

"Actions!" Willy crowed. "Actions speak louder than all these words, a far better expression for the occasion. Now let's get into the kitchen and celebrate Jenny's victory right." He came to the front of the couch, taking both his niece and wife by the hand. "On to the butter brickle!"

23

FORREST LET HIS NEW FORD PICKUP come to a stop in the bend before the ranch house, taking in the snowbound pines and pastures of his high country home. The Jackson Cattle Co. would once again have a genuine white Christmas, at least here in the hills, if not in the ranch house, where even mentioning Christmas was forbidden since his father died.

Turning off the motor and rolling down the window, Forrest listened to the falling snow hitting the pickup hood. A gentle wind blew, and either the wind or the heavy flakes made a shushing sound. Forrest let his lungs fill with crisp winter air. It felt good to see the land again. Seeing Granddad would be something a whole lot different. Forrest rolled up the window and started down the road.

Refusing the servants' help, Forrest came into the ranch house carrying his sports bag and wearing the buckle that marked him a world champion saddle-bronc rider for the fourth time. The buckle was showy, impressive, lined with jewels. But Forrest knew it wouldn't be enough, not for Sterling Sr.

Forrest's knuckle stopped just short of rapping on his granddad's study. On Forrest's next attempt, he hit the solid oak a trifle harder than intended.

"Yes?" came a reedy voice.

Forrest opened the door and walked in. "Hey, Granddad."

"We-ell, well. Just wondering where in creation you were. Expected you home days ago, young 'un. Thought we might have to postpone the New Year." Sterling slapped his grandson's shoulder.

Forrest took the seat next to his granddad's, a hard, thin-armed chair with curves in all the wrong places. It felt nothing like a saddle.

"So, you took the championship in riding. Early gift, seemed like."

Forrest nodded and waited, touching the brim of his hat in unconscious imitation of his former guardian.

"What happened in the roping?"

Forrest shrugged. "Carl couldn't hold on."

"Couldn't...or wouldn't?"

"Granddad, Carl wanted to throw more than..." Forrest searched for a good comparison, "more than I wanted to win the saddle-bronc title."

"Sure you're not working so hard on riding that you're letting your roping go to seed?"

"I'm sure." Forrest gave his usual answer.

"Your daddy always said riding *and* roping went together: timing, teamwork, balance. Always thought the same thing myself, when I was competing. Always thought maybe it was a Jackson tradition, even though I never got a buckle like the fancy ones your daddy got. Or that one you're wearing."

Sterling stretched his finger toward it. "Only thing better than that buckle is another like it. And one for roping. My solitary regret for the New Year will be that this wasn't a year of two world champion buckles." A tired wheeze drained out of him. "Next year." He fiddled with his bolo. "You'll be staying the week?"

"Just until after Chri — after the holiday."

"That'll please Annie. She's cooking up a real shindig for you."

And you? Forrest wanted to ask. *How do you feel about it, Granddad? How do you feel about...me?*

His grandfather apparently misinterpreted Forrest's keen look. "Hungry after your trip?"

"I had something down the road a ways."

Sterling snuffed. "Can't live on road food. I'll have Annie fix you up a plate. You just missed the meal."

Forrest nodded, knowing he had. Everything on the ranch went by the clock, and he had not forgotten the schedule. If things went well, he'd only have to eat a half dozen or so meals here before continuing on his way. There were lots of other places he could go that felt more like home than the ranch house of the Jackson Cattle Co.

Sterling pulled himself upright and moved to his desk, pushing an intercom button. Forrest listened to the authority in the old man's voice. Granddad hadn't changed, but then Forrest hadn't expected he would. His granddad would always be the same, just as Jen would: both iron-willed rough stock who did whatever they pleased, striking out at anyone who got too close.

The old man released the intercom button, his voice exhausted, and gestured for his grandson to follow him, not bothering to see Forrest obey as he turned and hobbled out of the study.

Forrest sat a moment, wondering what the old man would say if he didn't respond to the unspoken order as he always had. Then he rose and followed.

"Merry Christmas! Merry Christmas! And a fine one it is!" Uncle Barney held up his glass of eggnog and leaned forward to touch glasses with everyone around the Ivers' table. "Drink up," he urged Jenny, guzzling.

"Let us eat in peace, you old leprechaun. You've been speeding us up all night. It's Christmas Eve, not an eight-second event." Uncle Willy winked at Al. "You've got no schedule to keep tonight."

"And you quit your grumbling," Barney retorted. "You're just an outlaw. Wouldn't tolerate you for a minute if not for the legal sanction extended by that lovely wife of yours. Margaret, you still take after your brother." Barney gave Margaret a toothy grin. "Now hurry. I'm just trying to get all of you to the best part of the evening: the presents. Is everyone done? Good, good, bring your glasses to the living room. Another round, Margaret my lass."

They sat near the Christmas tree. Barney rested his back on the wooden nativity scene, then caught himself and peered into the tiny stable. "You've even got the wee babe in there. That's my Margaret. Everything for the occasion."

"Yes, I think that is everything," Margaret said. "Could you stand hearing the Christmas story before we open presents, Barney?"

"Can't say. I'll try, lassie. For you."

"Thank you." Margaret handed the family Bible to her husband. Willy paged through and began reading in a wonderfully slow, resonant voice as Margaret flipped off the light switch and turned on a small brass reading lamp near Willy.

Candles hardly noticeable during the feast now cast a scented, golden glow into the darkened living room, blending with the rainbow of lights on the tree.

"'And it came to pass in those days, that there went out a decree from Caesar Augustus, that all the world should be taxed....'"

At her place near Jen, Al listened. Years ago, she and her mother and father had spent Christmas Eve in the balcony of the Lutheran

Church, in deference to her grandmother's wishes. During the candle-light service, the minister had also read the Christmas story, in the same reverent voice, accented with joy.

"'And she brought forth her firstborn son,'" Uncle Willy continued, "'and wrapped him in swaddling clothes, and laid him in a manger; because there was no room for them in the inn....'"

Al imagined Joseph and Mary, coming into swarming Bethlehem, aching for rest. Aching, as she had been, on her trip from Wisconsin. When Al arrived, Aunt Marg and Uncle Willy had rushed around until both horse and rider were fed and comfortable. *How would it have felt to come to the end of a journey only to find nowhere to rest?*

"'And there were in the same country shepherds abiding in the field, keeping watch over their flock by night.'"

Every so often, Al and her father watched over a cow by night when the animal was known for difficult births. Al's father always awakened her, knowing she loved the event: "Al, it's time. Carina Thirty-three needs some help. Want to come?"

When the calf did emerge, wet and alive, the joy of birth overcame Al. New life: That was a part of farming. It was a part of veterinary work, too, a major reason Al had selected her future profession. She felt a twinge of uneasiness, knowing that she was straying from that path to follow a different dream.

"'And, lo, the angel of the Lord came upon them, and the glory of the Lord shone round about them: and they were sore afraid....'"

How did the glory of the Lord look? Like the candle near Aunt Marg's head, the one trickling its beams down her face? Or like the sun, hot and blinding? Was it like the lights on the Christmas tree, a blinking, vibrant display that seemed to laugh?

"'And the angel said unto them, Fear not: for, behold, I bring you good tidings of great joy, which shall be to all people. For unto you is born this day in the city of David a Saviour, which is Christ the Lord....'"

How could a baby be a savior? Such a confusing story. And how confused those shepherds must have been, sitting there, taking care of their animals, then hearing the voice of an angel —

"'And suddenly there was with the angel a multitude of the heavenly host praising God, and saying, Glory to God in the highest, and on earth peace, good will toward men.'" Uncle Willy paused. "I like another version of this sentence here, the one that makes it clear God's peace is only given to those he's pleased with."

Is God pleased with me? The question came forward, as it did on other occasions, when the night was silent. *Mom's not pleased. She'll never be pleased until I quit rodeo. Dad is. Is...God?*

Al turned to look at her aunt, radiant in candlelight, the red tones of her hair richly accented. Jen sat close by, and Uncle Barney sat clasping his knees on the floor. Uncle Willy bent over the book and looked at Al. "'But Mary kept all these things, and pondered them in her heart.'"

He smiled and continued, but his words repeated inside Al, ricocheting against the thought — *Is God pleased with me?*

Even after Uncle Willy finished reading and gave a long prayer of thanks to God, Al still wondered.

Strewn, torn paper, some almost shredded due to Barney's enthusiasm, littered the living room floor. "Well, and I must have been a good boy this year," Barney said, reveling in his booty. "Thank you, William, for giving me such a fine tie as this." He held up a gaudy green strip of shiny material, studded with red sequins. Jenny thought the thing was hideous, but she nodded when her father showed it to her.

"I'll be wearing it my first show as a commentator for the Chevrolet-Stetson series," he said, his eyes flashing.

"Daddy! When did you find out?"

Her father squeezed her. "Not long ago. But hard it was to keep it a secret until tonight as my special Christmas gift to you. Are you surprised, my girl? I told you I had a fighting chance, especially with all the Ex publicity giving rodeo a new life. And it happened. The Chevrolet-Stetson series will sponsor some of the finest rodeos in the country, and I'll be one of their television commentators. All because of my pretty face," he said, contorting it.

Jenny smiled, a lovely, rare sight. "In spite of your face, I think, Daddy." She kissed him. "Does this mean you'll have more time —"

"To haul you two girls around? I hope so. I should think we television personalities would get the red carpet, especially if our daughter happens to be the reigning barrel racing champion of the world, known by her trademark brown Stetson. It was you who turned it for me, Jenny, my girl." He laughed ecstatically. "You're my good luck charm, the key to my dreams."

"So if I hadn't won —"

"Mind you, I'm not saying that I wouldn't have gotten the job anyway, but your winning didn't hurt me. They like a gimmick, and a bit of the Irish made me stand out, but I believe your helping to make the O'Neill name famous and your endorsement of Stetson gave me extra punch at just the right time. It's a victory...for you and for me."

Jenny felt herself blushing. *If I hadn't won, Daddy might not have gotten his job.* All her father had lived for since her mother died was rodeo. *And I might have blown it for him. If I hadn't won, I would have buried him. What was I thinking? I'll never, never take my eyes off my goal again. No matter what anyone says, thinks...or writes.* Jenny recalled Forrest's note, then his grinning face, and hated every tooth of his smile. Or tried to hate them.

She took a breath and turned to see what the others were doing, hoping to rid herself of Forrest's memory, still stronger than her resolutions.

Aunt Margaret spoke excitedly to Al. "Thank you for the beautiful dress, Alison. How did you dare buy it? I'm so hard to fit, but this looks absolutely perfect!"

"Mom went with me to get it. You two are still about the same size. We planned on mailing it to you, but as long as I was coming down, I just brought it with."

"Oh, it's from your mother, too?"

"Yes, and Dad." Al looked troubled. "Doesn't it say that?"

Margaret rummaged through the paper at her feet. "I didn't see any card. Perhaps Barney covered it in his rampage."

"Oh, wait. I remember. I was supposed to buy the card." Al grinned awkwardly. "Sorry. I was planning on doing it later...."

"Never mind. You're my card." Margaret hugged her. "Why don't we call your folks to thank them and wish them a merry Christmas?"

"Al and I tried that earlier," Willy said. "Nobody was home. Just got the machine."

"Oh." Aunt Margaret quickly turned to Jenny, who was unveiling something. "What's that you have there?"

Jenny carefully undid the rest of the wrapping paper. "Shampoo from Al. Thanks, Al. I've heard about this stuff. It's supposed to be great."

"It is. Sanfrantastic." Al smiled at Uncle Willy. "I tried it on Promise, and I've never seen his coat so shiny."

"Good. I can't wait to see how it looks on Clover —" Jenny turned as she heard Aunt Margaret laughing. "What?"

Margaret shook her head. "You two, so excited about shampoo... for your horses." She laughed again, and Barney joined in.

"That's my girl," he said. "Always more concerned about Clover's looks than her own. Always more concerned about Clover's anything than her own."

"That's a barrel racer for you," Uncle Willy stated. "Horse first, everything else second. That includes the men, too. Am I right, ladies?"

Al and Jenny exchanged looks, but only Al smiled.

Eileen spent most of Christmas in her friend Rhoda's spare room. If her husband missed her, he didn't show it when she came back to retrieve some clothes and make sure he had dumped the scrap bucket underneath the sink. So instead of staying on a few days as she had planned, she packed a suitcase this time. A big one.

Harvey didn't offer to help her carry it to the station wagon. In fact, he hardly looked up from his paper as she lugged it toward the entryway. His inattention made leaving easier, but somehow, she couldn't muster up a shred of gratitude.

"Merry Christmas," she said, not looking at his face as she left. After catching herself from a stumble on the loose fourth step, she saw that he was standing, his paper dragging in one hand.

She gave him a chance to speak, a chance to move, but he did neither. He simply watched, as if in disbelief. She pushed the door closed and heaved her suitcase into the station wagon, then nearly backed through the bottom part of the garage door as it opened much too slowly for her.

24

"NICE ONE, AL, BUT THIS TIME, give Promise a little more inside rein," Jen instructed from her position near the timers. "Don't let him anticipate the turn. He's dropping his shoulder, getting off balance. Keep him centered under you. And use the leg cues. In those big arenas, he won't hear you."

Al walked her horse to the start/finish line and backed up so that he'd have a running go at the pattern. Thinking about which rein to use, where to direct Promise's nose, how much and where to apply leg pressure made racing much more difficult for Al, but Promise did seem to be responding well. As she cued him, he didn't shy or hesitate but did the pattern efficiently.

"Time?" Al asked when they finished.

"Sixteen point three-three. Great for a course this size."

Al scratched Promise's neck. "It didn't feel that fast. It just felt... smooth."

Jen nodded. "You and your horse become a machine. You work together, in total balance. Promise counts just as much as you do when it comes to doing the pattern. But you're the one in charge."

Jen's new system seemed awkward and artificial, but with two world championships to Jen's credit, Al had to try it herself. Already it was showing in her time. Under Jen's tutelage, Al was on her way to qualifying as the Ex's rookie racer.

"Thanks for all the help, Jen," Al said, hopping down from the saddle to rub Prom's nose. "I'm sure it was harder to teach me than it was to learn from you."

Jen had mounted Clover and was warming him up for his own run. "It's been fun, Al. Like...old times." Jen cued Clover and began the pattern.

Al and Promise watched them. The pair did seem to float, or slide, around the barrels. Their runs seemed nearly leisurely, except for the straightaway gallop. Yet Jen raced a steady average that hovered in the fifteens or low sixteens, depending on the course size.

"Fifteen-eight that time, Jen. You guys aren't any fun. You're too consistent."

"Have to be. So do you." ·

"We don't have to. But I want to." Al rubbed Promise down as Jen continued running Clover.

The two women had by now spent hundreds of hours training together, but Al was only beginning to understand how Jen ticked. She had changed since they rode together in the summers. All her energy was focused on racing, but whenever Al asked Jen about her plans for the season, Jen would speak no further than the upcoming rodeo. Even then Jen never bet on her own victory.

"Come on, Jen. Quit being humble," Al said one day after a grueling afternoon under the Oklahoma sun, particularly trying for a Wisconsinite only recently freed from a frigid northern winter. Al and Jen were practicing the pattern outside, so their mounts would be prepared for the variety of conditions and arena sizes they would soon have to face.

"Jen, you have to be a little bit confident. You have to know you're going to do well this season, just like you did last season. Your time today beat what you did in the NFR."

"No, Al," Jen replied, not even looking at her cousin. "It doesn't work like that. You can never count on anything. How you're doing today or how you did yesterday doesn't say anything about what'll happen tomorrow."

"But you have to have a winning attitude."

"Sure." Jen ran Clover through the pattern before she returned to where Al and Promise were resting. "A winning attitude is the attitude that you could win. You want to win. You see yourself winning. But you don't count on it. You don't ease up. You don't relax."

"Constant stress?"

Jen shrugged. "If you want to look at it that way."

No matter what Al did, no matter how she phrased the question, she could never get Jen to sound sure about anything in the future. Jen wouldn't even discuss the future.

Now Al's first rodeo as a member of the Women's Professional Rodeo Association was only days away, and she felt her own confidence plummeting. If Jen couldn't be sure of victory, how on earth could she?

Tom hung up the phone, standing in the middle of the Vandors' kitchen as if he stood alone in a wide pasture.

"Bad news, Tom?" Angie Vandor ventured.

"Yeah."

"But no one died? From the look on your face for a while there, I couldn't tell."

"Nobody died...but I might."

Angie plunged her hands into the soapy sink to finish the supper dishes. "You don't want to talk about it? That's fine with me."

"It's all right, Angie." Tom moved to the kitchen table, lifting the metal chair's legs so they wouldn't scratch the floor. "That was my uncle. He...sold the Circle H."

"Oh, I am sorry, Tom."

"Me, too." There had never been much chance of success with Al, but the Circle H seemed one portion of Tom's dream within reach. Until tonight.

"Well, it's not the only ranch around." Angie smiled and pushed through the kitchen's swinging doors, carrying a crystal bowl.

Angie soon reappeared, her hands empty. She walked to the sink and grabbed a damp dishrag, then came near Tom to swab the table, looking at his face as she wiped. "Don't let the Circle H worry you, Tom. It needed a mountain of work. There wasn't much left worth saving, though the land is beautiful. Doug and I rode the fence line a year or so ago. It's all broken down, like the buildings. Who bought it, anyway?"

"Sterling Jackson." Tom glanced at the phone.

"That so? Then maybe it was worth something after all." Angie finished the dishes and spread butter on the tops of the bread loaves she had just baked, tipping them on their sides and draping a dry dishtowel over them.

Tom rose. "Angie, do you mind if I use the phone again?"

"Not at all. Go ahead."

Tom walked back to the phone and dialed. The phone rang only once before a voice answered.

"Good evening, Jackson Cattle Company."

"Is Mr. Jackson there?"

"Mr. Forrest is on his way to a rodeo. Mr. Sterling is entertaining guests."

"Tell Sterling that Tom Rawlings is calling."

Tom saw Angie cast a surprised look in his direction. It wasn't like him to be so abrupt, but Tom felt no inclination to season his words tonight.

Angie turned Tom's way as she left the room. "Turn off the lights when you're done, will you, Tom?"

"Yes." He nodded, his attention riveted to the receiver he held with his shoulder.

A voice assaulted his ear. "Rawlings, that you?"

"What is going on, Mr. Jackson?"

"You planning on roping with Forrest now, son?"

"I'm calling about the Circle H."

"S'what I mean. You ready to play?"

Tom gripped the receiver and reminded himself that Sterling was a man to pity, not hate. "What's the game?"

"All or nothing, son. Now it's a gamble, after the trouble you gave me and my grandson. Missing that roping title." Sterling grunted in disgust.

Tom waited for the old man to show his hand, refusing to fall into a trap without first knowing its exact dimensions.

"Here's how it is, Tom: I'll give you a shot at the Circle H if you sign a contract I've just drawn up that says you'll rope for my grandson this season. And if by the last big show before the NFR, you have a total winning aggregate of, say, a hundred twenty-five thousand or more for a down payment, I'll hand over the Circle H mortgage. Fair enough?"

"The only way I could hope to make that much by then is if I roped and rode —"

"And did both good enough to make the top fifteen. Course I realize that, son. As a favor to your daddy, I'm giving you a chance at greatness. Since you're too dumb to take it yourself."

Tom turned the proposal over in his mind. Was Sterling giving him a chance or sealing his fate? *Lord, what should I do?*

"Let's make it a little more definite," Sterling said. "Let's see. Halloween would be a fitting date now, wouldn't it? You get that treat to me by October thirty-first, and I'll make good on your uncle's trick to cheat you out of your daddy's old ranch. I'll even give you five years to pay me in full."

When Tom didn't answer, Sterling said, "Don't try my patience, boy. Take any more time to decide, and I'll move the date up. Money, too."

Tom felt an urging in his spirit, and he responded. "I'll sign, Mr. Jackson — if you hand over the deed, not the mortgage, on the thirty-first — for one hundred thousand."

Sterling chuckled. "Guess you've got some brains. All right, it's a deal. It's about time you got back into the saddle. You should thank me..."

Tom pulled the receiver from his ear as the old man ranted about the evils of letting opportunity pass one by. The house sounded deathly quiet, and Tom guessed Angie had ascended the stairs to her bedroom where her husband, Doug, had gone earlier.

"Not a word about this to anyone, Tom, until the thirty-first. That'll be in the terms, too."

"I guess you can buy my silence along with everything else."

Sterling snorted. "My hand was forced, same as yours. Forrest spun out of here after you flat-out refused to rope with him. Said he was going to ask that fool, Winky Blackmont, to head his steers. No world championships with that has-been. Winky's drinking himself useless. I had to take the bit and run. Now you have to, if you want a chance at your ranch. I didn't do it all, son. Your uncle was fixing to sell out to the highest bidder before the new year. Didn't even have you picked out for a chance."

The old man's gravelly laugh increased Tom's ire. "He threw you over, boy. You should be glad I'm helping you out. Now get on over here and sign. My lawyer's right beside me. One thing more: You'll have to work out the timing on this, stop Forrest before he gets to Blackmont or anyone else. If he sets on another partner, our agreement'll be void." Sterling's laugh now sounded more like a coughing attack. "Forrest should get a chance to throw you over, too, don't you think? Adds a little more fun to the deal. A little justice. You'll have to hurry on over to California, Tom. I've got Forrest's number and the name of the place he's planning to stay in Red Bluff, if I can find it."

Tom heard papers shuffling and the sliding of wood on wood.

As Sterling searched, he kept speaking. "Red Bluff. Two-bit rodeo. The boy just won more than a hundred thousand at the NFR, and he can't win more than a thousand at Red Bluff, even with both riding and roping. Don't know why he's wasting his time on the road when he could be home. Ah, here we are."

Sterling rattled off the information Tom needed. Tom wrote it down and ended the call. He dialed Forrest's number, keeping the paper in front of him. He let the phone ring...and ring...and ring. There was no answer.

25

TIRED FROM HIS LONG DRIVE BROKEN ONLY by pit stops to fuel up, take care of Tamarisk, and try Forrest's number again, Tom stood at the entrance of the Old West Bar 'n' Grill before walking through the narrow entryway.

He approached the bar, keeping his body from touching the varnished wood as he looked at the patrons in the room. Tom was about to wave the bartender near when he spotted Forrest in a dark corner, quietly sipping from a glass and looking out the window across the room. A flashing sign above Forrest bathed him in intermittent red. A squat pyramid of half-crushed aluminum cans stood near his elbow.

Tom ordered a soda and took it to Forrest's table. The barroom wasn't crowded. A sprinkling of good-looking women had automatically smiled on seeing Tom enter, just as they would at the entrance of any halfway appealing man. Tom wondered why Forrest hadn't taken any up on their unspoken offers. Forrest usually had at least one or two gorgeous women in his company, or used to, after Jenny dumped him. But not tonight.

"Hey, Tom. What're you doing here?"

"Looking for you, cowboy." Tom set his soda down and pulled out a chair.

Forrest grinned, but his gaze strayed back to the window.

"Who are you watching for?"

Another grin slid across Forrest's face, and Tom saw several women smile in sequence.

"Nobody, Tom. Guess I'm watching for nobody." Forrest's eyes swept over the room. "A bar full of pretty women, and I'm staring out the window. And you're looking for me. Maybe we're both loco."

"Maybe," Tom had to agree, considering what he'd just done. "Do you still call yourself 'Forrest Fire', or have you settled down over the past two years?" Tom felt his friend needed a partial rousing before they talked business. No telling how long he had sat here, staring out the window, the beer and the isolation settling upon him like a stupor.

Forrest took a swig from his glass. "Why you here, Tom? Get thirsty way up there in the hills and suddenly crave a brew with your old roping buddy? Thought ranching couldn't make it without you."

Tom saw a glimmer of sobriety in Forrest's eyes and took that as his cue. "I can't make ranching without *you*, Forr."

"What does that mean?"

"I quit at Doug Vandor's. Tamarisk's in the trailer, behind the pickup I traded for my Silverado. I'm here to rope."

"You mean you just picked up and left? Packed all your stuff in your new pickup and took off?"

"New it's not," Tom said, "but yes, everything I own, after trading for the trailer and other things I'll need to rodeo, is in the pickup. Here I am." He lifted empty palms toward the low ceiling.

"Where're you staying?"

"For now, on the next block."

"You got Tamarisk in the trailer still?"

"I ran into Val Nolan at your hotel, and he's in the pickup, keeping an eye on Tamarisk and everything. Val's the only one I could find half-sober. I'd like to get Tam to a good stable tonight. So, how about it?"

"Well, sure. There're some open stalls where I'm keeping Canyon."

"I mean, how about roping?"

Forrest made a swipe at his chin. "You came here to rope with me? For the season?"

"Yes."

Forrest slowly shook his head. "I'm sorry, Tom. Told Winky this afternoon that I needed a partner. We're meeting in the morning to try some practice runs." He offered a dull apology with his steamy blue eyes. "Rodeo's tomorrow, Tom. Couldn't cut it much closer than that. Had to get somebody else."

Tom felt as if a bull had tossed him belly-first in the dirt. The air wouldn't come. Neither would speech.

"You all right, Tom?"

"I can't believe it," Tom squeezed out.

"I can't believe you're here." Forrest's eyes opened to half-mast. "Isn't like you to run off half-cocked; it's like the Tom I used to know. You really quit your job?"

Tom nodded.

"And sold your vehicle and everything just to come down here and rope for me?"

"Yes." Tom still felt it difficult to breathe.

Forrest laughed. "Bad move, cowboy. So what're you going to do now?"

"I don't know. I just felt that...this is where God was leading me..."

"Well, we all make mistakes, don't we? Even the Big Guy."

Forrest was still laughing, but sobered as Tom raised his eyes. "I am sorry, Tom. If I'd known sooner —"

"No." Tom regained his wind. "I should have thought it out better. I was just so sure." He shook his head again. "I really thought I was supposed to rope with you. I've been praying about it, and I thought God —"

"Don't worry." Forrest patted the table near Tom. "Have a drink with me. Then we can talk to God together. Tell Val to come on in. Tamarisk'll be fine."

"Val's had enough for one night." Tom's brain seemed clearer, but he still felt winded. "I shouldn't keep him out there any longer. Tamarisk, either. We were in Colorado not too long ago, and I didn't let Tam get out as much as I should have during the trip." Tom attempted one last save of the Circle H. "Your granddad didn't tell you I was coming down?"

"Haven't heard from him since I left the ranch, I'm tickled to say. Tell you what, Tom. You meet me at my room around ten tomorrow, and we'll go down to the arena together. I think I can find you another partner. You still heading, or thinking about being a heeler?"

"Heading, I guess. I don't know. Maybe I should just turn right around and leave." Tom attempted a weak smile. "Forrest, I have to think this out. I'm not sure where to go from here. I can't believe —"

"Don't worry about anything tonight," Forrest advised, peering at Tom. "You don't look so good. Get Tamarisk and Val situated and come back here. We'll figure out something." Forrest raised his amber-filled glass. "This solves all problems: past, present, and future."

When Tom didn't reply, Forrest drank deeply. He set the emptied glass down and winked at the barmaid, who smiled and took another can from the cooler. Forrest held up his hand to stop her momentarily. "Join me, Tom?"

Though Tom would have liked to drown his sorrows some way, the beer held little temptation. So far. "No, thanks, Forr. I'd...better get going."

"All right, then. See you tomorrow." Forrest waggled one finger at the barmaid, who put a single can of beer on a serving tray and approached the table.

Tom stood. "Okay. Tomorrow."

"At ten," Forrest called after him. "Don't do anything desperate before then, all right? You'll meet me?"

"Yes."

"All right, then. Bring Tamarisk, too. We'll see how he's doing."

As he left the bar, Tom sent Forrest an offhand wave through the bluish air, the forced laughter, the stink of alcohol saturating the wall and floorboards, overpowered by the stronger smell of loneliness. Even when he had been a bar hopper himself, Tom knew that last scent was more powerful than any tonic the bar offered to counter it. Still, like Forrest, often with Forrest, he had come, drawn like a ship to harbor, seeking warmth, safety, an end to his voyage — and finding none.

Tom shut the door behind him and gulped a big breath of city air, hardly an improvement over the bar's stench. He walked to the back of the horse trailer to check on Tamarisk.

"This might be the end of the trail, Tam." He rubbed the gelding's chestnut coat. "Guess we might as well get you comfortable for the night before we make the trip home." Tom withdrew his hand. "Home. Wonder where that is now."

The horse gave no answer, just a slight movement of one hoof against the trailer floor. Tom kicked at a crushed cigarette butt in the gutter before he climbed inside the rusty pickup cab.

Since the day Eileen packed her suitcase, she had only gone back to the farm to take away more clothes, more belongings. If Harvey's truck happened to be in the yard or in the garage, she merely drove back to Rhoda's.

Her marriage was over. The trip to the lawyer and the pieces of paper he'd helped her file merely testified to that fact. Eileen didn't know exactly how long divorces took, but since she doubted Harvey would contest what she had asked for a settlement, it probably wouldn't be long. Obsessive material generosity was Harvey's one gift, the one responsible for the farm's neglected condition — the one responsible for their becoming burdened with the farm in the first place. Eileen intended to be on the receiving side for once.

She'd asked for a fair settlement: half of all they owned at the time of sale. Knowing Harvey would never sell the farm although he hardly lifted a pitchfork to keep it, Eileen didn't plan to wait for her windfall. As soon as the holidays were over, she resolved to canvass the town and find a position — at the grocery store if she had to, but preferably the bank. She was good with figures, catching mistakes on her bank statements whenever they occurred. The tellers looked sharp when they saw her coming, and the bank president himself told her that she had missed her calling when she had become a farm wife.

"Let me know if you ever want a little part-time work," Lloyd had joked on her last visit, opening the door for her as she left.

As Eileen wrote "teller" above "cashier" on her list of possible occupations, she hoped the bank president wasn't completely joking.

Tamarisk trotted around the small, shoddy indoor arena, passing strips of daylight filtering through the wallboards. Tom cued his horse into a canter and circled the arena, keeping up a column of prayer to heaven as Tamarisk kept up a column of dust behind them.

Tom felt more hopeful after a night of calling out to God. Though he wasn't sure what to do next, he continued to pray with a growing sense of confidence. Somehow, he would get the Circle H. The land had always seemed a promise to him from the Lord, a legacy of his father and mother. Neither the train that killed him, the poverty that killed her, nor the greed that caused Tom's uncle to sell the land could take away what the Lord had promised. At least, Tom tried to believe it was so.

As he prayed, Tom built a loop with his lariat, feeling the rope in his gloved hand. He let the loop balance, slide, grow larger. He quit twirling and praying when the door at the arena's far end opened, and in walked Forrest.

"I don't know. Can't find him anywhere."

"Winky's not here yet?" Tom asked.

"Must have a hangover." Forrest mounted Canyon and nudged him toward the box. "Might as well try a round together." Forrest eyed the brown Corriente in the chute. "That steer looks like he needs a little exercise, Tom."

Forrest spoke to the cowboy whose job it was to set the Corriente free. "Soon as Tom gives the nod, you go ahead and let that steer loose."

As Tom got Tamarisk loaded, the chestnut horse's rump bumped the end of the left-hand box. Tom could feel his gelding's anticipation. Tamarisk had begun prancing once they entered the arena, and now that they were in position for the race the quarter horse loved above all else, Tamarisk's muscles bunched and his ears flicked at the slightest motion.

Tom pulled on the reins, reversing Tamarisk and allowing two other cowboys to fix the barrier string in front of him. Tamarisk followed every action with his eyes.

The cowboys stretched the barrier string across the box, making it ready to release when the steer had his head start. Tamarisk wedged himself into the box's corner, his body pointed forward, tensed for the blast out of the box once the barrier dropped.

Forrest watched from the other side of the chute, lariat in hand and an extra rope hanging from his saddle. "Tamarisk's looking good. I'm ready any time you are, Tom."

Clutching his own lariat with its drooping loop, Tom nodded.

The chute opened and the steer tore out. The barrier snapped free. Tamarisk charged. Tom's loop slid through the air as the horse drew into perfect position for the throw. Tom released, flicked, and the lasso settled around the Corriente's hooked horns.

Making a quick dally with the rope around his saddle horn, Tom expertly got his fingers clear as the rope went tight. He slowed Tamarisk and turned the steer to allow Forrest to make his throw.

Forrest's rope snaked out and caught both of the steer's hind legs. Tamarisk wheeled to face Canyon, and the steer stretched between the two horses, the ropes on his heels and horns taut.

"Well?" Forrest asked the cowboys who were acting as officials.

"Six point two — and clean on the barrier."

A smile started from the left corner of Forrest's mouth. "Nice, Tom."

Tom grinned back. "Slower than we used to do."

"Plenty good for a two-year vacation, cowhand."

"Don't start —"

"How'd you like a job, Rawlings?"

Tom was trotting with the steer back to the catch pen. His rope slipped through his fingers and trailed behind the Corriente, who was making straight for the hay in his pen. Tom watched the end of his lariat slithering in the dust. "You're not serious. You said Winky was roping for you this year. You told me that last night."

"Had to check you out first. Don't want any has-been roping with me. I'm going NFR this year, all the way to the world title. I need a partner who wants it bad as I do. That you, Tom?"

At first just a dot on the horizon, the Circle H came rapidly back into Tom's focus. "That's me, Forr. I want the Circle H."

"But do you want the championship?"

"Same thing."

Forrest nodded. "Glad we finally found the terms you'd take." He finished wrapping his rope and drew Canyon alongside Tamarisk. "Granddad said this was the only way you'd do it."

Tom stared, then shook his head, disbelieving. "You let me sweat all night, knowing you were going to take me on as your partner?"

"Only if you could still rope. We're friends, Tom, but this is the world championship at stake. I was sweating a little last night, too."

"You weren't sweating enough to ask Winky, though," Tom observed.

"No. Not that much." Forrest stuck out his hand. "Welcome home, partner."

CHAPTER

26

TOM WATCHED THE RED BRINDLE CROSSBREED trot into the center of the arena, his stride in time to his victory song. Vapor from dry ice curled around the bull. The spotlight followed each sway of the skin hanging beneath his thick neck, each thrust of his horns.

Another spotlight bathed a cowboy standing on a platform with his bull rope and chaps, facing the bull who made passes around the arena to the crowd's clapping.

The vapor, music, colored lights and human beat began stirring blood that had long lain dormant within Tom. "That cowboy looks like Lane, doesn't he, Forrest?" Tom asked, hoping to distract himself, hoping to keep old emotions from rising, old vices from returning to possibly overwhelm him. "Looks like Lane and Red Rock all over again."

"Lane Frost's dead. That's Casey Vollin from Salinas."

"I know. But he looks like Lane did." Tom rubbed the rope in his hand. *Concentrate on roping. Roping and riding. That's all you're here for.* "Old Red Rock still looks good. What a bull."

"That bull broke more cowboys."

"In more ways than one. Wonder if I ever could have ridden him. My daddy bucked off him once."

Forrest didn't reply.

The music increased in volume, quickened in tempo, along with the bull's gait, along with Tom's pulse. *Remember? Remember?* he heard the rhythm pound. *Glory, excitement, pleasure. All you want. All for you.*

He turned from the siren song. "Remember when Lane finally conquered Red Rock? I always hoped I'd get my turn at him."

"You still got bull fever, Tom. Sorry to say it."

Tom suddenly longed to give in to the fever completely, as he used to, as if it were the only thing in life that mattered. He tasted the temptation. Slowly his mind resisted it, gathering strength, steeling itself, like a guitar string being tightened until it played a true tone.

More to life, he reminded himself, and the thought broke the atmosphere's hold. *Much more. The abundant life, that's what I want, Lord. All you've shown me, all I'm beginning to savor. And more to come, blessings pouring down from the windows of heaven.*

Tom said a prayer of thanks before answering his friend. "Yes, I have bull fever, but I don't think it's fatal anymore. I wish I was riding, but it's going to take a lot of work before I climb on again." *Work both physical and mental.*

"Just be glad you're roping. This'll be a good place to test you. Remember to keep your fingers out of the way. Don't want to send you home to your ranch next year with a world championship buckle and no way to get it buckled."

"I'll watch my fingers. You just watch the steer." Tom's muscles relaxed slightly. They remained battle ready, but he no longer felt the old call to excess. There was an excitement entirely right and good, and another that could burn out of control as it had only two years before. Tom had wondered whether he could recognize the difference.

It was a spiritual conflict, one that Forrest could never understand unless he identified the opposing forces in this war of allegiance and chose, as Tom finally had, to serve the Creator rather than the destroyer. Tom wished Forrest was his brother-in-arms, a fellow soldier who would fight at his side and keep his faith secure, his resolve firm in the knowledge that all blessings, all real joy came from the Giver of life, not the taker. But Tom knew Forrest had not even begun to realize the existence of an arena other than the rodeo arena. Forrest had not yet sensed the supernatural skirmish or taken up his armor.

Tom had. And although the rodeo had scarcely begun, he had already won the first round.

When the lights came up and Red Rock retired to the catch pen, Forrest and Tom rode out to do their part in the opening ceremony. Since the announcement of the Ex, rodeo's grand entry parade had been revived nationwide, and all contestants were asked to take part.

Forrest sat absently in the saddle, watching the crowd. He'd slipped so completely into the habit that whenever he was among people, a part of him never ceased looking, searching, for —

"Forrest!" Tom said as they stopped in formation. "Is that Al over there? Alison Austin, down by the end?"

Forrest caught his breath. "And Jen." He couldn't add more because the line of horses moved into a pattern, and Tom slipped past him. Fortunately, Canyon followed his traveling buddy as they made their exit from the arena. Forrest let the reins go slack and craned his neck to watch the redhead on the black gelding. His eyes branded her image on his mind as they did every time he saw her, burning it deeper and deeper. *Jen. Who thought you'd ever turn up in Red Bluff?*

❦

"Jen!"

Jenny tried to move away through the crush.

"Hey, Jen!"

The voice was nearing, and Jenny saw Forrest shouldering his way toward her through a living maze of horses and dismounted riders. As he came closer, she fought to keep her appearance calm. "Hi, Forrest."

"I didn't think you'd be here. Glad I decided to come, now. I like the way the new year's shaping up."

Jenny looked over her shoulder. "We thought it would be a good place for Al —"

"So that *was* her. Tom!"

Tom headed in Forrest's direction, holding Canyon's reins in his hands. Riders around him were making their way toward the chutes or practice area.

"Come on over here, Tom." Forrest motioned. "Look who I found."

"Hello, Jenny."

"Hi, Tom. So you're back in rodeo. Good to see you."

"Thanks, Jenny. Is Al here? I thought I —"

"Right here." Al, horseless, ducked through the obstacles in her way and stood between Forrest and Tamarisk. "Hey, Forrest. Hi, Tom." She looked from one to the other. "It's so great to see you guys! I feel like I'm home."

Tom nodded, a wide smile spreading across his face.

"Are you riding bulls again, Tom?" Al asked. "Bet you'd love a shot at Red Rock."

He was slow to answer, though his smile grew stronger.

"I'm...just roping tonight, though I'll be in riding shape soon. The best I'm hoping for now is to win enough to pay my entry fees."

"Your fees? I paid for you, cowboy," Forrest said, "but only for roping, and I won't be doing it after this. And I won't even lend you money to climb on a bull."

"So you guys are roping together again." Al smiled, but Jenny noticed that she was really talking to Forrest alone. "And Jen and I are racing."

Jenny glanced at Forrest to see his response, but he was taking the reins from Tom and mounting Canyon.

"I was going to say it's like old times," Al continued, "but it's not, not yet, anyway. Ironside is gone, and I hardly know anyone on the circuit, not that Jen and I've had time for anything but racing lately." She bathed them all in a warm, wide smile brighter than all but Tom's. "It sure is great to see you."

As Al talked on, Jenny watched her, wishing she had Al's way of talking: free and easy, like a Dakota wind — no barriers in sight.

In the arena, announcer Sonny Florin was getting the crowd going, and the first bareback bronc was released from its chute. Jenny heard eight seconds elapse: eight seconds Al filled with talk, stopping only when the horn sounded.

"Did you hear that?" Al asked everyone, as if they all were deaf. "That cowboy got a seventy-six. Nice start."

"Not bad," Forrest agreed, shooting a look at Jenny. Again Jenny felt a rising heat that crept toward her cheeks. She struggled to keep it down.

"We'll all get together after the rodeo, okay?" Forrest asked. "I've got to get Tom here ready for roping now."

"You mean you've got to get ready for your saddle-bronc ride," Tom corrected. "I'm not up for a long time yet." He included Jenny in his smile, but Jenny's attention shifted to Forrest as he nudged Canyon ahead, his form soon blocked out by other riders and horses, none so high in the saddle as Forrest Jackson.

"Come on, Promise," Al whispered, maneuvering him into the position they'd marked out before the rodeo began. *How many strides is it to the first barrel? Think. Think! Don't blow it, not in front of four thousand people — and Forrest.*

Al heard the announcer say her name. She froze for half a second before cuing Promise to begin the approach.

They came into the arena fast, veering to the right and going a little wide on the first barrel. *Closer, closer.* Al remembered Jen's advice, keeping Promise straight until the last second and cutting the next barrel in a perfect circle.

Promise charged at the final barrel. Al cued him to take it tight and fast. He sliced in too close, too soon, and Al felt the barrel against her leg, felt it slam into her flesh and topple.

"Eighteen point eighty-two for Alison Austin," the announcer said. "The penalty on that last barrel really hurt her," Sonny continued, oblivious to Al's rush of emotions. "If not for the added five seconds, Austin would've been in the money. Next up is Charmayne Rodman on Scamper. Now this horse is a real champion, folks, just like his rider. Have been for a decade. Watch as they..."

Al tuned out the voice and walked Promise to his stall.

When Jen joined her after the rodeo, Al was still combing Promise while running through her failure.

"I won't tell you it's not bad to tip over a barrel, Al, because I know how I feel when it happens to me." Jen smoothed Promise's mane as she spoke.

"Can you even remember the last time it did?"

"Yeah, in practice the day we left Aunt Margaret's and Uncle Willy's place. Don't you remember?"

"I mean can you remember the last time it happened while you were competing?"

"Yes. At the NFR."

"You didn't tip over anything at the NFR."

"I did during the warm-up."

"That doesn't count!"

"Everything counts. What happens at practice is what happens in competition."

"I know, but —"

Jen laid her hand on Al's arm. "No. That's what happens. You're still letting Promise anticipate the turn. You're anticipating it, too. Wait for it to happen, then make it quick, tight. Don't lean into it so much. Don't let Promise drop his shoulder."

"Fine, Jen. Next time I'll try harder!" Al threw her curry comb. It bounced on the floor and landed under a clump of hay.

Jen bent down, but Al stopped her. "I'm sorry, Jen." Al picked up the comb herself. "I really blew it tonight, in more ways than one."

"Now that you know that, you can go on. Just remember, don't anticipate."

Al exhaled loudly. "I'll try to remember. It's just that we hit the first barrel too wide, and —"

"You were trying to make up for it on the last one."

"Right."

"Wrong. Wrong thing to do, although I did it a lot myself. But you can't race that way. Every barrel, every turn is new. You don't make one turn tighter because you went too wide on the other; you don't make it looser because you just tipped a barrel."

"You live in the present," Al said slowly. "That's what you do, isn't it, Jen?"

"What?"

"I've been wondering what the difference was between us, and that's it. That's why you acted the way you did toward Forrest and Tom when they showed up after the grand entry."

"What do you mean?"

"You know...there I am, remembering all the good times like they were yesterday, and there you are, sitting on Cloverleaf, cool as a rodeo queen to an old date."

"I wasn't...cool."

"Then what do you call it? Forrest was so glad to see you his eyes almost popped out, but you didn't give him anything to warm up to. I'd kill to get him to look at me like that."

"What about how Tom was looking at you?"

"Nobody notices me when you're around. Wish I was a red-head."

Jen looked at Al, her green eyes quiet. She watched silently as Al kept currying Promise.

After working out the last wisps of her anger through the thorough brushing she gave Promise, Al stepped back. "What do you think, Jen?"

"Prom looks...'sanfrantastic,' as Uncle Willy says."

Al laughed. "He does. I'm feeling better, too. Thanks for being patient. Think you'll be able to stand a whole year of my fits?"

"I do the same thing, though mostly I just work it out in my head, like you've been doing. I hang around Clover and try to understand what happened. By the next round, I'm usually ready to go."

Al gave Promise a final pat. "Well, Jen, now I'm ready to go...to the dance." She reached for her duffel bag. "Coming?"

"Not yet. I'll...meet you there."

"All right." Al lifted her bag. "I'm taking a shower first. If you get there before me, I'll find you. If we have any trouble, we can meet by the door."

"Okay."

Al started walking, talking as she went. "I told Forrest and Tom we'd bring in the new year together. Tom said he'd hunt us down and rope us if we stood them up. He was still pretty high from their victory. See you at the dance." She rounded the corner.

After a quick shower and useless struggle with her long mass of hair, Al gave up and shoved on her hat. She tried a little mascara on her lashes and ended up with a smudge under her left eye that degenerated into a red spot when she tried to rub it off.

She had better success with her outfit, a casual western look in new black Wranglers and a hand-tooled leather belt adorned with silver conchas and a buckle she'd won. As she tucked in her smoky gray long-sleeved, button-down shirt, she approved of the image in the mirror. "Not too flashy, but me."

When she reached the dance floor, she wished she had dressed flashier. Felicia Newcastle was gorgeous in a golden metallic shirt with fringes that set off her bleached-blond looks. Felicia had taken second in the barrel racing and was celebrating, a glass in one hand and two cowboys in the other.

"Hello, Al."

Al started at the voice so close beside her. "Tom!" She gave him a swift appraisal. "Don't you look spiffy."

He adjusted his hat self-consciously. "I overdid it? Guess I've been out of rodeo too long."

"No, you look great."

He did. Larger than nearly all the bull riders, Tom had the healthy, muscled physique of most good cowboys. The bronze-colored shirt with gold pinstripes brought out the highlights in his hair and the softness of his brown eyes. He, too, wore a winner's buckle, but his, for world championship team roping, outshone Al's silver barrel-racing buckle. He wore Wranglers, of course, their hems barely revealing the etching on his leather boots.

"I don't remember you looking so good, Tom. You must be living right."

He smiled. "I try. Want to dance?"

A slow country-western song had just started. Al nodded and Tom brought her out on the dance floor. He held her close, but only comfortably so, and as they danced, they talked.

Al hadn't realized how many dances they'd had together until the New Year's countdown began. She let go of Tom and looked anxiously around the room.

"What's wrong?"

"I told Jen I'd meet her, and I forgot! I've got to find her." Al began threading her way through people, making progress toward the door. She bumped into one woman who whirled and glared as yellow liquid from the glass she held spilled to the floor.

"Sorry. Oh, sorry, Felicia. By the way, congrat —"

"Forget it. Five...four..." Felicia spoke in unison with the crowd, resting her hand on a cowboy who sat with his back to her.

Al recognized the cowboy. "Hey, Forrest!"

He looked up from the table where he was nursing his drink. "Hey, Al. You seen Jen?"

Felicia gave Al an angry stare. "Two...One!" Felicia turned to collect her New Year's kiss from Forrest as the hall echoed with whoops, hollers, cheers, and party favor hornblasts. The band struck up a country version of "Auld Lang Syne."

Not quite knowing even afterwards if it was she or Forrest who initiated it, Al found herself in Forrest's arms, the beneficiary of a brief kiss.

Forrest released Al and laughed as Felicia stormed away. Sudden disappointment replaced Al's thrill at the touch of Forrest's lips. Now those lips were curled in laughter that perhaps was as insincere as his kiss. Al forced a half-hearted chuckle to hide her confusion. She watched Felicia's departure and stopped laughing when she saw the blond push past Jen, who was standing in the doorway. "Forrest! Is that Jen over there?"

"Where?"

Al pointed, but the doorway was empty.

CHAPTER

27

IF JEN HAD BEEN WATCHING BY THE DOORWAY, she never admitted it, not during the night of the New Year's Eve Pro Rodeo and Celebration at Red Bluff, California, and not in the rodeos that followed.

Al's performances improved steadily. She and Promise competed at several rodeos during the first weeks of January. In Odessa, Texas, at the Sand Hills Hereford and Quarter Horse Show and Rodeo, Al even placed third and won $1,339 with a time of 14.90. Jen took first with 14.67, a time that didn't please her considering the size of the arena but brought in $2,008. She and Al spent January practicing, traveling, competing, and traveling again, all the while looking forward to the big rodeos coming up. Neither mentioned the Ex.

They were "chaperoned" by Blarney as they drove into the Mile High City, buttressed by the Rockies. Al looked at the skyscrapers of metal and glass and wondered how the city had appeared when Denver was one of the busiest cow towns in the West.

"And she's a glorious sight now, isn't she?" Barney asked as he guided the pickup with its horse trailer through the city streets. "All spruced up with a new airport and convention center, too, looking shiny as a silver buckle to my eyes. Ah, Denver."

Jen kept reading from a worn book on barrel racing, but Al looked at the sights and quizzed her uncle about Denver history.

"Larimer Square was known for being the real hub of entertainment for cowboys in Wild West times," he said. "Rodeo was born some place or other like this, wherever cowboys had the leisure and cash to make competition interesting. After a long trail ride, the boys weren't above cutting loose a bit."

"Kind of like the cowboys of today after a rodeo," Al said.

"Sure, and there's not much difference between cowboys now and then where temperament is concerned, niece. But Denver has changed. She thrived in the old days because she was a major railhead, a place for the ranchers to send their cattle east by train. Nowadays there aren't many ranchers left, I'm sorry to be saying."

"But plenty of cowboys."

"For the next two weeks, yes. This town will be crawling with cowboys...and cowgirls, I'm thinking. And Larimer Square still pretends to be the Old West in the flesh." Barney looked thoughtful. "Are you girls sure you'll be all right traveling on your own after your competition?"

Jen looked up. "Fine, Daddy."

"Just like we were in Red Bluff. Right, Jen?"

Jen didn't answer.

"I am still regretting I wasn't able to be with you on New Year's. I would've liked to see old Red Rock for myself, if I could have finished taping my promos in time. I was there the day Lane first rode him, you know."

"Tell me about it," Al said.

"It was in 1988 during the Challenge of the Champions match rides at Redding, not far from Red Bluff..." Barney slipped readily into the tale, and Al, lulled by the voice of her uncle and the sunshine coming through the windshield, was asleep before they reached the building called the Coliseum, arena for the National Western Stock Show and Rodeo.

Six thousand people were expected to attend every one of the National Western Stock Show and Rodeo's twenty-three performances. Al's first words on stepping into the Denver Coliseum were, "Now I see why you told me not to use verbal cues, Jen. This place will be a zoo when we race."

Although Jenny shared Al's feelings, she hadn't replied. One cowboy, not three barrels, was occupying her mind. She hadn't seen Forrest since the night in Red Bluff, but no doubt he'd be in Denver, one of the top five PRCA rodeos of the year in total payoff.

Jenny had tried hard to forget the kiss she saw Forrest and Al sharing. She hadn't missed the shocked expression on Felicia's unnaturally white face, or Forrest's laugh when he let Al go. He only kissed her for an instant, probably just to pique Felicia, but Jenny still felt differently toward Al. It was painfully close to what had caused their breakup, and that betrayal still hurt too much to think about.

Jenny continued offering her cousin all the help she could, reminding Al to count out her paces, remember her cues, and above all, concentrate, but Jenny had begun freezing in places where she had partially thawed.

Al hadn't noticed Jenny's changed attitude. She was getting deeper into her riding, more focused, more natural, and less intimidated by her competitors. While Jenny was pleased with her student's progress, Al's growing success threatened her, despite Jenny's struggle to feel otherwise.

In Denver's National Western barrel racing lineup, Jenny had a good position in the first go-round. She was scheduled to perform near the first few runs, but Al would race toward the end.

"Watch that course," Jenny warned her cousin. "Try for a good time, but don't let Promise slip on you."

Al nodded and kept working Prom up and down the arena. When she passed close to Jenny and Cloverleaf, she asked, "Have you seen Forrest or Tom?"

"No."

"But they'll be here, right?"

"Everyone will be here. Everyone who's NFR-bound."

"And everyone who's bound for the Ex."

Jenny didn't take up that line of thought. The Ex was too far off for anything but dreams.

They trotted their horses around the arena, wheeling, turning, stopping. Jenny veered away whenever Felicia and Wellington came near.

On one pass, Wellington moved alongside Cloverleaf, rubbing shoulders with the smaller horse as he did so. Clover looked as if he might nip the bay, so Jen tugged on the reins to remind him who he was.

"Well, well. Jenny O'Neill. How's Clove?"

"See for yourself."

Felicia made an exaggerated examination of Jenny's mount. "The poor thing is all worn out from the trip."

"I don't think so." Jenny cued Cloverleaf into a trot, but Wellington matched the black horse's pace.

"And how's your apprentice coming along?"

"Pretty good. She might even give you some competition here, Felicia. That reminds me: Have you seen Forrest around yet?"

The blond's first answer was to kick her horse into a canter. "No. And you'd best tell your cousin to quit racing out of her league," Felicia sputtered before Wellington's long strides drew them away.

Two laps later, Al occupied the spot Felicia had vacated. "What was Felicia saying, Jen?"

"Something about telling you to stay in your league."

"My league's on the move. We may even make it to Felicia's level one of these days."

Jen let Al's words hang, looking at the arena floor before she asked casually, "How about mine?"

Al shook her head. "I can't see myself competing against you again, Jen." She let the reins slide in her fingers. "I don't know if I would even want that."

"Well, you'd better think about it. You're getting good, Al. Good enough to rile up Felicia."

"I don't think Felicia considers me a threat to her racing." Al squeezed Promise closer to Clover and leaned in the saddle toward her cousin. "She thinks Forrest and I have something going."

Jenny took a forced breath. "Do you?" She tried to exhale naturally and turned as if to study the arena layout before facing Al.

Al met Jenny's sharp look with a flustered expression. "I don't know what to think, Jen. Forrest — kissed me at the New Year's rodeo, but I think it was just to harass Felicia. You know him. What do you think? Is that something he'd do?"

"Yes." Jen felt ashamed of her eagerness to set Al straight. *So what if she does like him? Or if he likes her? I need to let it all go.* But Jenny knew how she had failed at doing that. *Maybe if I just accept that it's over....* "Forrest might use you to razz Felicia."

"I was afraid of that." Al's voice dropped to a shaken whisper. "He laughed after he kissed me, Jen."

"You like him?" she couldn't help asking.

"You know how crazy I've been about Forrest, Jen, better than anybody. Now that you've called it quits, I thought I might have a chance. I don't know. Maybe no one has anymore." Al slapped the dust from her denim-clad thighs, startling the horses.

"What are you talking about, Al?"

"Well, he isn't dating anyone. He doesn't seem...close to anyone. Even when he kissed me, there was nothing in it." Al quit speaking as another rider passed them. When she was well out of range, Al continued. "I've talked to some of the other women he used to date. Not Felicia, of course. They all say the same thing, even the ones who used to see him a lot after you broke up."

"So his heart's all in rodeo now."

"No, Jen," Al said, "I think his heart's still with you."

The two cousins continued their warm-ups without further conversation.

"Guess I'll find out if I'm really in shape or not," Tom told Forrest, his mind reeling. "I drew Moan 'n' Groan."

"That rank hunk of beef from the Swanson Stock Co.? I'll tuck you in bed when he stomps the daylights out of you — unless you get smart and skip your ride."

Tom shook off his shock. "I'm glad to get him."

"More scared than glad, I bet."

Tom smiled, though he felt anything but cheery. The irony was too perfect: an eliminator bull for his first draw. Rodeo knew no such thing as favoritism. Rookies and vets alike shared the same fate, unpredictability. Whether a rider found himself astride a ton of ignited dynamite or a dud, eight seconds were eight seconds, and he would be judged not by anyone else's performance, but by his own and a mercurial beast's. "I prefer to call it anticipation, not fear," Tom said, slipping into bravado.

"You and every other guy. It's good to be tight, though. The tougher the ride, the more adrenaline I need pumping through me, especially for some rank old bronc. But bulls are something else." Forrest slapped Tom's shoulder. "Sure you have to do this?"

"Let's go take a look at him."

Tom and Forrest made their way to the catch pen which held a large dun bull with a white blaze. Even eating hay, the animal looked menacing.

"That's him. Moan 'n' Groan. Quite a name."

"That's not his name." Forrest jabbed Tom in the ribs. "It's what they call a bull rider after he tries riding him."

Tom watched the bull, trying to recall the story on him in Red Bluff, where he blew out of the chute and almost hooked Brent Small before he could scramble out of the way. Moan 'n' Groan was a rank one, a bull where a high score was possible. Also possible was a trip to the hospital, but Tom put that possibility firmly aside.

"Don't be studying on this bull so hard that you forget about your roping, Tom."

"I won't." Tom ended his survey. "Just tell me you'll be there to help tie me on Moan, and I'll be there to loop a steer faster than anyone's seen, Lord willing."

"That's what I like to hear, 'cept for the 'Lord willing'."

"That's really the only part worth saying." Tom looked Moan 'n' Groan over again. "And it's probably the only way I'll ride this bull."

"I'd like it a lot better if you weren't riding at all. It's like watching my daddy all over again." Forrest's voice quieted. "Granddad should've put a no-bull-riding clause in that contract with you."

"I don't remember it bothering you so much before."

"Maybe I've learned a little since then. Hasn't been the same on the circuit since you left, Tom. I told Granddad to leave bull riding out of getting you back in."

"I wouldn't have signed then," Tom teased, seeing the bull make a sudden stab with his horns. "And you would've had to rope with Winky."

"Still might've been worth it." Forrest spat on the ground and sauntered off.

"Don't let him blow on you." Tom remembered Brent's words as he watched Moan 'n' Groan plow into the chute. Tom chafed his glove, wondering if he'd put too much rosin on it or on his rope. It didn't matter now. There wasn't time to do anything about it.

He tightened his glove, holding the end of the thong tie with his teeth. The buckskin felt good on his hand, like it should: a second skin, only much tougher.

Straddling the chute, Tom slid the braided bull rope down Moan 'n' Groan's side. Forrest helped bring it around the dun Brahma-cross's thick belly. The two heavy cowbells hanging from the rope jangled as the bull fidgeted, priming himself.

Forrest pulled the rope up and handed Tom the tail end. Tom put his riding hand through the handhold, took the end of the rope from Forrest, and laid it across his palm, wrapping it behind his hand. He gave the rope another wrap, pulled it in hard around his hand, then looped the free end neatly.

"You're not tied in too tight, are you?" Forrest asked, his brows drawn. "You won't forget to loosen the wrap?"

"No, I'm okay."

"You won't get hung up and let Moan knock the stuffing out of you?" Forrest persisted.

The thought wasn't pleasant, but a potential reality. *Am I in too tight? Will the wrap come loose okay?* It felt right, but it had been too long between competitions to be sure. Had this been merely another practice ride, Tom would've felt more secure. He tested his grip. "No. I'm fine." *I hope.*

Tom settled gingerly onto the bull's back, knees up, every muscle raw. The announcer rattled off his name and pre-ride information as Tom held the rail of the chute with his free hand, releasing it to beat his hat on, then grasp the rail again. *Dear Lord, please keep me safe.*

"Okay!" He nodded.

The gate flew open. Moan lunged with an angry bellow. Tom dug in with his spurs, trying to get a grip on the bull's thick, loose skin, trying to anchor himself to Moan's arching, flexing back.

The Brahma-cross threw his weight backward, then forward, springing from his hooves, hitting the earth. If not for the mouth guard, Tom's teeth would've been dust.

Up, high, twisting. Tom felt airborne, then he slammed against the bull's back. He slipped away from his rope as Moan kicked and curled inward, trying to force Tom onto his rope, off balance.

Straining, fighting gravity, Tom used his free hand to whip up momentum in the opposite direction. He pushed with one leg, pulled with the other, struggling for balance, struggling to keep up on his rope as the bull gyrated underneath him and jarred Tom's bones loose.

Moan went into his spin. Around, around, twirling the man on his back, trying to get him dizzy, to get his body forward so the horns that reached backward and speared the air could tear into flesh.

Tom stayed on, his free hand a counterbalance and his waist twisting with Moan's motion. Around and around, riding the twister, feeling caught up in power and motion, speed, skill, sensation. The ride. The ride!

The whistle. Tom came out of the spin and back to the arena. He heard the bull's grunts, the clapping of the audience, the force of Moan's cutting hooves landing and spraying dirt upwards.

In the midst of an explosive burst, Tom reached down and unfastened the wrap. The bull rope's tension drained, and Tom worked his hand loose as Moan gave another midair twist.

Tom tore his hand from the rope and jumped, passing a bull-fighting clown who touched Tom as if tagging off. Tom landed and the bullfighter went to work, distracting Moan long enough for Tom to reach safety.

Tom ran for the rails, his first steps unsteady, sinking, his legs bowed and aching. He grabbed for the rail and turned. Moan was chasing the bullfighters now, ramming the clown barrel with his horns, the flank strap whipping behind him.

A gate man collected Tom's rope and handed it to him, along with his hat, which Tom hadn't even realized was gone.

"Thanks, Cal." *And thank you, Lord. Thank you for keeping me safe, for the strength in my arms, for the power you have given your creatures, man and animal.*

The gate tender waved and walked back to his position as Moan trotted to the catch pen, brandishing his tipped horns at Tom one last time before the gate clanged behind him.

Forrest hung on the fence rails. Tom climbed over next to him and saluted the cheering crowd.

"What was my score?"

"Seventy-eight. Didn't you hear?"

"No." Tom still looked for Moan 'n' Groan, but the bull was out of sight. "Seventy-eight?"

"Yeah. Not bad, for a guy who's loafed two years. You would've got more points if you hadn't ridden like you was too scared to spit."

"I was...for a while."

"Then you got into the ride?"

"Yes."

The two cowboys stared past each other, playing back fantastic reels of bucking, flying, and spinning they had taped forever in the libraries of their minds: rides electric with energy they had harnessed, energy they had been part of. The ride. The reason for riding. There was nothing else to say.

28

"THERE YOU ARE. NICE RIDE, TOM," Al said, little realizing she made him feel more shaky than his ride had. "I didn't see it, but I heard about it. And you, too, Forrest. You guys are really cleaning up tonight. I saw your roping run, but I didn't hear how you placed." Al looked from Forrest's face to Tom's. "Well, what was it?"

Tom started to answer, but Forrest beat him to it.

"First. It's only round one, though," Forrest added.

"So what are your plans? Where are you staying tonight?"

"In the pickup," Tom answered, determined to make the conversation three-way.

"What's the matter? Can't afford the Stapleton's rates?"

"We'll be going down the road. There're a few other places I want to hit before the short round," Forrest replied.

"How do you feel about it, Tom?" Al asked. "Going to let this bronc rider bull you? You're the header of the team."

"We're going for the NFR, Al," Tom said, enjoying the legitimate opportunity of giving her his full attention. "We've got to go as hard as we can as long as we can."

"So do we. I mean, so does Jen, but we plan to stay here at least tonight. Can't you guys —"

"Does Jen want us to stay?" Forrest interrupted.

"I do," Al said.

Forrest touched his hat brim. "Thanks, Al. But we need to get going." He walked toward the alley.

"I could use something to eat before we leave," Tom said, taking advantage of his friend's departure. "And you deserve a free dinner. Nice job tonight, Al. You're doing much better than when I saw you at Red Bluff."

"Don't remind me."

"I'm serious about supper. Want to join me?" He saw her look in Forrest's direction. The movement was slight, and appeared sickeningly automatic. "No, Forrest wouldn't be coming. It'd be just you and me. Does that change your mind?"

He watched her hesitate and felt his heart drop, as it had when he first glimpsed her in Red Bluff. She was more out of reach than ever. His thought translated itself into language of its own volition. "You're hung up on Forrest, aren't you, Al?"

"What kind of question is that?" Al narrowed her gray eyes in what Tom knew was supposed to be taken for mock anger, but he saw her real disappointment. "I shouldn't even consider your offer now," she said.

A sprig of hope rose in his heart, slender and fragile. "Does that mean you will?"

The shoot grew branches under Al's smile. Tom had to concentrate on her answer, attuned as he was to his own responses.

"I could use some food, Tom. I'm starving. Jen says it's better to compete on a lean stomach. Keeps you alert, she says. I say it just keeps you hungry. Where should I meet you?"

"I'll pick you up." Tom tried to dismiss his euphoria and remain rational. Good grief! This girl made him feel downright intoxicated.

"What's your room number?"

"Fourteen. Give me a half-hour to get ready."

"That means our date will be only about a half-hour long." Tom recovered quickly, glad that he had even that long with her. "It's all right. I have to take care of Tamarisk and get everything loaded. Okay if I pick you up in the lobby? We'll save a little time that way. I'll call in the order right now. You still like Italian?"

"Love it. Bye, Tom."

"Good-bye." Tom watched her go, wondering if she was actually planning to meet him or hoping instead to bump into Forrest before returning to her hotel. Tom tried to ignore the ache that had nothing to do with his recent wounds in bull riding. If his feelings toward her were unchanged, so were hers toward him. He slung his bull rope over his shoulder and carried it past the vacating crowd. No one noticed the cowboy with the clanging bells, least of all Alison Austin.

"Forrest! You *are* coming with us." Al crossed the lobby floor in seven quick strides.

"No. Thought I'd look up Jen as long as Tom's set on wasting time with you. What room are you staying in? Is Jen there?"

"So that's what time with me is," Al said softly as he looked in both directions, in every direction but hers, as he always had.

"What?" Forrest glanced at her briefly before continuing his assessment.

"Nothing. Yes, Jen's in the room. Number fourteen." She scanned the lobby herself. "Where's Tom?"

Forrest thumbed behind him. "Waiting with the pickup in the driveway. Asked me to send you to him to save time." Forrest walked past her, then stopped and turned. "How's the fitness center they got here? Maybe I'll give it a try before we go." Forrest winked and flashed a grin before resuming his steps. "You two might have a little more time than an hour."

"Bye, Forrest," Al said quietly.

"No more than two hours," he called over his shoulder. "We have to go then. Tell Tom that."

Al walked out of the lobby without replying.

When Eileen looked at the clock again, only fifty-five minutes had passed.

This is ridiculous. I don't even know if she's got it yet, Eileen thought, but felt certain her daughter had received the letter she'd finally sent.

There was no reason to live the charade any longer: Her marriage was as good as over, and her daughter had a right to know, just as Eileen herself had a right to a new life. If only it weren't so empty.

She was getting good part-time hours as a teller, and a stint at the grocery store would have filled up all her spare time, but Eileen didn't feel she'd come quite that low. She was meeting her expenses without that. Besides, her mother-in-law wasn't doing well at Senior Manor, and Eileen spent many hours there, waiting for the inevitable day Janette would have to move on to the nursing home. The event looked close, but Janette refused to discuss it. Eileen wondered if she should alert Alison but felt that with the recent letter about the divorce, news of her grandmother could wait a while longer.

Alison. Alison. The young racer had written home several times, and Harvey always dropped off the letters at Rhoda's. Eileen was shocked the first time he did it.

He had stood there, hair black and gray — mostly gray of late — with a new growth of untamed whiskers, kicking the snow from the soles of his feet in an action born more of self-consciousness than need. "Thanks for coming to the door, Eileen. Wanted to give you this from Al."

"Rhoda isn't home or I wouldn't —" Eileen stopped the barb before it went too deep. "Well, thank you, Harvey." She took the letter. "Good-bye."

"Bye." He had stood on the stoop, his feet and bare head collecting snow. Eileen felt uncomfortable closing the door on him.

"Is there something else?" she asked.

"No, no."

Still he stood, hands in the pockets of his shabby overcoat. She wished she'd sewn up the right pocket before she'd left. It barely hung on; she could see stuffing next to Harvey's hand. And the night was cold.

She could hardly offer to fix it now.

But he looked so cold.

"Would you like a cup of coffee before you go, Harvey?"

"Thank you." He reached for the door and was beside her before she knew why she'd extended the invitation.

The thought of him sitting there at Rhoda's table comforted her now. He had actually attempted conversation, even asked her advice about one of the heifers he claimed to be treating. Eileen had sewn up the pocket while he drank his cup of coffee and talked. And talked. The miracle of it still surprised her.

She tried to include that episode in her short letter to Alison. Tried to explain that things were better now, that the impending divorce was better for all of them. And maybe it was, for her and

271

Harvey — but not for Alison, Eileen knew. Alison would never understand. And why should she? In her mother's heart, Eileen wished she could have spared her daughter this pain.

"How's your fettucine primavera?" Tom asked.

"Fine." Al took a sip of lemon water and refilled her glass from the carafe on the table.

"My lasagna is good, too." *Brilliant conversation, Tom.*

Al picked up another forkful and put it in her mouth. She looked out from the corner booth across the room of the small bistro. A half dozen or so patrons dined in the warm, candlelit shadows. Live plants decked the attractive wood textures trimming the room, cut flowers brightened each table, and hushed Italian music complemented the excellent food. The setting should have been romantic.

This is useless, Tom thought. *I should stick to rodeo. I probably won't get hurt nearly so bad in the arena.* He ate four bites of lasagna in silent succession.

"Did you order dessert, too?" Al finally asked.

"No. I didn't know how much you were into training."

"Not enough to miss dessert." Al signaled the waiter and placed her order. "Do you want anything, Tom?"

"This was enough. I'm not into sweets much anymore."

The waiter took the empty salad and appetizer dishes. Al rested one elbow on the partially cleared table. "What are you into, Tom?"

He smiled at the first interest she'd shown since leaving Forrest. "'What kind of question is that?' to partially quote someone else," he teased, glad to see a little liveliness in her eyes.

"My kind. I think you can answer it." She looked at him pensively. "Why did you leave rodeo and suddenly come back into it?"

"I could ask you the same question."

"You could." She took another sip of water.

"But you wouldn't answer?"

"Ask me no questions, I'll tell you no lies." She moved back as the waiter placed a large piece of chocolate pie before her. "Looks great. Thanks," she said to the waiter. "Don't tell Jen I ate this, Tom." Al poised her fork, ready to attack. "She wants to keep me on starvation rations. She read somewhere that it's healthier to never eat dessert. I try to keep all reading materials away from her now."

"I know what you mean. Forrest's got me popping vitamins and always wants me to join him in some new health fad."

"Forrest? I never thought he was a health nut."

"He's a success nut. He does whatever he thinks will help him win. He's put me on an exercise program, and he wants me to quit riding bulls."

"But you won't."

Tom pushed his plate away. "How did you know?"

"Everyone knows, Tom. It's…the way you ride, I guess…all out, actually enjoying it." Al looked at her plate. "Maybe I shouldn't say that. I only had the courage to watch you ride once, and that was years ago." She raised her head. "But I heard what some of the guys have been saying. You're even better than before. You're NFR-bound, aren't you?"

"In roping, I am."

"Not in bulls?"

"I'd like to be, but I'm going to take riding bulls —"

"One day at a time," Al said in a high, derisive voice.

"You don't approve?"

"I don't get it. That's what Jen always says, too. I guess it works for her. Can you really go on like that, without a goal? I need something to shoot for."

"And that is?"

"The Ex."

Tom leaned back. "I thought so. As long as we're quoting mottos, how about this: 'If you're going to aim, aim high.'"

"You think I'm aiming too high?" Al had finished her pie and brushed a crumb from her lips. "I'm going to do it, Tom."

"If you're going to, then you will."

Alison pushed her plate away and fixed her eyes on him. "I'm going to."

"I don't doubt it. There's an old saying in rodeo that the one with the most guts and try wins. It's proven year after year, around NFR time. It's not how I operate, but I've seen it work for a lot of other guys." He reached for the carafe.

"How do you work, Tom?"

"You really want to know, or do you want another motto?"

She gave him a half-smile. "I'd prefer both."

Why not? Encouraged by her smile, Tom plunged in. "Okay, then. I look to God for my direction. My motto is, 'Trust in the Lord with all your heart and lean not on your own understanding; in all your ways acknowledge him, and he will make your paths straight.'"

"The Bible, right?"

"Right. Proverbs three, verses five and six."

"Where have I heard that before?" Al closed her eyes, opening them after a brief silence. "That's how you ended the letter you wrote me. I remember now." Her voice grew softer as she receded into her memories. "You sent it and then disappeared from rodeo. I thought that verse might have something to do with it. I read it over quite a few times, thinking it might be some kind of curse. I planned to stay as far away from it as I could."

"Not a curse. A blessing. I wanted you to be the first to know that I had finally come to Christ, too." Tom thought back to the event. "I didn't know if you would remember that letter." He reached for her hand. "I'm glad you did."

Al looked at his hand on hers as if deciding what to do. Tom noticed her uneasiness and let go. "So that's how I work, Al, by Proverbs three, five and six, and other verses from the Bible as they come along. Proverbs three is my motto, though. What about you?" *Don't go too fast, Tom. She has to be ready. Just keep waiting. Aren't you used to it by now?*

"Oh, I work the same as ever, I guess," Al answered carelessly. "Keep my eyes on a goal and don't let anything get in my way." She held her glass at a slant with one hand, tipping it until water lapped the rim. "You still believe God exists, Tom?"

"I know he does. When I pray, I'm not talking to myself. I'm sure about that. Aren't you?"

"Not like I used to be." She set the glass on the table and pulled a balled-up paper from her pocket.

"What's that?"

"As long as we're on the subject of letters, I got this one today. From my mom." Al tapped the wad of stationery. "They gave it to me at the desk when I came down to wait for you. I was so happy to get it...at first. I hadn't heard from her since I left home. What *was* home."

Al took aim at the paper with her forefinger and thumb, and shot it off the table. "She's divorcing my dad."

Tom touched her shoulder. "I'm sorry, Al."

She drew her gray eyes level to his brown ones. "My dad does that." She laid Tom's hand on the tabletop. "Funny you should do the same thing just now." She smoothed out his hand and traced the scar that ended near his thumb. "Haven't lost any fingers yet, I see. This scar seems to be your only new injury."

"I'm very sorry about your folks, Al."

"Me, too." Her sudden smile barely masked the tears locked in her eyes. "And I'm sorry about your dad, too. Jen just told me today. And I'm sorry for dumping on you. I should have waited to tell Jen about my parents when I got back." She bowed her head. "I just can't seem to keep it in any longer."

"I'm glad you told me. Maybe I can help."

"How?" She asked the question sarcastically. "Going to turn God loose on me and my family? Or my ex-family?"

Tom's voice was gentle. "God moves however God decides to move. But I will be praying for you, for all of you. I'd like to help bear your burden, if you'll let me. I'll never give up on you, Al, and you shouldn't give up on your folks…or God."

He sheltered her hands with his. "I'll always remember the night you went forward at that Glory Seekers' meeting. Took me quite a bit longer, and a lot of sins later, but I finally gave my life to him, too. That's partly what made me drop out of rodeo, and that's when I sent the letter to you, to tell you I had found what you had."

Al's head was still lowered, and Tom let her keep the position, caressing her with his words, hoping to give her strength with his unspoken love. "Al, I'm not sure what's happened in your life between the time I saw you give it to Christ and now, but God won't forsake you, not even if you forsake him for a season. I won't forsake you, either. I know what it's like to feel alone. I'd like to be…" he made himself say it, made himself accept it, "…a friend. If you'll let me."

Her mouth opened, but the words took time to form. "Thank

you, Tom.... I could use a friend right now."

He moved toward her, and when one maverick tear escaped her eye, it landed on the soft fabric covering Tom's shoulder.

"So when will I see you again?"

"I'm not sure." Al flipped the lock of the pickup and opened the door a crack to reveal a quarter inch or so of white on the asphalt. It had snowed while they had been at the restaurant, but no flakes hung in the overcast sky at present.

"Forrest and I have to come back for the short round. I know you do, too. Maybe we can have lunch again? After that, we'll be up north for a while, then we plan to do Scottsdale and El Paso. Will you be at either of those?"

"Scottsdale, I think."

"Which days?"

"All, I guess. I'm not sure. Jen would know."

"Would you ask Jen to leave a list of addresses here? I'll pick it up during the short round." When she nodded, he continued, "If we're both at Scottsdale on the same day, how about going to see the Master Riders with me after the rodeo?"

"Fine." Al looked out the window.

Tom kept talking, hoping he'd say something that would draw her out of herself again and stop her from leaving. "Al, I'd like to get together sooner, but it probably won't happen. Our schedule's pretty tight. Sometimes Forr keeps me going so fast I wouldn't know which state I was in except for the road signs."

Al glanced at him in time to catch his smile. She didn't smile back, but she did look at him. "Will the horses hold up?"

"Forrest's got a couple of backup mounts we're going to use. We begin training on them next week, so Tamarisk and Canyon will have a break and be ready for Houston. Forrest's not taking any chances."

"He never did. Not with horses, anyway." Al opened the door and hopped down to the snow-covered pavement. "Thanks a lot, Tom, for the food. And for the company. I really appreciate...all you did."

"Wish I could do more." *So much more.*

Al nodded and was about to close the door, but Tom slid across the seat and stopped her. "I'll be praying for you, Al. And I'll be writing. Check for mail at your hotels...without fear."

He held out his hand, and Al traced his scar, the crooked X, with a swift, light touch. "Take care, Tom."

He closed his hand around hers. "God bless, Al."

CHAPTER

29

THE WILL ROGERS COLISEUM IN FORT WORTH sheltered Tom from something colder than Denver's snow: freezing Texas rain. The weather hadn't dampened the spectators' enthusiasm, however. They made their way past the lighted, sculpted-looking edifice in Amon Carter Square and entered it to find their seats. The grandstands supported thousands of rodeo fans, and on the ground level, behind the chutes, in the dressing rooms, and in the arena, teemed scores of cowboys. Not a barrel rider among them. That was the only fact marring the event for Tom, but that one fact carried more weight with him than the coliseum and all its fans.

He brushed his fingers over his scar, then tried to forget Al's touch and psych himself for his events. The Southwestern Exposition and Livestock Show and Rodeo was a good place for money, and if Tom had any hope of meeting Sterling's terms, he had to start making it. Now.

Tom looked at his competitors and friends congregating behind the chutes, wrapping yards of adhesive tape around old and new injuries, using it like a manmade ligament, praying it would keep bones together long enough to compete.

Some cowboys had black rings under their eyes from sleeplessness or bruising. Some looked like they'd gone on extended crash diets or fasts. Most were thin, short, weathered, gnarled, and hardy as piñon trees accustomed to bucking the wind.

Few led the privileged life Tom and Forrest were leading. Tom remembered well the days before he and Forrest won their world championship, days of endless miles and nights of bunking eight or nine to a hotel room — four to a bed, four to the floor, and one to a bathtub, when a room was an option.

Tom still had the maroon tent he and Forrest had worn out their first PRCA year of going down the road, the tent that let in wind, rain, and insects. He remembered cowering within it, unusually sober one frigid night in a campground by the Grand Tetons, when grizzlies were reported nearby. He remembered spending the night wondering how quickly a grizzly claw could tear through the thin fabric.

But even in those days he and Forrest had a cushion under them: Forrest's granddad. The old man was tight — stingy, actually — but Forrest managed to wrangle enough money from him, borrowed against his inheritance, to keep them both alive and active. Just when their stomachs went hollow, when the rusty white Ford's gas gauge hit empty, or when they had turned their pockets inside out and found only lint with which to pay the next entry fee, Forrest would procure a little something: just enough to keep them from starving, to keep the gas tank wet, to keep them competing. Sometimes, to keep them drunk.

But things were tough enough that Tom and Forrest grew the hardiness they needed to survive on the circuit. They could go without sleep, live on a hamburger a day, hock their dress boots at the most reliable pawn shop in town to scrape together an entry fee. They learned to live with uncertainty.

Rodeo broke many men, many women. But for Forrest and Tom, it was an adventure, an escapade just dangerous enough to be exciting. They experienced hardships, but not enough to crush them. They faced challenges they were capable of overcoming, if every tendon, muscle, and bone held. They lived the very best rodeo had.

The grand entry done, Tom waited for the bareback-bronc event to open the competition. Forrest would be up after bareback riding, and after that, Tom could ride his bull, Missile.

Among the cowboys, Missile was known as a bull that lived to seek and destroy, a "heat-seeking missile, fully armed," one veteran rider had told Tom as he stood at the catch pen to watch his draw. Missile had moves not even invented yet, designed to toss cowboys for the pleasure of sticking them once they landed.

In the pen, Missile did not look like a "hunter." His hide was dark with brown tiger-like stripes toward the haunches. His horns were long and curved, but nothing out of the ordinary. What made this bull was his mind, and as Tom watched him, he saw the black eyes sizing him up, returning Tom's scrutiny.

Though only shedding his rookie status in the PRCA circuit, Missile had the potential to become legendary. His intelligence and malice already marked him among the rodeo clowns. Bullfighter Suicide Sam, who would be protecting the cowboys this rodeo, had told Tom that Missile was one bull who didn't forget. "Try a fake on Missile once, it might work. Try it again, he'll be right on you," Sam assured Tom. "I did a step-through on him at Denver, after we got Jock McCarty safe to the rails. You can bet I won't do it tonight. Missile, he'd be waiting. When I turned my back, he'd go straight through me. Don't let him get your number, Tom, or next time, your number'll be up."

Sam knew his bulls, having fought them for a decade. He was one of the best current PRCA bullfighters, on his way to again becoming the choice protector of the cowboys for the NFR. "I've seen Missile blow at the gate, fake, spin, and do a stutter-step all at once, seemed like," Sam had said. "I've seen a few bulls as smart. Don't think I've seen any smarter. Watch yourself, Tom. If you buck off, keep moving. Get to the rails. Missile'll be right behind you, sure as shooting. And *don't* break a leg."

Tom reflected on Sam's advice as he looked over the arena. There would be no roping tonight, for Fort Worth had only five events: bareback riding, saddle-bronc riding, bull riding, calf roping, and steer wrestling. Tom and Forrest were in the top fifteen in the team-roping standings, third place at last glance, but it was worth a time-out for a chance at Fort Worth's $300,000 purse.

"Cowtown's the place to come in first," Forrest had drawled as they drove into Fort Worth, and Tom knew what he meant. The city was the site of many firsts in rodeo history: the first quarter horse show, the first cutting horse show, the debuts of specialty acts that spiced up rodeos with trick riding, roping, and rodeo humor. But humor was hardly tops on Tom's mind.

Tonight Forrest hoped to come away with at least six or seven thousand dollars when the rounds were finished. Tom was riding well and might pocket four thousand or more. If he kept winning, if he didn't get hurt, he'd fulfill his contract with Sterling. The NFR money, then the purse on the Ex circuit, would be enough to keep the Circle H running forever.

The NFR. The Ex. Though Forrest often talked of them, Tom had tried to keep them out of his vocabulary and his thoughts. Nevertheless, momentum was building for them both. Tom could feel it in this Fort Worth crowd, as he'd felt it at Denver and all the rodeos in between. The press was whipping up a rodeo fad, and grandstands everywhere were packed to the doorways and aisles. Rodeo wear was in, country music was in, and cowboys were the hottest thing going.

Whenever Tom turned on a television or picked up a newspaper, rodeo was front and center. Towns and cities bickered over who would host Ex rodeos. Even the tightest committees were offering added money previously unheard of. Everyone was looking forward to the NFR and casting bets as to who would make the Ex. After even the smaller rodeos, television crews singled out winners who would again be interviewed at the start of the next rodeo. Cowboy mania was hitting harder than the latest Asian flu bug, and right now the cure looked at least two years away. The Pro Rodeo Exposition was gaining the Olympic proportions rodeo sponsors and prophets predicted and prayed it would.

Tom wanted to be part of it — not only for Forrest's sake in team roping and not even for the Circle H, but for himself. If the Lord willed, Tom hoped to finish the season with a bid to the NFR and an invitation to the emerging Pro Rodeo Ex circuit. He would compete in the Ex, do his best, and come home to the Circle H. If Al somehow ended up accompanying him, it would be better than good. It would be the culmination of a dream.

By the time Barney, Jen, and Al reached Scottsdale, Arizona, for the Jaycees Parada del Sol Rodeo, Al had experienced her share of travel travail along with Promise, who had tasted the rigors of changing conditions in the arena and on the road.

Traveling kept Al's mind occupied. So did training, and Al was thankful for the distraction. It kept her from having to think about her mother and father's impending divorce. Tom's letters were a welcome diversion, too, as were his occasional calls. How he managed it, she rarely bothered to wonder, but she appreciated feeling that someone was looking out for her, that someone cared, even if it was only Tom.

As she and Jen checked into their hotel, Al noticed Jen was quieter than usual, which meant she had hardly threaded two words together during the day. "Anything bothering you, Jen?"

"Just thinking."

"What about? Seeing Forrest again?" Al avoided Jen's glare by checking for messages at the hotel desk.

"I don't plan on seeing Forrest, Al."

"No, but he'll show up at your door, just like he did in Denver. Isn't that what's keeping you so busy thinking?"

"No! I...I'm worried about...Promise."

"Promise?"

"Yes." Jen sounded more collected. "Are you sure Prom can keep up?"

"I'm not even sure I can. But what else can I do? I don't have a backup horse like everyone else seems to."

"You can borrow someone's."

"And pay a mount fee?"

"You're winning enough to afford it."

"Yeah. In that, I'm lucky. In that and in traveling partners. I couldn't make expenses without you, Jen. Not living like this."

"It's not me, it's Daddy. He's set on keeping his new image, and he figures that means helping us live like royalty, too. He keeps telling me to make you stop paying your expenses."

"I couldn't do that. `Always pay your own way,' my mom...."
Conveniently, as Al felt her throat constrict, the desk clerk handed

her a light brown envelope. Al recognized it immediately. "Look, Jen."

"What? Another letter from your mother?"

Al's stomach followed suit with her throat, feeling as if someone were drawing in a cinch too tightly around them. "It's not from my mom. I don't think I could stand another letter from her. This is from Tom." The postmark was from South Dakota. "So he managed to get one here, too." Al tore open the envelope and read the clear, plain handwriting. "He's going to try to meet me today." She checked her watch. "We should be done riding in time. Why don't we order a pizza and watch some television after the rodeo until he comes?"

"I don't eat pizza for anybody." Jen grabbed the key and led the way to their room. "Didn't you two see enough of each other at Denver during the short round?"

"We hardly had time to eat. I wish you and Forrest had come with."

"I don't barge in on twosomes."

"That's not what Tom and I are. But you could have made your own twosome with Forrest. It would've been like old times."

Jen opened the door to their room. "Forget it."

"Come on, Jen, I saw you two talking when Tom and I left. It's okay. As long as Forrest doesn't care about me, he might as well go for you. See? I'm getting into the spirit of pro rodeo." Al mimicked a western stance: her thumbs in her belt loop, her legs bowed, shoulders hunched, jaw out, and cheek full of a tongue meant to represent a chaw of tobacco. "I'd be just as happy if the other guy had won," she drawled. "That's what everyone says, right? Can they really mean it? Or do they mean it just when they win?" Al shed her western posture and stood straight at the foot of the bed, letting herself free fall onto the mattress.

"Don't do that, Alison! You could land wrong and twist —"

"Don't change the subject, Jen." Al's voice was unyielding. "Are you and Forrest getting back together?"

"Never."

"Never's a long time, they say."

"Don't give me your garbage." Jen kicked her suitcase against the wall. "Trade cute little sayings with Tom all you want, but don't give them to me." Jen glowered at Al before stomping off toward the bathroom.

Al followed her, hanging back just enough so the slammed door did her no damage. "I'm not kidding, Jen. I'm not advertising it, but I'm still very interested in Forrest, even if you aren't. Especially if you aren't. And if he ever shows even a glimmer of interest, I'll be there to glimmer back."

She waited for an answer. "Jen?" Al knocked on the door. "Have you got the fan on? Did you hear me?"

"I heard."

"So how do you feel about him?"

"Forrest and I aren't even friends."

"That's not what worries me. Do you have any feelings at all left for him? And don't say you hate him. Hate is close to love. That's about the only thing I remember learning in Psych 101."

Al heard the faucet running, and soon the door opened. Jen was toweling her face dry.

"What were you saying about hate?" Jen asked, her words frosty.

"It's like love: both strong feelings. You know."

"I don't hate Forrest," Jen said without passion.

"Do you love him?"

"Will you please quit bugging me?" Jen turned on the TV. "We're going to have to go down to the rodeo soon. I want to unwind a little first."

"Okay, Jen. But I'm going to ask Forrest out one of these days, if you don't mind. Do you? Jen?"

"What!" Jen gave a flip of her red head but kept facing the television.

"Is it all right with you if I ask Forrest out..." Al set a date in her mind, "...when we get to Houston?"

Jen turned her face from the screen, her green eyes already taking on the haze of television. "Al, do whatever you want. Just leave me out of it."

"That's all I wanted to know."

CHAPTER

30

IT STARTED WITH A CUP OF COFFEE, but it wasn't ending there, and Eileen wondered if it should.

Now Harvey came in for a cup every time he brought the weekly offering of Alison's letter. Alison still wrote faithfully, although her letters had changed from being chatty to being mere sports updates. Harvey brought each over even before he read it himself. Since she'd moved out, Eileen was seeing more of her husband than when they were living together.

The two would discuss Alison's letter, then Alison, and progress to the weather or town gossip or whatever topic they hit on. Lately they were trying to unravel problems with the farm and Janette's health. Never did they talk about themselves, but otherwise their conversations were long, surprisingly pleasant, and incredibly regular. Harvey's visits were becoming a ritual, one that Rhoda seemed to think perfectly natural.

"We're getting *divorced*, Rhoda," Eileen stressed after Harvey left his cold cup of coffee on the kitchen table. "He acts as if we're dating again."

"Maybe you are."

Eileen answered by hurling Harvey's cup into the sink.

As Rhoda checked the porcelain for damage, Eileen spoke. "I'm sorry, Rhoda. I won't be staying here much longer. I'm hoping to get a job in the Eau Claire branch, perhaps go on to Madison from there, once I take some college courses. That's what I should have done long ago." She stooped and wiped up the spilled coffee.

"You're telling me I should look for a new boarder?"

"Not yet. I'll stay as long as Janette needs me."

"Which you don't think is going to be long," Rhoda supplied. "Are they talking about sending her to the nursing home?"

"If by 'they' you mean the administrators at Senior Manor, yes. They haven't made it a formal request yet, but they are talking. Harvey isn't, however. Neither is she." Eileen scowled. "That old lady is as stubborn as her son."

Rhoda laid a hand on her friend's back. "You're very good to her, Eileen. I'm sure both she and Harvey appreciate all you're doing."

"I've known her for twenty years, and for at least half that time, she was as much my mother as Harvey's." Eileen looked across the table to the chair Harvey had so recently vacated. "Besides you, Janette's been about the only person to listen to me in this town. One doesn't walk away from friendship like that."

"Or love?" Rhoda suggested.

"Or love." Eileen glanced guiltily at the sink. "I really do apologize for tossing the cup, Rhoda. I'll replace it."

"No need. It isn't broken."

"It isn't?" Eileen rose to see.

"Some things can take a lot of abuse, withstand a lot of pressure," Rhoda said, "and still not break." She handed the cup to Eileen, withholding the thick homemade dishrag that had saved the cup from death, but Eileen's sharp eyes detected it.

"You're not on the verge of a Bible lesson, are you?" Eileen asked, resuming her seat and laughing inwardly at her friend's harmless deception.

"I could be." Rhoda held up the rag. "But I don't know how to work this in as part of the parable. Guess I'll leave the lessons to Janette. She seems to be doing a good job."

Eileen rubbed her thumb over the porcelain cup. "Janette's got me listening to her memory verses now and doing all her reading for her because she claims she can't see the words clearly anymore. What a crafty mother-in-law I have!"

Eileen sat at the kitchen table and watched the snowflakes descend as Rhoda unfolded the newspaper and read. When Eileen excused herself and went to her room, still holding the porcelain cup, Rhoda made no comment.

As Al waited for Tom, she shaded her eyes from the waning Scottsdale sunshine, looking through a gap in the arena railing to see a large, upright saguaro cactus and spreading, bush-like ocotillo.

She walked toward the fence, mentally reviewing her ride. Third place. Pretty good for PRCA. Not only that, but she had come in fourth in the average after taking another third to Jen in the first go-round.

Now, as she killed time, Al let herself bask in her victory. It was ever so much warmer than sunshine.

"Hi, Al." Tom ducked into view, skirting the side of the bleachers. "Thanks for meeting me. You're even early. I take that as a compliment."

"I could say you're late, but you're not," Al answered, hiding the strange shock she always felt at seeing a cowboy without his horse under him. Tom was no exception. He looked different from the way he appeared while roping. Less intense, maybe. Definitely smaller. But then, every cowboy lost a few feet of height when he dismounted. "So you and Forrest beat your idols today. How did it feel?"

"Always feels good to win. And to win against Leo Camarillo and H. P. Evetts makes it incredible." He took her hand. "Ready to go?"

"Where? To see the Master Riders, I know, but is it some kind of riding seminar or a country-western group?"

"Kind of." Tom smiled as he walked.

They came to a tan canvas tent and stepped in, taking a pair of the many seats before a raised plywood platform on which a small band played.

Two men plucked guitars, another handled the percussion, two female singers provided background vocals, and one woman played the keyboard. The group swung to the music, their stops and starts polished, every chord, every beat on time. They were professionals, but their brand of western apparel made them look more casual than many rodeo fans.

"So Master Riders is a country-western group, just as I thought," Al said as the song ended and the crowd clapped.

"Kind of," Tom repeated, smiling ambiguously over the heads of the people in front of them.

Al knew the reason for Tom's smile when the band finished their set.

"Welcome!" the lead guitarist said, taking off his white hat and waving it in the air. "Congratulations to those of you who won in the rodeo. Condolences to those who bucked off or finished last."

The speaker placed his electric guitar in a metal holder and fanned himself with his hat. "How many of you here love rodeo?"

The hundred or so people in the tent responded by throwing

their hats in the air or waving their hands. Almost everyone whooped.

"Well, all right," the speaker responded, wiping his forehead with his thick forearm. "And how many of you rodeo?"

Half the crowd rose this time, but they made up for their cut in number by cheering even louder. A score of hats became frisbees that ricocheted off the tent ceiling and walls, falling into the crowd who good-naturedly handed them back down the rows to their owners.

"Rodeo people are my favorite people, whether or not they actually compete," the speaker said, sitting on a stool one of the backup singers brought out. "I used to ride myself. Bulls."

A couple ki-yis from the crowd seemed to imply other bull riders were also present.

"They used to call me 'Rank Rick,' 'cause everyone knew I loved to ride a rank bull. The ranker, the better." Rick made his voice low and scratchy, breathing menacingly into the microphone.

More whoops from the audience. Not from Tom, though, who sat in apparent introspection.

"Then one day I got on the rankest son-of-a-heifer you ever did see. His name was V-8, and all the boys said the V stood for velocity, and the eight was for what he did to cowboys when he bucked them off. And they were right, 'cause when he came out of the chute, he blew like nothing I'd ever been on. I'd taken the championship a few years earlier, and in all them ten rounds put together, I'd never felt a bull so strong or fast. He was twisting me one way, then the other before I even knew which was my outside leg. When his head came up, same time his back end did, one bonehead met another."

There was nervous laughter from the crowd and some blank

292

expressions on those who had personally experienced what Rick was talking about and wanted to forget.

"When everything went black, I knew I was in trouble. And something in me cried out. Yeah, I was scared. I knew I was in a bad spot. Knew maybe I was hung up, being dragged to death or maybe trampled on. But the thing that scared me more than V-8's invisible horns or hooves was the blackness."

Rick set his hat in his lap as he held the microphone so near his mouth that it rubbed his black goatee. "See, I knew I wasn't in the arena anymore. So I figured I must be dead. All around me was blackness. No crowd. No cameras. No beer mamas. You cowboys who've tasted the glory of this world know what I mean. I was alone. No one cared that I was a world champion because there was no one around to care. For once, and for the first time in longer than I could remember, I was alone."

Alone. Rick let the word sink into the crowd. The tent, which had rocked so recently with lively country tunes and riotous cheers, was silent.

"Hey, let's hear some music, Rick," someone said, attempting to sound untouched by Rick's narrative; the quaver at the end of the cowboy's voice betrayed him.

"Sure, friend. More music coming up." Rick stood to retrieve his guitar.

"Wait!"

"What happened?"

Not everyone was ready for a musical interlude.

"Finish your story."

"Yeah. Finish!"

"Well, all right." Rick slung the guitar over his shoulder and remained standing. "I was alone. Me and the blackness. And I didn't like it. Goin' down the road, you kind of forget what being alone is. There's your travelin' partner on the seat next to you all day. Nights there's your buddies or women to keep back the lonelies. In the arena, there's moments you feel alone, like when the gate opens, but that's not real. Sure, you're in your own little world for eight seconds — or less — but the bull's there with you, and you know the crowd is all around. But this, what I was experiencin', was utter *aloneness.*"

He paused. "Some people, that's what they find at the end of the road. They never get out of that darkness." He paused again, this time for slightly longer. "But I did. I'd like to tell you how it happened, and if you don't mind, I'd like to tell you about it in the way I know best." He hit a chord on his guitar and smiled.

Applause swelled from the crowd. Those who feared Rick's darkness were relieved to hear the air filling with music, and those who craved an ending to the story knew they'd soon be appeased.

The keyboard player started the music, a melody in minor: slow, dreamy, country. Not foot-tapping music, more like heart-stirring. It reminded Al of the last summer day, when you hear the call to share in its passing beauty: Take one last dive from the bridge over the river, have one last picnic near the purple fireweed, ride through the green field grass one more time before fall tinges everything with brown.

Rick's guitar added a wistful counterpoint to the melody as he sang. The other band members quietly accompanied.

The song was the story of Rick's life, focusing on three events, one for each of the three verses. First Rick sang about the death of his mother when he was a child and how his father had to go away in an attempt to support him and his grandmother when jobs in town grew scarce.

The music built to a crescendo after the verse. Percussion, back-up vocalists, and guitars strengthened the melody while the keyboard followed its own tune, the counterpoint Rick had begun. Everyone sang the chorus:

> *Why is it that the good ones ride away?*
> *Where do they go, and why can't they stay?*
> *I'd ride on out after 'em, if I only knew the way....*
> *Why is it that the good ones ride away?*

Chords softened, diminished. Rick sang softly, the keyboard harmonizing, describing the joyful but short reunions with his father, now a professional bull rider:

> *The days when I could see him ride, seemed our good times hadn't ceased.*
> *Grandstand hot dogs with my daddy were to me the greatest feast.*
> *Though he never won the most pay, he never won the least,*
> *And he might've won the big one, if not for one big buckin' beast.*

The music built, and then slowly, slowly, the sound floated down. The keyboard was again the center. The drums hardly vibrated; all singers fell mute. Several bars more, and the keyboard faded. Rick picked up the melody, his voice conveying deep but controlled emotion about his father's bull wreck:

> *I held my daddy's hand, looked in his lifeless eyes,*
> *He said, 'Son, hold tight onto the truth, don't fall for foolish lies.*
> *You'll still have a daddy when I'm gone, One who never dies,*
> *'Who wipes away every tear his loved one cries.'*

The music swelled, quickened. Death, life — they were in the music, intermingling, surging, struggling, until life triumphed. The plaintive thread that had run throughout the song in Rick's counterpoint, in the keyboard's harmony, became the melody, expressed at last:

> Took me years to understand what my daddy tried to say,
> That my Father up in Heaven will never go away.
> He'll go with me down each lonesome path, every briary way.
> You can know him as your Daddy too, today.

All voices returned to the refrain, the original melody:

> Now I know why all the good ones ride away.
> In heaven they all shed their miry clay;
> In Jesus Christ they find the path, the blessed, holy way.
> The good in them was his, and his to stay.

The band kept playing, and Rick looked at the audience. "This was my hope in that blackness: my daddy's words, my daddy's testimony of the life in Jesus. I cried out to my heavenly Father, asking pardon for the wrongs in my life that had kept me in darkness. And then, then there was light!"

Rick put his lips to the microphone and rode the waves of sound. Some in the crowd began clapping, trying to sing along with the full-voiced band. Some stood, swayed, and raised their hands.

> Now I know why all the good ones ride away.
> I know why on this Earth they cannot stay.
> The good in them was Jesus Christ, who died to make the Way.
> You can know him as your Daddy,
> You can know him as your Lord,
> You can know him as your God this very day....
> This very day....
> This very day.

Suddenly the song was over, like the last plucked note of a harp. Al did not join the wild clapping.

She stayed planted in her seat for several more sets and testimonies given by other members of the band. Then came the dreaded moment.

"I invite you tonight to come to know the Savior," Rick said, "to know the Master Rider. Let him teach you how you ought to ride through life. I met him in the midst of blackness. You can know him tonight, and escape the darkness of your life. The Bible says in Romans ten-nine, 'That if you confess with your mouth, "Jesus is Lord," and believe in your heart that God raised him from the dead, you will be saved.' I invite you to come to him. Pray by yourself, pray with one of us, stay in your seat if you want. Confess. Believe. And be saved."

Tom held Al's hand and leaned over as several men and one barrel rider she recognized walked down the aisle to the front of the tent.

"What is greater than seeing people coming to the Lord?" Tom looked even more excited than when he took his victory laps. "This is what it's all about."

Al felt tied to her chair, condemned to relive another altar call, her own personal purgatory. She remembered too clearly the Glory Seekers' meeting and the prompting in her heart that caused her to leave her seat many years ago. She had gone as if in a trance, walking that long, long aisle to the front of the tent. That night the pastor had said what this man said, talking about God's love and free gift. Again Al's heart stirred. Again her mind slipped into numbness.

I can't! Too much...to give up. Too many dreams...My life. Mine —

"God, be merciful to me, a sinner," Rick prayed from the platform, his hand on a kneeling man who had asked him how to pray.

"Please forgive me. I know that when Christ died, every sin I ever did or will do was nailed up there with him, that I might taste life eternal. Thank you for your love, Jesus. Thank you for your salvation."

"Good to hear the gospel, isn't it, Al?" Tom broke into her memories. "I remember when I said those words myself, when I first believed and Jesus erased all my sins. You did it years before I did. Sarah Bower walked up there with you. I was watching from my seat. Remember?"

Al remembered her confusion, the pastor's urging, the words that Sarah, next to her, had said, then Sarah's lit face as she cried and repeated the words she claimed had given her salvation, freedom. To Al those same words seemed the essence of slavery.

Sinner? I'm no sinner. I do my best! I try so hard!

"Remember, Al? Remember those blessed words? 'Be merciful to me, a sinner.'"

Tom looked so full of expectancy. How could she tell him that she had never managed to say those words herself?

31

AL'S EVENING WITH TOM CAME TO AN ABRUPT END due to Forrest's appearance in the Master Riders' tent. Caught up in the emotion of the prayer meeting, Tom met his partner with a partial hug from which Forrest recoiled.

"Glad you could make it, Forr! Didn't think I'd see you here tonight."

Forrest looked at those kneeling on the platform and the small groups huddled in prayer. He wore the same expression he had the last time Al had seen him bucked off.

"Had to get you. We have to be going, Tom." Forrest swung his eyes agitatedly around the room. "Thought you said you'd be done here an hour ago."

"I did, but the meeting went on. By popular demand." Tom jerked his head toward the platform. "That's Winky over there. Think team roping will ever be the same?"

"Not if he takes religion serious as you. Hard to imagine him living sober, though." Forrest stared at Winky. Even from where they stood, Al could see lines down the cowboy's face, tear tracks.

"We can go in a minute, Forr. Just want to welcome my new brother." Tom left, and Al watched Winky receive the bear hug Forrest had refused.

"Tom's pretty psyched." Al edged closer to Forrest, sensing an ally.

"Yeah."

She evaluated Forrest's reaction and decided her own uneasiness was at least matched by his. "Want to wait for him outside?"

"Yeah. Yeah, I sure do." Forrest's voice took on life as they moved away.

Due either to the city lights or a heavy blanket of clouds, no stars shone in the heavens. Al felt soothed by the open space above her, black as it was. She tried to forget Rick's message about blackness.

"Feels good to get out of there." Forrest leaned against the fencing and tilted his face upward. His eyes looked dark, his face hard and handsome, like some hero's sculpted visage.

"Yes, it does feel good." Al stood next to him, grateful just to be under the same sky. "So you're leaving tonight?"

"Sure, there's another rodeo in —"

"Don't tell me." She smiled. "It doesn't matter where, does it? You really love going down the road."

His face relaxed. "Just part of the job."

"Really?"

"No." He laughed. "Sometimes, it's the best part."

"What about going home?"

"Sometimes that's the worst part," he said in a tone Al hadn't heard him use before.

She never asked the question in her mind because Tom chose that moment to emerge from the tent.

"Okay, Forr. We'll bring Al to the hotel, and then I'm ready to go."

Forrest nodded, but he thrust his hands in his back pockets and began walking away. "You bring Al back. I'll be waiting at the trailer.

Got to give everything the once-over. Meet you there." Forrest didn't wait for his partner's answer.

Tom slowed his steps and watched Forrest cross the parking lot, ducking in and out of lamplight. "Sure wish he'd come to the whole meeting, Al," Tom said, reaching for her hand. "Someday."

He smiled at her, and Al felt her face burn under the joy radiating from him. *He thinks I'm just like him. He thinks I'm one of those born-agains, just as Sarah did.* Al felt the corner of her mouth twitch, and she bit it while searching for the words to disabuse him. "Tom, I'm not sure... I mean, don't think —"

"Don't worry, Al." His voice was gentle. "I won't push anything. I'll wait until you're ready."

Relief. He knew, then, that she was as far from knowing the alien joy on his face, the light Rick had spoken about, as Forrest was? And he accepted her? Without question?

"I know you're busy with rodeo, Al. Just leave me a little room in your life now and then, okay?" When she didn't answer, he continued, "I don't want to add more pressure to what you're already under. I only want to be what you need me to be."

He talked a little more about the meeting as they walked, and gradually switched over to which rodeos were coming up. Al let his words wash over her as she, too, turned her thoughts toward the arena.

"See you on down the road, then?" Tom asked when they stood at her hotel room's door.

"If you're around when we are."

"I'll do my best to make that happen." Tom gave her another of his beatific smiles before he left. "If we don't meet in the meantime, I'll see you for sure at Houston. Or the Dodge National Circuit Finals."

"See you at Houston. Or Pocatello," Al said, letting the door come between them before Tom had turned down the hall.

Blarney O'Neill had gotten tied up at a rodeo too far east, and Jenny and Al were on the road again, bereft of chaperones. Jenny longed to hear some country-western as she drove, but Al was asleep, and the radio would wake her.

Curled against the door, Al's hands made a pillow, but her hat was ready to flip off anytime. She stirred in her sleep and the hat tumbled to the floor where it came to a rest upside down.

Upside down. Jenny's own hat had fallen like that once. She had awakened to find Forrest grinning at her.

"If this was a convertible, you'd have just lost one fine Stetson," he said, handing back her hat and kissing her nose.

Jenny had stretched comfortably into his arms, her eyes green slits that watched the landscape flying by, made into barely recognizable blurs by Tom's driving.

Into Jenny's ear Forrest whispered a prophecy of many, many pleasant things to come: matching world championship buckles, top-of-the-line travel trailers, and above all, the luxury of years together. At the time, it had all seemed possible.

A white ranch house and yards of spreading picket fences had streamed by. "We'll have a ranch, just like that one," he said, apparently reading her thoughts.

Jenny had smiled. "With miles of fences for you to paint?"

"Miles. Miles and miles and miles. . . ."

And miles. Jenny felt a muscle spasm in her right leg and an answering decrease of the accelerator. She had been dangerously close to sleeping, falling too deeply into memories.

Al yawned and tipped her hat with one foot where it lay on the floor. "Where are we?" Another yawn misshaped her words.

"About a hundred miles farther than we were when you dropped off."

"I can drive now." Al reached for the map. "How far do we need to get? Where did you say we are?"

Jenny glanced from the road to point a finger. "About there, I think." She pushed her palms against the steering wheel, stretching her back into the seat.

"I'll take over. You look as if you could use a rest."

Jenny nodded and eased her foot from the accelerator. As she pulled the pickup over and slid across the seat, her boot ticked Al's hat, setting it to rocking. The motion brought back her daydream, but Jenny tried to forget, glancing through the windshield to see her cousin cross in front of the truck and climb in.

"All ready to go?" Al asked as she fastened her seat belt.

"All ready." Jenny reached for the radio and hit the auto-tune, surrounding herself with steel guitars.

Forrest returned from the lobby desk defeated and empty. *Did you think she'd write?* he asked himself, trying to get the stupidity of that thought through his skull. He held in his hand a letter addressed to his roping partner, not, as he'd hoped, a letter or even a note from Jen to him. Forrest shook his head, wondering why he had let himself get so carried away with the notion. Even when they were together, Jen had never written a single letter of the alphabet to him. So why was he setting his heart on a letter now?

First place where we've been long enough to have an address since the season started. Doesn't seem to matter a whole lot.

What was it for, anyway, this mindless movement from state to state, arena to arena? The buckles, sure. Fame, maybe. Money? Forrest had seen all that money could do, and he wasn't overly impressed. His grandfather had oxcarts of the mighty dollar, and it hadn't done him much good.

There was the ride. That made up for much of the rest of life's insignificance, but it was hard to hold on to eight seconds and release the rest of the week's meaningless hours. He knew well that the glory of the ride would only last while he was young. His father had died in the height of glory, but Tom's father had kept trying, kept drinking, breaking bones, and tearing ligaments until he was too beat-up to be taken seriously. A train had stomped Bob Rawlings to death ten years too late.

What is there for a cowboy when he can't cowboy anymore?

Every once in a while Forrest wrestled with the question. It tortured him only when he was alone, sober, and tired enough to let doubts have their way with him.

What else? If not rodeo, what?

The answer was easy: nothing. All Forrest had ever achieved was tied up with rodeo. Jen, recognition, all of it had to do with how well he could ride a bronc or swing a rope. Unlike Tom, Forrest didn't see anything else in life worth...living for. Not anymore.

Once he had contemplated life beyond the grandstands, but that was only with Jen beside him. Alone, he knew if he was ever caged in four walls of a ranch house or four corners of any kind of fence, he would go wild, like some Brahma with boiling blood.

For there was anger inside him, and something worse than anger. Forrest Jackson, heir to the wealthy Jackson Cattle Co., two-time world champion of team roping and four-time champ of saddle-bronc riding all at the tender age of twenty-three, had tasted glory and found it...tasteless. Insipid as Sunday beer, although that discovery had taken longer. The realization had been dulled by the initial excitement of fame, of so many doors swinging open to him, so many signs with his name flashing, red and blinking. Only later had Forrest realized the lights were a warning.

No matter how many miles he logged in one season, how many shiny buckles he brought home to Mr. Sterling Jackson Sr., how many victory laps he took, none of it would bring Jen's or his granddad's love, the two prizes Forrest poured out his life to win. And would continue to pour out his life to win. And would never win.

Never.

And that cold truth cut through all he was.

CHAPTER

32

RODEOS CAME AND WENT, including the prestigious Dodge National Circuit Finals Rodeo, where Al swept through four rounds in a fog, barely able to recall what happened even at her celebratory dinner with Tom. The dinner was a rushed hour-long affair, much like the entire DNCFR seemed to Al. After Tom was gone and she and Jen and Uncle Barney were off to another performance, Al hardly believed the money she'd won. For the first time, she had more than enough for expenses.

Jen acted as Al's rudder, evaluating her performance, directing practice sessions. When Barney protested that Al had done well enough to skip a lesson or two, Jen acidly suggested that perhaps the riders at Houston would think differently.

To Al's surprise, she met Houston's ground rules and was eligible to compete. Her last win edged her twenty-five dollars ahead of Sarah Bower, who formerly occupied the number seven slot. Al had just made the cut.

The Coliseum in Denver had seemed big to Al, but the Houston Astrodome, with its countless tiers of stacked seats and cavernous roof that towered over the huge arena floor, seemed monstrous.

Barney O'Neill stood with his niece and daughter at the edge of the arena, yards of empty space in front of them, a wide Texan expanse.

Al walked toward the arena's center and stood in the dirt and sawdust mixture. She rotated in a slow circle, viewing all the seats. "How many people will be watching?"

"An average crowd is around fifty-four thousand," Barney said.

"And I'll be riding here."

"And I'll be commentating here...at last. What are you thinking, Jenny my girl?"

"I can't remember where the restrooms are."

Barney laughed. "Always the practical one, while Al and I are the dreamers." He pointed. "They're that way, I believe, the ladies' a little beyond the men's."

Al continued her circle, raising her arms with the bag they held and going into a spin. "The dome!"

"The eighth wonder of the world, some call it. I think I'll say that a few times during the performances. Eighth wonder...." He reached in the pocket of his green sports coat for a pen and a scrap of paper, and began scribbling.

"How many performances will you be doing, Uncle Barney?"

"Every one." He tucked paper and pen away. "I've been wanting to do Houston since I started announcing. The Houston Livestock Show and Rodeo is second only to the NFR, Alison. You'll be riding in a rodeo with a purse totaling more than half a million dollars."

"Sanfran-tastic!" Al pirouetted again.

Barney picked up his bag from the dirt where he'd set it. "Three people will be aching to share one seat. The scalpers will be having a heyday. So will the media, I'm betting. Television cameras from at least two networks will be here for all eighteen performances."

"Three rounds, eighteen performances...."

"One a day."

Al stood still. "Do you think I can do it?"

"What, niece?"

"Compete against the top six racers this year and the top fifty from last year? I feel like I'm almost in the NFR."

Barney turned from watching his daughter disappear. "You almost are, yes. And yes to your other questions, although the day you beat my Jenny, I'll be hard pressed to figure out who to cheer for."

"Don't worry. That'll never happen."

"I won't worry. But the day could come, Alison. Will come. Maybe soon. You were looking awfully good at the Dodge National Circuit Finals. Awfully good. You had better be thinking about how you would handle a victory lap. I know Jenny is worrying about it."

Al's bag slipped from her hand. "No, she's not."

"Oh, yes. Just as she is thinking about winning tonight, about what score will put her in first, in the back of her mind, she's wondering when her cousin will become her toughest competitor. She's telling herself no one can beat her. But somewhere, a voice is whispering your name."

"I haven't beaten Jen in years, in eons, and I'm too far behind to be a threat now. Jen's not worried about me. She'd tell me if she was, and she hasn't."

"What Jenny tells you may not be what she thinks, Alison. In her heart, she may feel otherwise."

"I'm seventh, Uncle Barney. Seventh! Jen's first, way ahead in the money. I barely made seventh! No one's even in position to touch Jen's place, and after Houston —"

"The newspapers may link your names. Or one of you may come up on top."

"One will: Jen."

"Well." Barney picked up his bag and walked toward the entrance. "She'll be coming back soon, so hold your tongue. But Jenny won't always be coming out on top. At some rodeos someone else will take the victory lap. It may be you. It may be someone like Felicia Newcastle. Out of the two of you, which would you be choosing to take Jenny's place?"

"Me." Al didn't hesitate an instant.

"And that was well said. But if they ask you in front of the cameras, don't you be admitting it, my girl. Everyone rides for himself in rodeo, but if asked, he'll always be 'tickled pink' or 'purple' or any of a dozen colors to see another man win. And the ladies say the same. Don't you be saying any different."

"So that is just a line. And the one about never saying you're going to win is another line?"

"My girl, you have to be knowing you will win. Down in your marrow, you have to be feeling it. Believing it. But never admitting it. That's the cowboy's creed: Praise your mount, your partner, the judges, the crowd, your grandmother if need be, but never yourself. We're a humble lot, we rodeo folk. But mixed in with that is an equal measure of determination — and no small amount of pride. Learn with your eyes, Alison, not your ears, and you'll be seeing things as they really are."

"So it's all an act: The camaraderie, the —"

"No, no. The camaraderie is real. There's no sport like rodeo for that. Even your worst enemy will generally do all he can to help you: cinch you up in the chutes, share hard-won information about your mount. But everyone wants to be winning. And why not? Those who believe something else aren't being honest with themselves or won't have to worry about winning for long because they won't. Winning is try, talent, and talk. Mental talk. Telling yourself you can do it until you can. Jenny knows that. I thought you should be knowing it too, my girl." He took a few paces. "Remember — ride to win. You're champion enough to be competing in Houston. Start acting like it. And let the world see what Alison Austin can do."

Tom found her just before the grand entry. "Al!"

"Hey, Tom." Al reined Promise out of position. "When did you get in?"

"Just now. Forrest's still outside. Talk to you after the entry?"

"Grab a horse and come with. You're part of the show tonight, aren't you?"

"Not without Tamarisk. Houston is his arena, but we got in too late to get him and Canyon unloaded in time."

Processional music began. The line of horses moved toward the arena, breaking into a gallop as they entered.

"Tom, I've got to go."

"See you after the entry, then, all right?"

Al nodded and resumed her place in the queue.

As she came onto the Astrodome floor, Al scanned the crowd. Row after row of black, brown, even green and blue cowboy hats, bare heads with bleached-blond manes, gray sprinkles of hair, a whir of faces in a myriad of skin tones decorated the grandstands. Banners, drapes, festoons with stars and stripes or the Houston logo, capped with a cowboy's hat, adorned every level of the dome.

Fifty-four thousand people. Looks like a million. Promise followed the horses ahead of him as they loped in formation, slowing to a trot, then a walk as they made one lap and lined up in the middle.

Al sat, her hand on the saddle horn, feeling fifty-four thousand people looking down on her. Those highest in the grandstands were indistinguishable. *I hope no one throws anything from up there. Could be deadly.*

The announcer was speaking, but Al couldn't concentrate on his voice. She heard instead the orchestrated breathing of the crowd, could imagine the collective sigh of air from fifty-four thousand pairs of lungs. And the eyes: some behind horn-rimmed glasses or jeweled frames, some bloodshot and bleary from beer, some bright and anxious, some peering over the arena barriers, close and demanding. They all wanted a performance. They had come to see a show. And it had better be good.

"Al!" Jen whispered. "Come on!"

With her heels, Al touched Promise's belly, and the horse followed behind Jen's black gelding. The grand entry was coming to an end. After the anthem, Al would soon face the challenge of proving herself to thousands who had little if any idea who she was.

I'm a champion, she told herself, struggling to keep her head high as they left the arena. *I'm a champion. That's why I'm here — to race with...other champions.*

She picked out a few of her competitors: Janet Ballenter riding a sturdy paint; Nona Ellsen mounted on her white burst of lightning named Flash; Colleen Lockhart atop palomino-colored Chameux; Felicia Newcastle, proudly astride the imposing Wellington.

And Al Austin, on Promise. I'm like them. I'm just like them. I could win here. Prom and I could win.

But never in her twenty-one years of existence had Al felt more like a nobody.

"Al, are you okay?"

She was leaning against the walls of the alley where soon she and Promise would race toward the barrels. Tom eased beside her, full of concern.

"I still look bad?" Al gave him a quavering smile. "Thought I was doing better."

"Did the crowd scare you?"

"Uh, you could say that."

Tom grinned and reached for her hand. "Going to faint? I'll catch you."

"No, I'm not going to faint." Al snatched her hand away.

"That's better. I was wondering where the old Austin spark was. Didn't take much kindling to get it going. I remember you were like this at that big rodeo in Montana, too —"

"Let's not reminisce about my past failures right now, okay?"

"Failure? You beat Jenny that night."

"I did?"

"Don't you remember? You do the best when you're all riled up, Al. Most of us do."

"What are you talking about?"

"Nerves. Being scared...feeling a strong sense of 'anticipation,' as I always like to call it. Forrest calls it getting 'up' for a ride."

"You two feel like this before you compete?"

"Everyone does. Only some don't admit it."

"And I've been trying to be calm and cool. That Uncle Barney!" Al snorted.

"It's his fault you're nervous?"

"He told me to act like a champion, to tell myself I could win until I believed it. Right."

Tom leaned against the wall near her. "Some people swear that works. I'm not one of them."

"Me either." Al's voice held a trace of its former decisiveness. "It's too…artificial."

"Or prideful?"

"That doesn't bother me."

"It should. The Bible says, 'Pride goes before destruction, a haughty spirit before a fall.'"

"Then I guess it does bother me. I don't want to self-destruct out there. Or fall."

"You won't. How about a date after your run?"

"To celebrate or as a consolation prize?"

Tom looked at her solemnly. "If it all depended on you, Al, I'd say to celebrate." He put on the white cowboy hat he'd been holding. "How is Promise doing?"

"Running faultlessly. Not even Jen has any more pointers for Promise."

"I take that to mean she still has some for you, then?"

Al laughed. "I don't think she'll ever run out. Even that night in Montana when I beat her, she —"

"And you said you didn't remember."

Her head came up defensively. "Now I do. I didn't before. What's with you, Tom? Are you here to get me calmed down or fired up?"

"Both, but you can probably do it all by yourself. I bet you're thinking about your ride right now. You're running the course in your mind, thinking what cues you'll feed Promise, remembering how many strides between barrels, where to turn on the speed, where to slow. You've been thinking about racing the entire time we've been talking, haven't you?"

"Yes," she said sheepishly. "It's not that I'm not glad to see you, Tom, but…. This is Houston! And I would…I'd like to…."

Tom let her wrestle with words for a while. "It's okay, Al. I know the signs. Your heart's lost to rodeo, right?"

Her eyes showed surprise. "No! This minute I'm thinking about how I'm going to do, but rodeo's not my whole life. Not like...like Jen or...someone like...Forrest. I'm only in this for the Ex. After that, I'm going back to college to finish my degree. And then I'll do my graduate work."

Tom folded his arms.

"You don't believe me?"

"I'd like to. After this rodeo, you'll know how it is to win two, three, four thousand dollars in exchange for less than a minute's work. Do you think you'll feel the same? It's hard to walk away from rodeo, Al."

"You did."

"Yeah. Look how far I got."

"This is only for the Ex, Tom, for my hometown, my dad." She noticed his grin. "All right. It's for me, too. I want to get to the NFR, to the Ex. Then I'll be satisfied."

"Okay." Tom kept his arms folded.

"Give me two years. If I don't quit after the Ex, I give you full permission to drag me away."

"You promise?"

Al stuck out her hand. "I'll even shake on it."

Tom clasped her hand but didn't shake it. He held it, looking at her, imprinting her gray eyes in his mind. "Al, it may not be fair, but I'm going to hold you to your word."

"Fine. I meant it."

"Two years. Okay." He held her hand a moment longer. "I'll meet you here after the show."

"Fine." She turned to leave.

"God bless, Al." He touched her shoulder, wishing he could tell her all he was thinking, all he was feeling. "Ride well."

33

As THEY RODE INTO THE ARENA, almost like the open range, Tom felt Tamarisk tremble. It wasn't a bad tremor, not a start or jump or the beginning of skittishness; the big horse's body was contracting, tensing, coiling like a rattler before its strike. Tamarisk was preparing himself for that burst out of the box, when he would have to rate the fleeing steer and put his rider in a position to throw a loop around the Corriente's short horns.

The steer was a good draw, Tom knew: a fast runner, but a straight one. No fakes or stalls. This steer would watch for the chute to open, then tear out. Tamarisk would need his nervous energy to catch this Corriente, and Tom was glad to feel his horse tightening.

Tom backed Tamarisk into the box and glanced across the chute to Forrest, who held one lariat at his side, another on his saddle. Canyon danced, ears pricking forward, then back, responding to the pressure Forrest exerted on the reins as he set him for the run.

Tom felt time slipping into low gear. The steer in the chute kicked, and Tamarisk strained, bumping his rump against the back of the box. Tom repositioned Tamarisk, holding him back until the steer quit fighting and straightened, ready to race, his energy focused ahead. Then Tom nodded.

Slam! The chute opened, the Corriente rushed. Tamarisk flinched. The barrier swung clear and Tamarisk lunged after the steer, lining himself up for Tom's throw, gaining ground, gaining speed.

The rope slipped through Tom's gloved hand, the loop building as it had the moment Tamarisk left the box. Tamarisk drew behind the steer's left hip. The rope sizzled over Tom's head. He lowered it and threw with authority, his arm following through, pointing at its mark.

Slicing the air, the loop found its moving target and settled, the figure eight dropping over the Corriente's horns as Tom pulled the slack tight and dallied the end in one swooping motion. Tamarisk slowed, absorbing the jerk and swinging the steer into a turn to allow Forrest the widest space possible for his toss.

Behind the steer, Canyon's eyes wide and Forrest's hidden under his hat brim, another rope whistled, cutting the air, reaching for the Corriente's hind legs, finding them.

Tom watched the loop go snug. He cued his horse. Tamarisk wheeled to face Canyon, stretching the steer between them, then releasing it. The catch had taken 5.3 seconds, if the arena display wasn't lying — incredible for the dome's size.

"Five point three seconds!" The announcer's mid-rodeo accent slipped in his frenzy. "Five point three, folks!"

The mike registered a mad static sound, as if the announcer had gone into convulsions. Then his voice boomed, "Never have I seen such a run here in Houston! Let's pay off these two pros from Colorado: Rawlings and Jackson — on their way to another world title this year, if this run is a sample. Ain't it good to see these boys together again? Show 'em we're glad to have 'em back, folks."

Thunder, lightning, and rain was in the crowd's response. The clapping and shouts didn't die down even after the two men cantered out of the arena behind the steer, which still carried Tom's loop like a crown.

Al went over her equipment once more, checking Promise's gear for wear, rubbing a frayed edge of leather, adjusting the cinch, examining Promise's boots. She walked the gelding back and forth in the space behind the arena, trying to work out her own jitters rather than her horse's. Being "up" was one thing, being a wreck another. Al had to summon a little class before she faced the million-eyed monster that Jen and everyone else casually called "the crowd."

Jen had been her usual pre-performance self: withdrawn, distant. Uncle Barney had been downright irritating before the show, bouncing around like a large, happy leprechaun. Al was glad to be away from both extremes, here, alone with her horse, herself. Even Tom's company, though reassuring, had been a distraction.

Mentally, she ran the course, feeling every angle, turn, and sprint. She gauged the distance between barrels, recalled the unmarked spot she'd set for Promise's approach. Tom had been right when he said she was racing while talking to him. Once she stepped onto Astrodome soil, she found it difficult to quit racing in her mind for anything. If Forrest himself proposed, Al felt she would have to pause the better part of a nanosecond before consenting.

Forrest. Next to the divorce, Forrest was burr number two under her saddle. Al had promised herself she was going to ask him out once she reached Houston. So far, she hadn't even seen him. Tom always seemed to be the one who sought her.

Not a bull rider, Al told herself as she recalled Tom's kind, brown eyes. *A cowboy, but not a bull rider. Tom is great. A perfect friend. But anyone who falls for a bull rider is crazy, asking for a heartache on horns. Not that I ever would...or that he would ever fall for me. A bronc rider, on the other hand....*

Tom, even though out of the picture, gave her some time, some attention, while Forrest, if he wasn't trying to avoid her, at least made himself suspiciously scarce. The New Year's Eve kiss, which Al had held onto for so long, was dissolving. She needed something else from Forrest, something real. Maybe tonight she'd get it.

Tonight. After the race. After I win.

Had she really thought it? Was there a possibility she could win the go-round? Here, in Houston? Against the best in rodeo? Against... Jen?

Maybe. Yes.

The thought was strong, outweighing other considerations, but insane. *I should try to survive Houston, not win it,* Al counseled herself, grabbing at the reins of reason. *If I can keep an even pace, I'm almost sure of a place in the Ex. Stay safe, like Jen says. No risks. Besides, there's no way I can beat Jen. I don't even want to. Felicia, yes. I'd love to beat her. And maybe I will. But winning the round? Impossible.*

Still, other thoughts nipped at her. *Wouldn't a win at Houston prove...something? To Forrest? To me? To...God?*

Prove what? At what cost? An injury, either to her or to Promise, could torch all her dreams. Al remembered a racer who had slipped under her horse when he fell in an earlier show. Joyce Noonan, a pick for last year's NFR, had ended up in the hospital as a result of reaching too hard for the Houston pot of gold. Joyce's horse had to be destroyed.

And what about Promise? What if Al ran him too hard and something went wrong, a pulled muscle or a strained tendon? Why risk the whole season for Houston?

More and more Al knew Jen's urgings to invest in a second mount were sound. Promise was holding up well, but eight or nine additional months of going down the road could put him out of commission for the NFR even if they did get a chance to ride in it.

But how could Al pay for a backup horse? And how could she split her love between two mounts? She had never entertained the idea of getting a relief mount for Ironside, but this was a different circuit. She couldn't have an unreliable or overly tired horse now. Promise could lose big. Worse, he could fall — and Al with him.

After tonight, Al thought. *I'll start saving up after tonight, after I ride, after I talk to Forrest.*

Al nudged Promise into a trot. So much depended on this rodeo. It was almost as if she stood at a crossroads.

I'll ask Forrest. Al slowed Promise as her heartbeat accelerated. *I'll ride. I'll beat Felicia. And then I'll ask him.*

And deep within her, Al knew she would do both.

She had memorized the lineup prior to her turn: Jen would race first, then Felicia, and then Al. The peroxide blond who ranked number two in the world standings was just bringing a smug-looking Wellington down the alley as Al readied herself for her run. Felicia's smirk indicated that she had done well.

"Al-li-son." Felicia swung Wellington's head high, so that it almost hit Promise's nose, but the brown gelding hopped back unscathed.

"Watch it, Felicia. Prom needs his nose for a little while yet. I'm next."

"Can you-all beat an eighteen-twelve? That's what I just did."

For Houston, the time was excellent. "We'll give it a try." Al moved Promise past Wellington, into position, facing the slot that led into the arena and the barrel course.

"I suggest you give it more than a try." Felicia fought her short breaths to get the words out. "I already beat your kin."

"You did what?"

"Jenny did an eighteen-fifteen." Felicia shrugged. "Figure it out for yourself."

An official gestured to Al. Al waved and gave the course a once-over. "Eighteen-ten, Felicia," Al said over her shoulder, her eyes trained on the first barrel. "Figure that out."

"What-all are you talking about?"

"My time." Al squeezed Promise and began the approach: Felicia, the crowd, and even Forrest temporarily erased by velocity.

Jenny brushed Clover, careful to follow the hair making a three-sided swirl on his solid chest.

I...lost. Twice.

She knew it was coming, knew it from that moment in Scottsdale when Al had said she was going to ask Forrest out.

And you said you didn't mind!

Jenny's scores had been sliding since then, although she had managed to stay near the top of the slope for a while, probably due to Clover, who thought only of racing and eating. He was never distracted, but she had lost her focus. She might as well admit it.

The curry comb dropped from her hand.

"Jen?"

She closed her eyes.

"Hey, Jen."

He was near enough to pick up the comb and hold it out to her, Jen saw when she wearily lifted her lids.

She accepted the comb and put it to Clover's hide, beginning a long side stroke all the way from his withers to his flank.

"Jen, I just came to tell you how sorry I was about you losing —"

"I don't want to talk about it." She moved to Clover's tail, farther from Forrest. Her vigorous strokes made the horse crane his neck to look at her, though he continued chewing his mouthful of hay.

"Okay." Forrest inched closer. "If you ever do…" He left his sentence open suggestively.

She laid a hand on Clover's flank and faced Forrest. "Look, not every woman considers you God's gift."

"I never said —"

"No? No, you're right. I guess it was Al who said it. Or was it Felicia?"

"Who cares what —"

"Don't pretend you don't. If Felicia hadn't made me see what you were, I bet Al would have. How many more were there, Forrest? While we were together, I mean. I don't expect you to keep count since then." Jenny turned to rip at a strand of Clover's tail.

"Jen…." Forrest took a long time to find his voice. "It was Felicia that made you break up with me? What did she say?"

"Say?" Jen whirled to look at him, holding the curry comb high, a strand of black hair dangling from it. "Would I believe anything she said? Or anything you said? I saw you, Forrest."

"Saw me what?"

"Saw you…with her." She countered his shaking head with her own.

"No." Forrest stepped forward but Jenny shook off his arm. "Not while we were together, Jen. I never went out on you. Ask Tom. The worst I ever did was drink too much when you needed me most. I never touched anyone else until we broke up."

A partial admission. If he had been with Felicia afterwards, why not before? Cowboys were notorious charmers, Forrest in particular. Jenny had known his reputation and still been stupid enough to love him, believing for years that she was the only one, as he always told her. She'd believed. Until she saw otherwise. "Forrest, there's nothing you can say. I know what I saw. Why don't you just leave me alone?"

Had Forrest glimpsed her churning, flaming insides, he would have listened. But he came closer, laying his hand on her shoulder. "Jen, you're wrong about me and Felicia. I know you and she have this thing going, but I never —"

Jenny's internal temperature soared. "I'm wrong? Me? Yeah, I am — in ever believing a single word you said. That was where I blew it, Forrest. That's where I went wrong. That, and thinking you and I had ever, or could ever...." She faltered, remembering her dreams for the two of them. Those dreams had been snuffed out like a candle. A single candle. In a darkened hotel room. The memory inflamed her. "Give it up, Forrest, and get out of my way. I've got my own life now, and there's no room for you in it. Ever. So go."

He stood there, his mouth open but no words escaping.

"Go. Don't waste my time anymore, cowboy. Nothing you can even think of saying will ever change my mind about you. It's over. Save us both a scene, and get back to wherever you came from."

"Jen, I know sometimes I gave you a rough time, but now I just —"

"Get out of here, Forrest." Her voice was rising, barely controlled by the time she came to his name. "Get out now."

When he was gone, she doused the embers of her rage with tears that burned far more than fire.

34

"HEY, FORREST!"

Still raw from Jen's lashes, Forrest was slow to acknowledge the female voice calling him. He had just finished loading the horses in the trailer outside and was looking forward to going down the road as soon as Tom got done with his fool ride. Forrest left his hand on the door as he glanced at the woman walking toward him. "Hey, Al. Heard you did pretty good tonight," he said without any feeling.

"I think so."

Al neared him, looking as if she didn't plan to speak again but was waiting to respond to him. A partial smile hung on her lips, ready to mature. That was Al: a welcoming face. Quite a switch from the face Jen had shown him tonight. Forrest moved to open the door. "You going outside?" he asked for lack of anything else.

"If you are."

He held the door for her. "I've got to check on the horses. We're about ready, soon's Tom gets his brains shaken loose. Missile didn't scramble 'em enough at Fort Worth, I guess. Now Tom thinks he can lick anything on hooves."

He opened the horse trailer and climbed inside. "Hey, Canyon. How're you?" Forrest tugged on the short lead rope securing his horse. He gave Tamarisk a pat before backing out of the trailer.

"You're leaving tonight?" She was leaning against the side of the vehicle.

"Sure. You...and Jen...staying?"

"I think so."

"You don't know? What's wrong? Isn't Jen talking to you after you beat her?" Forrest felt himself wishing Jen hadn't talked to him either.

"I beat Felicia. Beating Jen's time just happened. It wasn't my goal."

The tone of her voice made Forrest stare. Al sounded like a champion. No reason she shouldn't, now that she was riding like one. Al finally was beginning to scale the heights he, Jen, and Tom had known for years she was capable of reaching. "So you did it all because of Felicia. Guess any goal's okay, long as it makes you win. You and Felicia butting heads?" Forrest tried not to think of the last time he'd said something like this, tried hard not to think of the person he'd said it to.

"Wellington and Promise almost did, before the race. At Felicia's instigation," Al answered. "That had quite a bit to do with my time, I think. I won't know until another few performances how I'll stand, but so far, our time is first. Promise earned his oats tonight."

"I know." He hopped down. "You got an eighteen-oh-seven. Pretty hot."

"You don't miss much, do you?"

"Not a lot." Forrest closed the trailer door and began checking the tires. He had already done so before loading the horses, but in big cities like Houston, a tire or two was often known to go flat, the prank of young locals proving their manhood. Tonight Forrest was tempted to slash a few tires himself.

"So...." Al stuck behind him as he moved around the white pickup and trailer. "Were you satisfied with your time in roping?"

"Have to be. It was better than what I did in the bronc riding, anyway. Had a good draw, too, but Silverwind caught me at the gate. I marked him out okay, but my timing was off the rest of the ride. Just couldn't spur him right. Took all I had to hang on."

"I know. I saw."

Forrest straightened. "You don't miss much, do you?" he echoed.

"No, I don't." Al smiled. She leaned against the trailer, her hands tucked in the pockets of her denim jacket, a washed-out color approaching gray.

That jacket almost matches her eyes. The thought surprised Forrest. He'd never noticed Al's eyes before, maybe because they couldn't compare with Jen's green ones, eyes that could glow like a traffic signal and did, whenever she turned rank...as she had less than an hour ago.

Forrest shunned that thought and again considered Al, remembering Jen had said something about Al being interested in him, Forrest's first criterion for any woman...except Jen.

Al had clear, healthy skin with an athlete's high color, a straight, well-shaped nose, well-formed lips. Though Jen's looks were far more striking, far more in the mold of classic beauty, Al had a magnetism of her own tonight. She looked approachable, even appealing. Or maybe it was just because of the reception Jen had given him. After that meeting, probably even Silverwind would seem friendly. This gray-eyed young woman leaning against his horse trailer seemed downright hospitable.

The tension Forrest carried in his shoulders released slightly. *Good old Al. Always a kind word and a smile.* He saw her lips move to a full smile under his gaze. *She's not a bad-looking woman.*

She wasn't bad at all. Standing there, under the soft lights of the lot, her long, brownish-blond hair in its usual unruly curls about her face, she looked actually pretty. Not pretty like Jen, in a way that made Forrest's blood pump, but pretty in a way that made him want to keep looking at her. Al would never stomp a man to death, that much Forrest was sure of.

"What is it?" Al put her hand up to her head and touched her hair. "I don't have any arena awards still on me, do I? No clumps of dirt or...anything else?"

"No." Forrest rested his back against the trailer. "Winning's something, isn't it? Especially at Houston. Gets you all revved up. Gets you thinking about the NFR. Bet you'll make it."

"I'm not making any bets yet. The NFR is a long way off."

"I know, but...." He rubbed the knuckles of his left hand over his chin.

She lifted her own chin as she waited for him to finish his sentence, and Forrest noticed the contours of her face, emphasized by shadow and light. *Why not?* he thought. *Jen never wants to see me again, and I'm tired of being alone, tired of waiting....* But he couldn't do it. He couldn't use Al just to spite Jen, just to ease the ache of missing her.

Al spoke, startling him. "How about dinner at the next rodeo we're both riding in to celebrate Houston and plan for the NFR, Forrest? I've been dying to talk about that with —"

Though Al didn't finish her sentence, Forrest knew she was referring to Jen. He forbade himself to feel guilty. Jen already thought he was guilty anyway, in regard to Felicia, Al, and probably every other woman in the circuit. What was he risking? Jen didn't care about him anymore. She'd told him so point-blank minutes ago. Maybe if he did move on, Jen would begin to think, begin to care again.

"Anyway," Al said, "I'd love to have supper with you, Forrest."

Suddenly, he felt nervous, as if he was about to blow his last chance with Jen. He bucked himself up. *This is my only chance. I've got to see Jen again, got to stay close.* He looked at Al, seeing little family resemblance. *At least she's staying in the same room with Jen. If I see Al some, I'll have a reason to see Jen. This might be exactly what I need.* But his uneasiness increased.

"Forrest?"

He looked at her, but he couldn't reply.

"Would you like to have supper with me?" she pressed.

"Let's go on back to the arena and see if my partner's still alive." He saw the persistent question in her eyes and felt her resistance when he took her hand to lead her. She clearly wasn't moving until she had her answer.

"Supper, Forrest?"

He took a breath, answering as he exhaled. "Sure. Sure, why not? Let's get back now." He tugged at her hand and was surprised at the happy little squeeze she gave him as she walked alongside.

Tom missed Forrest's presence in the arena, but old bull riding friends were quick to offer their assistance in the chute, and soon R-4 was set to go.

The black bull showed more of his Brahma heritage than most, sporting the large hump on his back and the thick, hanging folds on his neck. His muscled appearance was more formidable than his reputation. R-4 used to give a challenging ride, but this season, the young bull seemed determined to get out of rodeo. Every once in a while the dynamite would return to his bucks, but he had disappointed several cowboys present, who assured Tom that the only thing he had to worry about was a low score. R-4 was going down-hill.

"This next rider took a two-year vacation but is back with what looks like a bid to the NFR and the Pro Rodeo Ex," the announcer said as Tom straddled the chute and prepared to settle onto the bull's back. "There's old cowboys comin' out of the woodwork since the Ex got the go-ahead."

Tom lowered himself on his bull, not letting the announcer's words bother him, though some of the boys in back of the chute uttered oaths of disgust.

"Don't let 'im rile ya, Tom," Brock Issacson said, climbing the back of the chute like a ladder. "He's just tryin' to pick up the crowd. He knows ol' R-4 ain't likely to do the trick."

"Show him up, Rawlings," urged Newt Ringling, currently number five in the standings. "I been on this bull before. Seen him buck last week, too. He's got some surprises left. Better get yourself a good handle."

Tom checked his grip. It felt tight, but right. Strong. He hoped R-4 would show a little spirit. He almost felt up enough to handle Missile.

He finished wrapping himself in as the announcer's chatter trickled to an end.

"Ready?" asked the chute boss.

Tom set his body. "Ready!"

The gate jerked open.

R-4 stood there.

"Give 'im some spur!" someone advised, but Tom beat the words with his heels, and R-4 took a walloping jump into the arena, skittering across the dirt, faking, stalling — throwing every nasty bull trick in the book.

When R-4 went into his spin, Tom was recovering from a violent twist. The bull nearly had him in the swirling well of gravity inside the spin, but Tom resisted, pulling himself back into balance.

Where's the whistle? No ride ever seemed longer, more violent, and yet the spin went on and on. Tom's hand and back and legs and tailbone cried out as the spin jumbled his brains, taking away clear reasoning, leaving only pain.

The bull's head came up, his rear end followed suit, and the combined force flung Tom straight toward a skull-crushing impact.

Suddenly, the bull's hindquarters twisted, lurching Tom to the side and pitching him over, nearly slicing the side of his face with one curved horn but saving him from splitting his head open.

Tom hit dirt with his feet, then the ground was pulled away. A searing bolt of pain ripped through his arm.

Hung up! No! Lord!

Tom yanked his hand and pulled the bull rope with the other, but nothing came loose. His body lifted and smashed into the ground with R-4's bucks.

The bullfighters moved in, attempting to free him, but the wrap cut into Tom's hand and wouldn't give.

R-4 lunged, ducked, and Tom felt himself nearing unconsciousness, falling into the blackness that meant death. *Lord! Lord God!*

The bull made a seesaw buck, rocking on his front and back feet in a sharp whiplash motion. Tom felt his body twisting helplessly, his head nearing the hooves — then jerked away.

He was in the dirt, face first, his hung-up arm extended in front of him and the other underneath him. Where his legs were, Tom had no idea.

❧

"Hey, hey. You okay?" Shapes hovered over him, Tom could tell. But he couldn't move.

A clang of spur against metal, someone vaulting the fence rails nearby.

"Tom! Tom, it's Forrest! Hey, buddy!"

The biggest response Tom could muster was to move his tongue along the grit inside his mouth.

"Get a stretcher," Forrest commanded. Then, "What happened to him?"

"Got hung up. Did a cartwheel out of it."

"Take any kicks?"

"Don't know."

Apparently the stretcher had been coming before Forrest's order, for Tom felt careful hands probing and moving him.

"Hey, I'm...I'm all right." It was all Tom could manage.

"You're okay?" Forrest had heard the diagnosis, but he didn't look like a believer.

"That's what they tell me." Tom rested a hand on his hip, cautiously moving it up his bruised side to his riding arm. "I am okay, but it doesn't feel like I am."

"You're alive." In monotone, Forrest affirmed the miracle.

"Thank you, Lord. Yes, I'm alive." Tom nodded. "Hanging up: terrifying thing." He tried to grin, but the side of his face was too swollen. "Didn't even make the whistle. That was one ride that definitely wasn't worth it."

Forrest looked at him woodenly.

"Sorry to worry you." Tom hadn't seen Forrest's father die, and Forrest never mentioned the bull wreck, but Tom knew it hung heavy in his mind. He could read it in Forrest's eyes now, see it replaying in Forrest's head. "I'm not sure what happened."

"You tied in too tight, and when the bull threw you into your arm, the wrap end wedged. I told you not to let that happen."

"Not this time you didn't." Tom overlooked his friend's anger, knowing it was directed to an event long ago. Tom put his hand to his neck and tried to rub out one of the many golf-ball-sized knots. "Where were you, anyway?"

"Outside. Getting ready to go."

"Are we ready, then?" Tom was eager to get the conversation off himself.

"You're not. Doctors think you should stay the night for observation, so we're staying." Forrest wandered from the bed, his back toward Tom. "Al'd like to see you, and there's a reporter outside, if you feel like company."

"What's the reporter want?"

"Same old thing. 'Super-Cowboy Defies Death at Houston' or something like that. Got his article already written, I bet. Just needs a few quotes to slap in. Should I tell him to take off?"

"Yes." Tom hardly felt adequate for an audience with Al, let alone an interview with a stranger.

"What about Al?" Forrest still wasn't facing him.

"Let her in." Tom practiced moving his arm without groaning.

Forrest walked to the door. "I think...Jen's out there too. I'll let them both in." He paused. "Sure you're okay? You going to be able to compete, or should I call in and cancel your next ride?"

Tom felt his limbs unbend as he gingerly moved them. "Just tell me when. I'll be ready."

332

35

EILEEN APPROACHED THE LEATHER-BOUND BOOK warily. It looked innocuous enough sitting there on her mother-in-law's bed table, but if not for Janette, Eileen would have tossed the black book and all like it into the pink garbage can at the table's side before she ever considered opening it. She knew a little about the false balm within its pages.

"Go on, Eileen," Janette urged from her rocker. "I need to hear the Word today. Something from Mark or John, if you don't mind. Those are two of the gospels."

"Yes...Matthew, Mark, Luke, John...." Eileen flipped through the wrinkled pages.

"So you know the books of the Bible."

"Some." Eileen located the beginning of John and seized a hunk of pages, putting her finger on verse one of the first chapter on the first page that caught her eye. "I had a devout Catholic for a grandmother. She taught us a little catechism when mother wasn't looking."

Janette nodded. "You've mentioned a bit about that before. I imagine she used to read to you while you climbed all over her lap, waiting for the gumdrops that would be the reward for learning your lesson."

"Lemon drops, actually. Shall I begin?"

For an answer, the old woman closed her eyes and leaned back, starting the rocking motion that would continue all the while Eileen read.

""Do not let your hearts be troubled. Trust in God; trust also in me. There are many rooms in my Father's house; otherwise, I would have told you. I am going there to prepare a place for you.""

"John chapter fourteen." Janette's mouth split into a happy smile, although her eyes remained closed. "A perfect choice. Go on, dear."

""And if I go and prepare a place for you, I will come back and take you to be with me that you may also be where I am."" Eileen glanced up, but Janette's eyes were still closed and the rocking had not ceased, both signals that she wished to hear more. ""You know the way to the place where I am going." Thomas said to him, "Lord, we don't know where you are going, so how can we know the way?" Jesus answered, "I am the way...and the truth and the life. No one comes to the Father except through me.""

Eileen read on, looking up occasionally to see the lidded eyes and pendulating body. Finally she read without halting, keeping time with the rocker and beginning to think about the words.

""If you love me, you will do what I command. And I will ask the Father, and he will give you another Counselor, the Spirit of truth, to be with you forever. The world cannot accept this Counselor, because it neither sees him nor knows him. But you know him, for he lives with you and will be in you. I will not leave you as orphans; I will come to you.""

The rocker stopped its motion; Janette's eyes opened but their focal point was far away. "I've been foolish, Eileen; I'm sorry."

"What?" Eileen shifted the thick book to her lap as she looked at her mother-in-law.

Janette reached a hand to her nose and picked off her spectacles, letting them hang from their braided string. "The administrator paid me a visit this morning. She asked me to consider giving up my little apartment and taking a room at the nursing home."

Janette's hazel eyes rested on her. "The board has decided I'm no longer capable of caring for myself. Meals-on-Wheels does all my cooking, and I'm sure you've noticed how often I have to ask you to do the cleaning anymore." Janette sighed. "I'm afraid that goes for this old wineskin as well. There've been times lately when I wondered if I could step out of the tub once I stepped in. Though it hasn't come to that yet, I almost did pull the alarm chain. I have to say I know now why they have it there. I considered it an affront to my dignity once; now I know it's there for my safety."

Eileen wished Janette's gaze would release her, but the old eyes looked steadily into hers. Casting about for something to reply, Eileen moved her hand across the old Bible's textured hide.

"Open it again, Eileen, and read that last part over, dear. 'A Counselor,' the Scripture says. I'm mightily in need of a counselor. I'm so glad the good Lord led you to read this passage."

Eileen repeated the last few verses, reading until she came to the end of the section.

"Please continue, dear. Then I must talk with you a bit."

Eileen read, ""'Before long, the world will not see me anymore; but you will see me. Because I live, you also will live. On that day you will realize that I am in my Father, and you are in me, and I am in you.""'

"'I am in you,'" the older woman murmured. "Well, I guess that's as good a guarantee as I'm ever going to find. Eileen," Janette said, drawing herself straight in her chair with much effort. "I'd like you to help me move into the nursing home this weekend. Mrs.

Netherstahl says they have a vacancy and would be happy to give it to me."

"This weekend?" Eileen repeated stupidly.

"It's difficult for me to believe, too, dear. But it's time for me to go at last. Been holding out as long as I could. Now I see it's nearing disobedience to the Lord." Janette lifted her head and looked at the knickknacks adorning the apartment's walls and cupboards. "Don't know why I've been so tenacious about staying in this place. Like a spider in a crack, I've been. Neither rain nor sunshine could budge me. Help me stand, dear?"

Eileen assisted with a firm arm on her mother-in-law's rubbery flesh. A tottering step later, Janette sank to the refuge of her bed. "Thank you, dear. You will tell Harvey, won't you?" She inched toward a reclining position. "He's been fretting about me, and I'd like him to know I'll no longer be a problem child. I need to nap now, but how I've enjoyed your visit, blessed daughter." Janette smiled.

Eileen bent to kiss her, and the old eyes closed. Eileen stood above her an instant longer before she walked away and shut the bedroom door after her.

The ancient Christmas cactus bloomed in Janette's living room window, a minor miracle, this time of year. Eileen stepped toward the pink flowers and picked up the watering can to give the plants a drink before she left, taking comfort in the chore she'd performed many times. She nestled the slim spout among the leaves of the African violets, careful not to leave moisture on the foliage, no brown spots to spoil the furry leaves.

Does the nursing home allow plants? Eileen turned the question over in her mind as a way of considering Janette's move indirectly, a way to accustom herself to the idea of her lively mother-in-law residing in a place of the living dead. Eileen could hardly absorb

Janette's news, so she contemplated the plants, the sunlight streaming through the window above them, the verses she had read —
anything for a temporary diversion.

"'Do not let your hearts be troubled; trust in God, trust also in
me.'" These words had paved the way for Janette's decision. She had
submitted to the board's decree. Had she chosen to fight, she might
have gained a month or more of semi-independent living before
being forced to move. No great amount of time, but any stay of
decision would be a victory. Anything would be better than living in
a nursing home. Eileen had often heard Janette say the same, to
Eileen's secret agreement. But Janette had chosen to go.

"'There are many rooms in my Father's house...I am going there
to prepare a place for you.'" The passage Eileen had read by chance,
Janette had received as an oracle, and the confrontation Eileen had
been dreading was waylaid. Because of an old woman's fancy that
whatever passage Eileen happened to read to her from the Bible was
straight from the mouth of God.

Such a strange, blind faith. Childlike. Childish, Eileen decided. As
she let herself out of the apartment and left the halls of Senior
Manor, Eileen couldn't help feeling she had been used by some
higher power. Used. And she didn't like the feeling at all.

Though Al had been noticeably anxious when she informed Jenny
about her date with Forrest, Jenny's reaction deceived her. Jenny
accepted the news in the same manner in which she accepted Al's
big win at Houston: stoically. After a heart-to-heart conversation
with Al doing all the heart baring, Jenny assured her cousin that no,
dating Forrest was fine with her and that, no, she didn't mind losing
to Al in racing, either.

"Do your best. That's what rodeo's all about, Al. Besides, I'd rather lose to you than Felicia," Jenny said. And Al had hugged her and gone on to do even better.

Although Jenny tried not to begrudge Al's success in and out of the arena, she couldn't squelch her anger, an anger as slow-burning but persistent as a peat fire. Part of her hoped Al would notice and try to help put it out, but Al hardly spent time with her cousin anymore. It seemed she was either racing, sleeping, studying racing, planning strategies, practicing, accepting her awards, or…with Forrest.

Between rodeos, Jenny and Al still occupied the same traveling space, the same seat in Barney's new F-10 pickup that now hauled a new horse trailer with living quarters in the front. But more and more, the two women were becoming silent traveling partners, each dwelling in her own thoughts.

Al's hot streak continued as her fear of crowds diminished. At the outdoor Austin-Travis County Livestock Show and Rodeo, she took first in the first go and in the short round, leaving Jenny to feel she was experiencing a rerun of Houston. Al came away with $3,188 and Jenny with $2,524 — far less than their takings at Houston, however.

Jenny's position continued to drop as the weeks and months passed. Al and Promise outstripped Jenny and Cloverleaf, and everyone else. Al Austin was garnering considerable attention from the media and competitors alike.

At the unseasonably cool outdoor Oakdale Saddle Club Rodeo in the "Cowboy Capital" the beginning of April, Al won $1636, despite encountering difficult ground conditions, while Jenny was left with $1,295. While Al took her victory lap, Jen concentrated on the beauty of the nearby Sierra Nevada foothills and wondered why in heaven she had ever thought something good would come of Al's return to racing. Something had come of it, all right, Jenny knew, thinking of Forrest. But if it was good, it didn't feel much like it.

Al didn't perform well in her next outdoor rodeo. Forrest had promised to take her out afterwards, but not even this incentive helped. She didn't place. She couldn't say what had gone wrong and was unwilling to ask Jen, who had taken first in her stead.

After her shoddy performance, Al hung around the arena, listlessly watching the other racers, disinclined to return to the solitude of Promise's stall where the clamor of her thoughts would be deafening. She stayed to watch the bull riding, which turned out to be her greatest mistake of the night. Even in the twilight of the rodeo's aftermath, with Forrest at her side, Al couldn't forget what she had seen.

"Let's not go to the party tonight, all right, Forrest?"

They were sitting in the bleachers, watching the crowd dissipate. The air was warm. Stars showed up in the sky despite the glare of the arena lights. It was the equivalent of a balmy summer night in Wisconsin — minus the mosquitoes.

"We've got to celebrate, Al. Tom and I aren't moving on until Sunday. And that bronc I rode left me pretty thirsty."

Forrest's grin made no dent in her gloom, and apparently he comprehended that. "All right," he said, leaning against the bleacher. "I know you didn't do so well tonight, but everyone's luck runs out sometimes. You'll do better on down the road."

"It's not just my time, Forrest."

"Something else? Shoot. I'll listen." He grinned, and again his smile made no impact on her. "What do you want to talk about?" he asked with a bit more sincerity.

Al reached for his arm, and he obliged by laying it across her shoulders. Despite his lady-killer reputation, Forrest hadn't evinced a hair of wolfish behavior toward her, to her frequent irritation, especially tonight. Couldn't he see that she needed to be held spontaneously for once? "Forrest, I watched the bull riding." She grasped his hand. "Didn't you see it?"

"You mean Newt's wreck?"

Al could still hear the indescribable sound of a man's body being tossed and trampled against the rails. "What happened, Forrest? Why couldn't he get away?"

"Got hung up." Forrest actually moved his hand in a soothing motion across her shoulders. "Like Tom did in Houston."

"Like Tom? I didn't know Tom's was that serious."

"That's why I made him go to the hospital. Easy to get internal injuries, all that knocking around. That's what happens when you get hung up. Everything gets banged. Happens in bronc riding, too, you know. Part of the deal."

"A man almost dies — is dragged to the ground and nearly mashed to death — and you say it's just 'part of the deal'?" Al stiffened as Forrest's hand stopped its movement.

"Happened to my daddy, too." Forrest sat completely still. "Sometimes, when I close my eyes, I can see it happening."

Al thought she felt Forrest tremble but knew that was impossible.

"Only this time," Forrest continued in a voice slightly above a whisper, "I'm in the arena with him, helping him, and he doesn't die. He doesn't die."

Pain saturated his words, or perhaps now Al could better hear it. She touched his shoulder, wishing she'd dealt with her horror on her own instead of adding to his. "Forrest, I'm sorry. I didn't think —"

"Saul Branger got hung up last year, Brock Issaccson last week. But they died, like my father. Thrown around like a sack of feed." Forrest's head shook almost imperceptibly. "I heard a kid got it last Friday. A kid. He was fifteen. Name was Sully Thompson. Died all because he wanted to ride the bulls."

"They should ban it."

His head whipped up. "What's with you? You never seen anyone die before? Happens every year. You're not new to this sport. I remember one time when the four of us were in California. We saw two guys —"

"I didn't see." Her voice contained no anger now.

"I guess it's true you never watch. I know Jen and Tom saw it."

"I was with Ironside, as always. I never stayed with you three to watch. Never did like the rough stock events, especially after hearing how my dad got gored." Al paused. "I couldn't appreciate most of the clown's routines once I began understanding them: too coarse and sexist. And I've always hated steer wrestling and calf roping, so that didn't leave much else to stay for."

"Anything you do like?"

"I like the chance it gives to fine animals who love to buck and would otherwise be slaughtered. And I like racing. And team roping." A tail of a smile moved the ends of her lips before they went straight again. "I've only seen Tom ride a few times before tonight. I'm so glad I didn't see him hang up at Houston."

"But you watch me ride."

Al looked at him steadily. "Now, I do. I watch...and pray."

"You sound like Tom." Forrest laughed. The sound echoed in the stadium. "Look, Al. Nobody pays cowboys to risk their lives. They want to do it. They have to do it. I have to. My daddy hoped he'd die riding. He used to tell me that. I don't happen to feel that way, but I respect it. You ban rodeo, you ban some people's lives. My father would've killed himself if someone'd banned what he lived for."

"But it's so dangerous —"

"So is skydiving, boxing, race car driving. So are motorcycles. So are airplanes, automobiles. When you get down to it, so's the bathtub."

"A bathtub doesn't turn on you and hunt you down. A bathtub doesn't trample and gore you."

"I'm not crazy about bulls either. Used to beg my daddy to quit riding. I lost him to them, Al." Forrest quit talking, but Al's touch must have encouraged him to go on, his voice low. "I don't want to lose Tom. If I could talk him out of riding, I would. But he loves it. As much as I like riding broncs, he likes bulls. Maybe more. You can't take that away from someone. People have to make their own choices. In any sport, you're going to get hurt. In any job, there's that risk." Forrest's voice took on a hardness. "And we all end up dead anyway."

Al stared at him. "So it doesn't matter?"

"I don't know. But I wouldn't go around telling people what they can or can't do. That's playing God."

The last of the stadium lights went out, and the sky seemed to close in. Millions of stars scattered across the heavens, some hardly visible, some in distinct patterns.

"Forrest, do you believe in God?"

"Sure. I've even prayed, sometimes."

"Really?"

"Yeah. One time in Vegas, when I came down right under a horse."

"And you were okay?"

"Not a scratch, but pretty sore. Like Tom at Houston. Guess all four hooves missed me. I still wasn't seeing straight when they pulled me out of the arena." He stood and raised Al with him. "Now I'm really thirsty. Let's go. Tom and Jen are meeting us."

"Tom and Jen? How did that happen?"

"Jen and I had a little talk after her ride. I was looking for you. Found her instead. We straightened up a couple things we had messed up in Houston. Tom came by, and when he saw us talking, said we should celebrate the reunion." Forrest looked past Al and talked steadily, oblivious to her stricken face. "So starting Sunday, we're all traveling together, just like old times. Tom says we should stop on the way and see this real pretty place —"

"What about Uncle Barney?"

"He's cutting you two loose. You should be glad for some menfolks to take care of you." Forrest started down the bleachers, holding Al's hand so that she was forced to follow. "Now we can spend more time together," he tossed over his shoulder.

She struggled with her footing and emotions. "Forr, you're not.... You didn't get this whole thing going because you...."

"What?" He turned just as she knocked herself in the shin. "You okay, Al?" He touched the hand she clasped to her leg, attempting to lift it and examine the wound as though he would be able to see the bruise beneath the denim. "Was I going too fast?"

"Yes, Forrest." Al took his hand away and rubbed her shin. "You went way too fast."

CHAPTER

36

THE COMPANY OF FOUR SPLIT DURING THE DAY, though they would meet in the evenings before Jenny and Al went to one room and Tom and Forrest went to the other. They ate and exercised the horses together, but since it took two vehicles to haul four horses, sometimes the women rode together, followed by the men, or sometimes Al and Forrest would ride in the white pickup with its trailer, ahead of the red pickup and its trailer. Tom wasn't sure which way was worse.

He never thought Al would actually gain Forrest's affection. Though he'd long suspected her of being infatuated with Forrest, he figured his partner's seemingly exclusive devotion to Jenny would keep Forrest and Al safely apart.

Seemingly. That was the key word here, perhaps. Tom leaned his forearms on the steering wheel and cast a look at Jenny. She had been staring through the window, lost in thought or enjoying the greenery and California sunshine, when she caught his motion and turned.

"Time for me to drive, Tom? I'm ready."

"No, I'm fine." Tom rotated his neck to loosen the vertebrae Tigertail had compacted on his latest ride. The eighty points had

344

topped the go-round, but the ride had left Tom shaken in body and spirit. He'd come far too near the bull's left horn. It was too close to what had happened at Houston.

The impending rodeo at Red Bluff featured some notoriously rank bulls. Tom hoped he would draw one of the non-hunting variety, and he focused on the scenery to dispel a growing fear. "Sure looks different around here since last time, doesn't it?"

"Sure does."

Spring and warm weather had touched the California soil, and Tom knew just what the air would smell like when they stopped to give the horses a break near the grassy roadside. "No chance of exploring the Shasta-Trinity Recreational Area this trip, I bet. Did Forrest say where the next pit stop is scheduled?"

"He's probably planning on going all the way to Red Bluff. Maybe we'll stop near the lake or river a few minutes. Forrest likes that country."

Tom made no comment. He kept the pickup humming down Interstate 5, obediently following his traveling partner and Al, who were just ahead, right where he was forced to think about what they might be talking about or planning in the privacy of Forrest's pickup cab.

Had he not felt guilty about it, Tom would've prayed his partner wasn't serious about the gray-eyed woman who had lately become Forrest's most steady date. *Al and Forrest together.* Tom exhaled in frustration. This was nothing like it had been when they traveled together so long ago, nothing like what Tom had hoped would happen when he first sighted Al at Red Bluff almost four months earlier. Though Jenny was a pleasant traveling companion, a lot more so than Forrest, riding with Al would be heaven. Watching her riding with Forrest was...well, the opposite.

"Jenny?"

"Yeah?"

She turned from the window. The sun streaming through it made the edges of her hair an auburn fire. Jenny O'Neill was one beautiful woman, but she was not Al, and though Tom could appreciate God's workmanship in Jenny's features, he knew the Lord he worshiped had no place in her heart. That set the lovely barrel racer further out of bounds than even Al seemed to be at the moment.

"What, Tom?"

"Do you remember that trip we all made north of here to Mt. Shasta? When Forrest said we had to see Lake Siskiyou?"

"I remember." Jenny watched his face as if it were a screen replaying memories. "I remember," she repeated. "The iris were blooming. Blue flags, Forrest called them. Said they were prettier than anything he'd seen in any opening ceremonies."

"And there was still a lot of snow on Mt. Shasta. We stopped at the dam."

"Like Niagara Falls, Forrest said, only...what was it? Three times higher than Niagara?"

"And Al said she was going to jump."

"I remember that!" Jenny laughed. "She didn't place in the rodeo, and she said she was going to end it all. Got that look on her face that Aunt Margaret gets sometimes when she's being dramatic. And you wouldn't let her out of the pickup unless she allowed you to rope her."

Tom laughed, too. "I kept that rope safe around her middle the whole time we were up there."

"She wasn't going to jump, you know. It was just another one of her jokes."

"I know. I guess I know."

346

Tom shook his head. "Suicide's not something to joke about. I felt better knowing I had some way to haul her back if she really did get any ideas."

"Al wouldn't. She's practical as they come."

Tom slowed to cross a bridge over another river. "Maybe Al is practical, but even I get funny ideas when I'm near heights, especially bridges or something with water flowing underneath. Something about it...."

"Makes you want to jump?"

Tom stared at her. "You, too?"

"Sometimes." Jenny scanned the landscape outside her window. "Remember the old steel thing we had to cross one time in Idaho? Forrest said he was going to climb the bracings and hang right over the river. We were all standing on top, looking at the rocks so far below and the water spraying against them, and I felt like I could jump. I almost wanted to. I wondered if that was going through Forrest's mind, too. I was so glad when you wouldn't let him do the climb."

"He was a lot madder at me for stopping him than Al was about my roping her at Shasta Dam."

"He didn't know why you did it. Maybe she did."

Later, Tom wondered why he said what he did next. Jenny would have let her statement go. Even as he spoke, Tom felt he was exposing himself to injury. Probably unnecessary injury. "And why did I do it for Al, Jenny?"

"You love her."

She said it so simply, as if Tom's existence weren't tied up in those words. Jenny wasn't even looking at him but at the passing scenery. Tom was thankful she couldn't see his expression. "You

347

think so?" He tried to keep his voice calm.

Jenny faced him, her lips in an honest line. "I know so."

Tom only glanced at her, concentrating on keeping the pickup between the tar's dotted and unbroken lines. "Does she...know?"

"You're good at hiding it, Tom." When Jenny spoke again, her voice was quiet. She turned toward the window. "Like I am."

Tom let the words sink in. "With Forrest?"

"With Forrest." Jenny shook her head in slow denial. "I still can't believe it, and I don't want it, but it's there."

"Why don't you tell him?"

"Why don't you tell her?" Jenny countered. "It's gone a little too far to say anything now, hasn't it?"

"I guess so. I wish I'd said something before, something she understood. I thought I told her how I felt. Well, kind of told her."

"I said too many things to Forrest I still don't understand." Jenny's green eyes brimmed, but she held back the flood. "What makes us do it, Tom?"

"Ruin our chances for happiness, you mean?" Tom knew the answer but didn't want it to sound trite. "Sin," he said carefully, watching the road but reaching out with his scarred hand to show Jenny he meant what he said. "Sin is what separates us from others. From God."

"Wondered when you'd get God in on it." Jenny gave Tom only her profile to look at. "I don't like your sermons much." She glanced at him, and her voice became kinder. "You've been making Al pretty nervous, too."

"Al?" Tom almost hit the brakes. "She feels the same way I do."

"No." Jenny's tone left little room for doubt. "You just think she does because she doesn't say anything. Don't you ever wonder why?"

Tom stared at the back end of the horse trailer ahead.

"Al can hide things, too, Tom, just like we can. She doesn't want to hurt you, but I think she feels exactly the same way about God as I do. I know God gave me a life to live, and I'm living it the best way I know. So's Al. So's...Forrest."

Jenny silently challenged him to say otherwise, but Tom felt no strength to argue. If what she said was true, it explained a lot. Had he imposed his own salvation experience on Al? Was that part of the hesitation he always felt around her?

"I'm sorry, Jenny," Tom said at last. "Sorry to be so pushy."

Jenny softened. "We forgive you, Tom. I do, anyway. You're just trying to share what's most important to you, what you think is the most important thing in the world, for everyone. Why shouldn't you tell us about it? You wouldn't be any kind of friend if you didn't."

Once again, Tom heard wisdom in her words. Evangelism: it was an act of sharing, sharing the most important thing in the world with friends. Sharing the news, the "good news": the Greek meaning of "gospel." Tom longed for the day when Jenny would accept it, when Al would accept it, if she hadn't already. "Thanks, Jenny."

"It's okay." She turned away.

"And Jenny?"

"What?" She stopped her window-gazing to look at him.

Sharing the most important thing in the world with friends. He wouldn't forget it. "Brace yourself. Because I think I'm going to feel a whole lot more urges to share real soon."

"S'all right," she drawled, almost smiling. "We all have skin thicker'n a buckin' bull's. And I can sleep through 'most anything." She reached to pull off her boots, drawing her feet underneath her. "Wake me up when we get to Red Bluff, or whenever things start getting good." She paused, looking at the white pickup ahead. "Though that might take a while."

Jenny later wished Tom had let her sleep until June. Al took all at Red Bluff, and when Tom and Forrest left to hit some rodeos toward the south, Al again beat the stuffing out of Jenny's standings. When the men returned, no one mentioned traveling together, though before they left, Forrest did treat everyone to a sirloin steak dinner at the Cowboy Cantina, a favorite spot of his and Jenny's when they had dated.

Jenny wore her new empire-style crepe dress, watched herself during dinner, tried to be civil, and felt afterwards she had succeeded. When Forrest said that he and Tom would probably be going down the road for a good long time before they all saw each other again, Jenny could have sworn he looked for her reaction. She didn't know what he saw in her face, but she hoped at least it had not been indifference.

If Forrest had planned to get her attention by dating Al, it was working. In a big way. Jenny couldn't deny her feelings for him, and she was having second thoughts about burning any more bridges, too — in case she someday wanted to cross all the way over to him.

When the men left, Al continued to keep Jenny on her toes. After messing up two runs in one rodeo, Al came back at the next performance to make Jenny and Clover earn their first-place prize. Toward the end of the month, at Clovis, California, Al edged Jenny out of the first-place take of $1,037, undercutting her time by four-hundredths of a second. Jen was beginning to think California had it in for her, but wins elsewhere boosted her morale.

During the beginning of May, in Guymon, Oklahoma, Al slipped around the third barrel and had to settle for a paltry fourth place, while Jenny and Clover claimed the victory lap and the $1,083 in prize money. This made it easier for Jenny to be congenial at the "Welcome Home" party Aunt Margaret threw the following day.

Green had returned to Oklahoma, replacing the brown grass over which Jenny and Al had raced in December, when they had seemed to be close friends again. As her father turned his blazing red pickup down the dull red driveway, Jenny tried to drive the sadness from her heart. She hadn't seen Forrest in weeks, and when she did, he would probably be across the table as Al's date.

Jenny frowned inwardly and concentrated on the events of the day. Why was she suddenly so obsessed with the future, anyway? It was best let alone, just as the past was best buried. "What do you think Aunt Margaret made for you this time, Daddy?" she forced herself to ask.

"Let's see...it was lobster last time, so I'm guessing my dear sister will be waiting for me with her famous Mutton O'Neill."

"You remember every meal she makes."

"And why shouldn't I be remembering?" her father huffed. "Sure and you two are craving home cooking as much as I. Especially a taste of the homeland."

"Sure and we are," Al answered as the vehicle rolled into the yard where Aunt Margaret, in a red short-sleeved dress, wiped her hands on the white apron tied around her middle.

"Welcome!" Aunt Margaret tried to hug them all at once. "Supper is ready. I've got —"

"Mutton O'Neill sitting on the table, all ready," Barney said, kissing her cheeks.

"That's right." She made a tch-tch sound with her tongue. "I hate aging. It makes me so predictable!"

"Dependable, my girl, that's all. And my stomach is thanking you in advance."

Aunt Margaret waved them all inside to a table spread with entrees in gleaming glassware.

They spent the evening on the porch, talking their supper away, grateful for the cool of night seeping in as the sun sank. A few birds crisscrossed the sky, catching a bedtime snack.

"I hear you're making your presence felt on the circuit these days, Al," Uncle Willy commented as his brother-in-law lit up his cigar.

Al tried to move upwind before she answered. "We're on a hot streak." She laid an arm on the porch railing and set her cheek on it, breathing deeply. Such clean air. So often now it seemed she was breathing the smoke and manure vapors of the rodeo world. Just for tonight, she wanted to leave it. Just for a moment, she wanted to feel rooted to the land, to taste the flavor of home — but the rolling red-earthen hills of Oklahoma were nothing like Wisconsin's hills, and Al didn't even know the names of the birds she watched.

"Any bets on your making the NFR, Al?" Uncle Willy seemed determined to drag her back to rodeo.

"I'm not making any bets," Al hedged, thinking of a similar conversation between her and Forrest.

Al wondered where Forrest was...and whom he was with. Though he hadn't revived the notorious black book which he'd created after losing Jenny, Forrest made no promises he wouldn't. He still dated Al when their schedules allowed, but she wondered why he bothered. His kisses weren't much better than the one he'd given her on New Year's, and although he always tried to show her a good time, he rarely opened up to her since the rodeo of Newt's bull wreck. She felt she knew more about him through Tom's letters than through her talks with Forrest himself.

It was Tom who kept her up to date on their traveling, when the next rendezvous might be, what their wins and their few losses were. Both were performing well. Tom's hang-up at Houston, apart from causing him great expense in adhesive tape, hadn't hurt him in the standings, he joked in his letters. Al kept every one in her duffel bag. They were at least second-hand news of Forrest.

The only thing I have resembling love letters are from Tom, and even that's stretching it. Al was tempted to work up some resentment toward Forrest but knew it would be unfair. What did she expect? To blot out Jen's memory within a few months of dating Forrest? She should be thankful she had come this far. Forrest was attentive, in his own way. He wasn't much of a talker, but she'd always known that. He showed his affection in other ways: in a rose he once handed her before a grand entry, in ordering her favorite foods at rustic restaurants once or twice when they secured the luxury of being alone, in making sure she was safe from his rowdier cowboy friends at the parties he loved to attend — the unfortunate sites of most of their dates.

Even amid the noise and chaos of spilled drinks, blaring nasal heartbreak songs, and contorting bodies dancing out of rhythm to the music, Forrest gave her *most* of his attention. Occasionally a well-turned woman would catch his eye, but those mesmerizing blue eyes always returned to her. He really was quite thoughtful, if distant. So distant. Sometimes Al wondered if Forrest's preference for her might only be due to her affiliation with Jen. When he had suggested traveling as a foursome, Al was sure he was trying to get Jen back, but nothing had happened. Sometimes Al almost wished it would. Then, at least, the suspense would be over.

Whenever Forrest picked Al up at her hotel room, he always greeted Jen as well, making small talk that didn't change after he was alone with Al. But was that a fault? Really, Al knew she should be glad Forrest wanted to smooth things over with Jen, if that was what he was doing.

Everything was going so well with her. The NFR and the Ex bobbed on her horizon, like the birds swooping in the sunset over the Oklahoma hills. Forrest, the epitome of everything cowboy, the superstar in Wranglers, was dating her. Al's dreams were coming true.

"No, I haven't talked with Eileen since last week," Al overheard Aunt Marg saying to Uncle Barney in low tones, "but the hearing was Tuesday. I'm sure the divorce is final by now."

Al closed her eyes, blocking out the birds, the sunset, the hills. If this was happiness, it felt...strange.

37

AL DISLIKED CALLING RHODA'S NUMBER to speak to her mother. While she held the receiver and waited for Rhoda to get her, Al nearly hung up.

"Alison!" said a faraway voice.

Al put the receiver to her ear. "Hi, Mother."

"It's so good to hear from you, darling. Where are you calling from?"

"Another rodeo. I don't have much time, but...I wanted to talk to you." Al tried to shield the mouthpiece from the noise of the crowd and animals, knowing she wasn't succeeding. *I should have called later,* she thought, but the urge had come so hard that Al felt she couldn't compete until she had talked to her mother. "So, how are you?"

"I'm fine, Alison. How are you?"

"Fine."

"And Barney, Jennifer? How are they?"

"Fine, fine. All fine."

"That's good."

Her mother didn't sound nearly as strained as Al did. "How's dad?" Al asked, hoping this would fuel the conversation until she could calm down.

"He looked fine when I saw him as well. We had a talk about you over coffee the other day. He's very proud of you." There was a long pause. "I'm...so sorry about the separation, Alison."

"So am I."

"Sometimes I wish I.... Well, I left initially because I felt I couldn't stay on the farm any longer. You were going off to start your life, your father was happy with his.... I was the one going mad, going nowhere. I didn't want to hurt anyone. I tried to explain that in my letters, Alison. It really has nothing to do with him...with either of you."

That is the definition of a no-fault divorce, isn't it? No one's fault. No one gets hurt that way.

"Alison?"

"Yes?"

"I am sorry. So very sorry."

"I know." Al tried to sound more chipper. "Thanks for the letters."

"You're welcome. I hope to see you this summer." She sounded more cheerful. "If all goes well, I'll be staying with my friend Eva near Cheyenne around the time of the rodeo. If you let me know when you're riding, I'll be sure to come."

Wow! This is something new. "I'd love to see you there, Mother. I'll check with Jen. She keeps the schedule."

"Fine. Let me know, please, Alison...with enough time in advance so that nothing gets in the way."

Like Dad? Al attempted to push the hurt down inside her, but it kept welling up. *Mom's trying to make concessions. Give her a break.* "I'll do my best to let you know in time. You'll be staying with Rhoda until then?"

"For a while. Alison...your grandmother isn't well. We've had to move her into the nursing home. She's doing fine emotionally but not physically. Do you think it would be possible for you to make a short visit? Just to see her for a day would mean so much, for both of you. Try to come home when you can, won't you?"

"I'll try, but that's a long trip. We keep mostly in the southwest. Is Grandma...dying?"

"She's eighty-four," Eileen sidestepped. "Her heart has been bad for years. I suppose she could die at any time. I don't know if this latest bout means anything or not. The doctors say she's doing well enough, but to me, she looks so much weaker. I knew it would be hard for you to come, but I wanted to let you know so you could make your own decision."

Al heard the briskness of her mother's last statement, as if she were verbally dusting her hands after completing a difficult chore. *Is Grandma really sick, or is this another attempt to manipulate me? Is that what the divorce was, too?* "What do you think I should do, Mother?" Al asked, testing her.

"Darling, I really can't say. Grandmother could be with us another five years or more, I suppose. What you do is really up to you. Perhaps I shouldn't have mentioned it. I felt you should know, though, in case.... It's really impossible to say what her condition is. Perhaps nothing's wrong. I may be overly anxious. At any rate, please don't let it affect your riding."

I won't let it affect my riding any more than your divorce did. "I'll try." Al could hear the steer wrestling starting. After the bulldoggers, Forrest and Tom would be team roping, then it would be her turn to compete. "I should go, Mother. I...love you."

"I love you too, honey. I hope you do well. Good-bye."

"Bye." Al hung up the phone and turned toward the wall, hanging onto the silver metal siding of the phone box. *How can it all be so casual? Our family...demolished.* Then a new wave of pain hit her. Grandma. Dying.

"Al?"

She wiped at her eyes before she left the comfort of the cool phone booth. "Oh, hi Tom." Al swallowed to relieve the ache in her throat. "Shouldn't you be getting ready to rope?"

"Soon. You all right?"

"Fine. Racing jitters again, I guess."

He didn't look like he believed her. She tried again. "Really, I'm okay, Tom. Just some bad news. Where's Forrest?"

"With the horses. Want me to get him for you?"

"No. You know how he is before his event."

"I sure do." Tom reached toward her, then pulled his hand back and stuffed it in his pocket. "Feel like talking about it with me? I'm still your second pick, aren't I?"

His statement, or maybe the way he said it, made her think. *Am I doing to Tom what Forrest is doing to me? Treating him like leftovers? Am I hurting him?*

Tom's face gave her no answer. His brown eyes were mild as ever, his forehead unfurrowed. *Don't exaggerate your appeal, Al. If Tom ever did love you, it was a long time ago.* "I'm okay, Tom. Thanks. You have to go, and I should, too. Do you see Jen anywhere?"

While Tom's attention shifted from her, Al took another swipe at her eyes, removing the last bit of moisture.

"I thought I saw Jenny by the concessions. Want me to check?"

"No, I'll go. Or maybe I'll just see about Promise instead."

"I'll go with you. There are still about six more bulldoggers up before I have to get ready."

Al cut through the crowd, appreciating Tom's presence. Usually it was difficult to get through without a few fans or even a few men trying to stop her. With Tom at her side, she made good progress.

They walked to the practice area behind the rodeo arena, where Al had left Promise. She unhitched the reins and held them. "Thanks again, Tom." She felt a twinge of wistfulness. "You always seem to be around for my dark times."

He laid a hand on the railing. "You were talking to your mother?"

"How'd you guess?"

"I thought it was someone from home...process of elimination. Is she okay?"

"She says she is. My grandmother's not, though."

"I'm sorry."

"I'd really like to get up to see her. I just don't think it's possible."

"Afraid you'd lose too much money?"

"That — and no wheels."

"I'd take you if I could. We've got a few days' rest coming up, but not enough to make it to Wisconsin and back." He considered the problem. "How about going by Amtrak?"

"That's an idea. Or I could always ride a bus."

"Don't take a bus. I'll gladly pay the difference. I don't think it's safe for someone riding alone — especially someone like you. Some jerk would take one look at you and think he struck gold."

"Are you saying I can't take care of myself?" Al pretended to bristle, knowing that wasn't his implication.

"Sorry. That's not what I meant. Just...be careful. And please don't go by bus, all right? I meant my offer."

Al looked at him closer. Was this typical cowboy banter, or something else? She decided to try to find out. "Are you making that kind of money now that you can throw it at any woman who comes along?"

"I can throw it at you if it means keeping you from riding a bus alone. It's the least a friend could do. Let me know, all right?"

A friend. That's all he considers himself, then. "All right, Tom. I don't need your money, and I won't take a bus. I think I will try to get home for a few days, though."

"Good. Just get back soon." He looked around him. "I should go. Forrest's probably pacing by now, cussing me out."

"Probably."

"Bye, Al."

She returned his wave and mounted Promise, dismissing their conversation before she'd completed one pattern.

What Forrest missed most about Al, besides her sparkle, which had lost a few volts anyway, was an excuse for running into Jen. He was in a race with time. Soon the summer rodeos would begin, and there would be little, if any, opportunity to win Jen back. He'd be too busy trying to win the titles. First they'd go to California for the rodeo at Redding, then up to Canada to compete at Cloverdale, then Vegas for the Helldorado, Fort Smith in Arkansas, back to California, and so on, with assorted rodeos in between right on through the Fourth of July, known ironically as Cowboy Christmas, when things really got busy.

Have to break out the Cessna then, Forrest thought. *Even with the plane, there won't be much time for anything but rodeo.*

Today, however, the thought did not entirely dismay him. The latest issue of *Pro Rodeo Sports News* had come out, proclaiming what he already knew. He and Tom were in the PRCA's first-place Crown Royal team roping standings, and Forrest was first in saddle-bronc riding.

Forrest stretched out, feeling the sun on his face and squinting against it to see Tom exercising the horses.

He glanced back at the standings, and his face clouded. Forrest watched his partner lead first Canyon, then Tamarisk back into the trailer before he said anything. "Seen the *News*, Tom?"

From inside the trailer came Tom's voice. "No. How are we doing? Still on top?"

Forrest couldn't decide if Tom was faking his ignorance or not. "Yeah, we still are, partner."

Tom stepped down and joined Forrest on the ground, where he leaned against the trailer tires. "So what's wrong?"

"Didn't say anything was."

"You didn't have to. What is it? Not missing Al, are you?"

Forrest surveyed Tom coolly. "How long've you known you were in the top fifteen?"

"What?"

Forrest scrunched his hat down until the brim hit his nose. He thumbed at the paper on the ground. "Take a look."

Opening the first page, Tom ran his finger down the listing, stopping unsteadily. "Twelve! I am in there, Forr!"

"'S'what I said."

"Hey, I didn't know."

"Right."

Tom set the paper between them. "Wow."

"You really didn't know?" Forrest peered from behind his hat.

"I was keeping track of the money, thinking about the ranch. But I didn't think —"

"You didn't." Forrest stood and dusted himself off. "Now what? You going to concentrate on roping or riding?"

Tom's mouth hung ajar, then the corners of his lips lifted. "I think I'll do just what you do, Forr." He put one palm on the ground and raised himself. "Which event do you give the most to? Saddle-bronc riding or team roping?"

Forrest did not smile as he answered. "Okay. I get it." He pulled one hand from the pocket of his Wranglers and with it opened the pickup door. "But from now on, you're driving, hotshot."

38

AL SPENT ONLY THREE DAYS AT HOME: one to arrive, get settled, and see her grandmother at the nursing home, and two split between her mother and father, with additional brief visits to Grandma.

Her mother met Al at the train station, then drove her to Gilman, keeping the conversation alive by filling Al in on the news about her father and grandmother. Eileen referred to herself only in asides relating to the other two.

When they pulled up to the nursing home after a lunch of pasta and salad at the only cafe in town, Eileen laid her hand on Al's wrist. "Darling, I want to prepare you a bit more before you see Grandmother."

"She's not going to know me," Al said flatly.

Eileen hesitated. "She may. But she has her good and bad days. I never know how I'm going to find her." She looked past the blue dash to the darkened window in the building ahead. "It's just like me to be negative, isn't it? This could be one of her clear times. I hope so."

Grandma's room was dim as they stepped inside, past the woman lying like a mummy behind the first partition. A green curtain hanging from gold hooks split the room in half.

As Al peeked around the curtain, she felt the atmosphere change. Her mother — or at least Al assumed it was her mother — had done a fine job recreating Grandma's bedroom at Senior Manor. Pictures hung on the walls in almost perfect simulation of their old positions. Al saw the woodcut of the Swiss villa where Grandma and Grandpa had spent their fortieth wedding anniversary. There was the old flour sack picture board, where photographs of nieces, nephews, children, and grandchildren, along with many adopted members of these categories, smiled down at the old woman lying in the hospital bed.

Al looked past the bed, where plants lined the large window ledge: the ivy with its great green and silver leaves; the Christmas cactus, its segments shining, Al was sure, from a recent milk bath administered by her mother; and several pots of African violets and other small plants.

All that had really changed was Grandma herself. Al stared a moment longer at the familiar, eternal mementos before she could rest her eyes on Grandma's sleeping face with its sallow skin and limp folds that had been full the last time she'd seen her. Al wanted to keep looking at the knickknacks in the corner shelf instead of that ancient death mask.

"It's all right." Eileen motioned Al forward, her arm around her. "Grandmother knows you're coming. She asked to be awakened if she was sleeping. Go ahead."

"What do I do?" Al felt cold, almost frozen.

"Call her name. Bend down and give her a hug or kiss her cheek. Take her hand. Do whatever you're comfortable doing. She'll wake up eventually."

"Grandma? Grandma, it's Alison." Al stroked her hand. Flesh hardly covered the protruding knuckles and bones. "She's so thin,"

Al whispered, looking up at her mother.

"Alison?"

Grandma's voice hadn't changed. Neither had her eyes, a golden hazel, enlarged by thick glasses.

"It's me, Grandma." Al kissed her cheek.

"Dear Alison." Grandma turned her head to take in Eileen, standing behind Al. "So good to see her, isn't it, Eileen?"

"So good." Eileen placed her hand inside Grandma's open palm so that the older woman could touch both Eileen's hand and Al's.

"How long are you staying, child?"

"Three days. We've got another rodeo coming up that Jen says I can't miss." Al looked at the new concaves in Grandma's face. Her mother had been right. Grandma was slipping fast. "Maybe I can stay a while longer."

"Don't you dare." A light came into Grandma's eyes. "You do what you have to do, Alison. Don't come home until you're finished with rodeo. For good." She smiled serenely. "Isn't that right, Eileen?"

"Whenever you're ready, Alison. If you ever are," Eileen added. "I've told Grandmother how well you're doing."

"No surprise," Grandma said. "I thank the Lord you've had no injuries. Is Jenny doing as well as you are?"

"Better. She's switched to racing Banner now, to give Clover a rest, but she's riding just as strong." Al thought uneasily of Promise, wishing she had arranged for another mount before she'd left. He looked good, but he was favoring his right foreleg. "I should have taken a few more days for this trip. I should have brought Promise home, let him rest. That would've given me another reason to come back."

"Do you need any, dear?" Grandma struggled to sit, and Eileen moved to the other side of the bed to assist as Al tried awkwardly to help.

"Thank you, girls." Grandma touched the pillow behind her back. "That's better. I was saying? Oh, I remember. How long are you staying, dear?"

"Three days." Al shot a look at her mother, who was pulling up a chair and missed Al's visual inquiry.

"Oh, that's right." Grandma half-closed her eyes as she sucked in a slow breath of air. "It's so good to see you." She applied the tiniest pressure to Al's hand.

The conversation dragged for another fifteen minutes before Grandma asked Al for the favor of reading the Bible to her in her mother's place. Al gave her mother a questioning glance as she opened Grandma's nightstand drawer and took out the heavy black book. "What would you like me to read?"

"Anything, dear. It's all God's word, even the begats. You just page through till you come to a place where you feel like reading, and I'll be praying that the Lord will direct you to what he wants read today."

The left side of Al's lip twitched, but Grandma apparently missed this sign of Al's agitation, as did her mother.

Al shifted the book to the edge of the bed. Page after page turned in her hand, but Grandma did not move. Al turned another section of pages, then saw a chapter heading. Her mother's face gave Al no clues as to whether they should continue their stay or not, so she read, trying to assume the reverent tones she remembered Uncle Willy had while reading the Christmas story. That was the last time Al clearly recalled hearing the Bible narrated.

"'As for you, you were dead in your transgressions and sins,'" Al read, flinching. *Nice one, Al. Great deathbed passage.* Before Al was able to turn elsewhere, Grandma's hand gave her another squeeze.

"Perfect, perfect," Grandma murmured without opening her

eyes. "What a lot Paul has to say in this section. Thank you, Alison. Please continue."

Al's lifted brows lowered, and across the bed, her mother smiled encouragingly. "'…in which you used to live when you followed the ways of this world and of the ruler of the kingdom of the air, the spirit who is now at work in those who are disobedient.'" Al tried to make the words ring as Uncle Willy had.

"Alison, dear?" Grandma's eyes opened.

"Yes?"

"Please read in your own voice." The old eyes closed.

"'All of us also lived among them at one time, gratifying the cravings of our sinful nature and following its desires and thoughts. Like the rest, we were by nature objects of wrath.'"

Grandma nodded slightly, so Al continued. "'But because of his great love for us, God, who is rich in mercy, made us alive with Christ even when we were dead in transgressions….'" Al halted.

Grandma's heavy lids lifted. "What is it, dear?"

"What does it mean?"

A smile slowly moved Grandma's lips. "So now you're thinking about the words instead of how to read them? Good. That's the best way to read. What part don't you understand? I wouldn't blame you if nothing made sense. It's a difficult saying."

"The…" Al looked guiltily at her mother. "The dead-alive part." Al marked the phrases with her fingertip. "'Dead in your transgressions and sins, dead in transgressions…alive with Christ.'"

Grandma's eyes hinted at a smile. "A good question. And what comes between the death and the life?"

Al consulted the passage. "God?"

"Mm-hmm. How does the Scripture put it?"

"'But because of his great love for us, God, who is rich in mercy, made us alive with Christ..."

"Yes?"

"'Even when we were dead in transgressions'?"

Grandma chuckled. "I don't think the Scripture has a question mark there, but that's how I read it, too. Or used to," she said, casting a look at Eileen. "Yes, Alison, you've answered the riddle. The love of God is the bridge between death and life. Understand?"

"No."

"Then keep reading." Grandma's lids shut.

"There's a parenthetical expression here: '...it is by grace you have been saved,'" Al said. "Should I go on?"

"Mm-hmm."

"'And God raised us up with Christ and seated us with him in the heavenly realms in Christ Jesus, in order that in the coming ages he might show the incomparable riches of his grace, expressed in his kindness to us in Christ Jesus. For it is by grace you have been saved, through faith — and this not from yourselves, it is the gift of God — not by works, so that no one can boast....'"

"Something else?" Grandma asked softly.

"Yes."

Grandma roused herself to open one eye. "Try reading just the phrases of that last section which begin with 'by.'"

Alison separated the phrases, reading them aloud.

"Now, you tell me what it means, dear," Grandma said when Al finished.

"It says you were dead in sins, but because God loved you, He saved you by..." Al picked out the verse, "'by grace through faith.'"

"Yes." Grandma sounded supremely contented. "And why did he save 'you'? Not because of anything you try to do yourself, not by any kind of work — God prepares all the good works that we do beforehand. Why does he save you, Alison?"

"'Because of his great love.'"

"Quote, unquote," Grandma remarked. "That's his gift." She unveiled her eyes. "We studied that some time ago, didn't we, Eileen?"

Eileen smiled indulgently, and Grandmother turned to Al. "Hand the Bible to me, please, dear." She found the passage and handed it back. "Romans ten, verse nine says, 'That if you confess with your mouth, "Jesus is Lord," and believe in your heart that God raised him from the dead, you will be saved.' Here's the cornerstone, verse ten: 'For it is with your heart that you believe and are justified, and it is with your mouth that you confess and are saved.' Your mother and I have been studying this."

Al recalled that the verses were the same she'd heard at the Master Riders concert, and she felt a vague anxiety.

"There's nothing we can do to earn salvation," Grandma said. "Just believe God raised our Lord Jesus from the dead." Her eyes closed with finality. "We come to our Lord as sinners. We have nothing to offer him. Yet our belief and repentance please him, and he gives us...everything. More than we could ever hope to possess ourselves. The greatest treasure...."

Eileen gestured toward the door, and Al slipped the Bible into the nightstand's drawer. Grandma's eyes didn't open even when Al took her hand from the elderly woman's grasp.

Only the hair at the base of Harvey Austin's neck remained pure black. The rest was mixed with gray. He said his graying was due to worrying about his mother, but Al noticed that he talked about her own mother far more in the time she visited him.

They were sitting at the kitchen table when he dropped his bombshell. "I'm selling the farm, Al."

Before she could recover, he went on. "I've never been much of a farmer. Ed Vlasky down at the hardware store says he can use me to do handyman jobs and some clerking part time. Pay's good. What do you think?"

"Is it what you want?"

"I don't like living on this place by myself." He glanced at Al, then stared at a spot on the table, running his hands through the thinning hair above his ears. "Maybe if I'd done this ten years ago, your mother never would've gone."

Al didn't answer.

"How did she look when you left her?"

"I don't know. The same."

"I saw her in the grocery store Monday. She looked good. We talked a little. I plan to see her again this week."

"Did you tell her about selling the farm?"

"We already talked about what price to ask, so I won't say anything more until I do sell it. She knows me good enough to also know that what I say isn't always what happens, exactly."

Al checked her watch. "I have to go now, Dad."

"Need a ride to the station?"

"Mom's taking me."

"That her new car you drove over here?"

Al heard the sadness in her father's voice but knew no way to comfort him. "Yes. She got it this week."

"I know. She's making the payments with her job at the bank. I tried to get her to keep the station wagon, but she said she couldn't." He looked at the floor. "Funny she's staying around, isn't it?"

"What?"

"Your mother. I thought she'd go back to the city, but she's staying here in Gilman. She sees Grandma every day. Can't thank her enough for that. Grandma's been calling her 'Patsy' now and then, when she's tired. That was my sister's name. She died when she was three." Her father stared at the table, then pushed on it with his palms and stood. "Sorry to go on like this, Al. I know trains don't wait. Thanks for coming to see your grandmother. Now go on back and make us proud, like you have been."

"I will, Dad. Love you." She kissed him.

"Love you, too." He hugged her a second longer than she did him. He watched her put on her windbreaker and walk to the door. "Alison...."

"Yes?"

"Think your mother would like to come down to the station with us to see you off?"

"I...guess you can ask her when we get to Rhoda's, if you want." Al started down the stairs so he wouldn't see her surprise.

"Sure. We can ask her."

As they clumped down the entryway steps, Al felt something was peculiar, missing, but not alarmingly so. It wasn't until she boarded the train and waved at her parents from the window that she realized the farmhouse's fourth entryway step was no longer loose.

39

WITH SUMMER CAME THE GREAT RODEOS at Santa Maria, California; Reno, Nevada; Greeley, Colorado; and the wild scramble for big bucks on the Fourth of July's Cowboy Christmas. Toward the end of July the famous Cheyenne Frontier Days Rodeo arrived, but not Al's mother. Grandmother was getting worse, Eileen said when Al called, and Al only wished that she, too, could be near to help her grandmother leave life.

Al's performance at Frontier Days made her regret she had spent the time in Wyoming instead of Wisconsin. She hadn't placed, which wasn't a new experience lately. The strain on Promise finally demanded her attention and action, but with the busy summer schedule, finding another good barrel-racing horse was as difficult as getting a good night's sleep.

Tom and Forrest rode in and out of Al's days and nights. It seemed she was always saying good-bye, getting the horses loaded for another rodeo. The romance with Forrest, or whatever it had been, dwindled back to friendship. Or maybe it had never gone past friendship at all. While Al still longed for what she had made him in her heart, she knew the flesh-and-blood Forrest had nothing to offer her. The searching look in his blue eyes that had drawn her was something probably only Jen could fulfill, if anyone could.

What little Al saw of Forrest was in the arena. Like Jen at her racing, he rode and roped as if every rodeo was the NFR. And maybe it was. Maybe it had to be. Rodeo was one continuous moment, with every body cell programmed for victory. Victory or...nonexistence, at the least.

Traveling in the summer traffic and heat severely tested both riders and horses. Air conditioning only created extremes in temperatures harder to bear. Promise's fatigue, or perhaps her own, caused Al to slip out of *Pro Rodeo Sports News's* printed standings, though she dipped in and out of the top twenty. While Al didn't feel ready the day she left Promise under Aunt Marg and Uncle Willy's care, she left him anyway. Jen told Al all the way to Oregon that it was the only way she could hope to finish the season, but Al remained unconvinced.

Blue Sky, Al's new mount, was a tough Montanan horse of nondescript brown. While he didn't have Promise's speed or finesse, he had the heart and intelligence to learn Al's signals quickly, and although he suffered many losses in the interim, slowly Al and Jen taught him how to fly.

"Looking good," Tom commented after Al came in from her run at the Pikes Peak or Bust Rodeo in Colorado Springs.

"Isn't he?" Al cooled Sky down as Tom walked alongside. "I'm pretty sure we'll make the short round. How about you and Forrest?"

"First in roping, second for Forrest in riding so far."

"And what about your riding?"

Tom appeared not to hear. "Where's Jenny?"

"I'm not sure. Probably near Uncle Barney."

Al had finished walking Sky and put him in his stall. Tom

helped curry him. "So how are you doing, Tom? I haven't seen you in a while."

"I tried to catch you in Dodge City. Where did you go after your run?"

"I was with Sky, then Jen and I visited some friends of hers. Sorry I missed you. When are you leaving this time?"

"I didn't ask." Tom worked on Sky's mane, the horse's only claim to beauty, besides his tail. Both were long and shiny, a rich color darker than his body. Tom gave Sky a few more strokes. "Would you like to have supper with me, Al?"

When she hesitated, Tom rephrased his question. "We don't have to go anywhere. How about a hot dog at the concession stand? I'm hungry."

"I am, too. But a hot dog?"

"We used to live on them, remember? But I suppose now Jenny would beat you up for eating something like that."

"Yes." Al smiled and made up her mind. "Let's go."

The hot dog led them to a Baskin-Robbins for an ice cream chaser. Al stood before the glass display case, pointing out three different flavors, while Tom chose two scoops of blueberry and raspberry. He and Al sat at a small white table just outside the shop to eat the cones, speaking between licks.

"I never get ice cream cones," Al said for the second time. "Thanks a lot, Tom. I'm going to make this one last."

"Hope it's worth getting into dangerous waters with Jenny."

Al bit into her cone, crunching on chocolate chips before she answered, "I haven't been in any danger with Jen since I quit dating Forrest."

Tom looked surprised. "Did she say she —"

"Not a word. I can tell, though. She didn't mind losing to me half so much as she minded my going out with Forrest." Al licked pensively. "I don't think I did, either. I never knew how hard dating him was until it was over."

Tom said nothing, though Al noticed he paused in mid-lick.

"It's much easier like this, Tom. Forrest and I...I'm just glad I didn't get hurt...too much. You should have told me I was out of my mind. What kind of friend are you?"

"Not much of one." He rested his hand on the table, ice cream melting down his cone in colored trails. "Al, have you been reading the Bible I gave you?"

"Some."

"Have you thought about it? Is there anything you'd like to ask about? I've been trying not to be too pushy."

Al selected her words. "I read those verses in Ephesians you underlined." She felt heat near the corners of her eyes and stopped speaking, knowing tears were seconds away. "They were the same ones I read to my grandmother the last time I saw her."

Tom dropped his gaze. "How is she doing?"

"A little worse, my mother says. I wish I could go and see her, Tom. As soon as I race at the Cow Palace, I'm going home and not coming back until the NFR...and then only if I make it."

"You sound like you've had enough of rodeo."

Now safely past the tears, Al spoke more freely. "Maybe rodeo's had enough of me. I nearly ruined Promise before I let him go. I just hope Sky can make it until Prom has recovered. He was a big expense, but I had to do it." Al looked at her remaining scoop, counting off the chips as if they were days and weeks. "Before we know it, it'll be September. Maybe I should just go back to school."

"What about the NFR? What about the Ex? How will you feel if you leave them behind?"

Al tilted her cone and watched the ice cream run into her napkin. "They were so important to me. They still are, but not in the same way. I guess Forrest was part of that dream." She looked up. "Do you think he and Jen will get back together now?"

"Maybe, as this season winds down. If Jenny can learn to forgive and Forrest can learn —"

"What about you, Tom?" She could see that she had brought him up short, but she persisted. "What about the NFR? What about the Ex?"

"Forrest and I will do the best we can —"

"I see." Al stood, not wanting to hear another word about Forrest. She felt strangely let down that Tom was still obviously following his partner's lead, afraid to determine his own future himself. "Jen's probably asleep by now. I should get back."

"Wait a minute." Tom reached for her hand. "Please sit down, Al. I have to ask you...something."

"I have to sit down for you to ask me?"

"I'd rather.... It would be easier."

"All right. What?"

Tom leaned forward, still clasping her hand. "Al, maybe you don't know how I feel about you —"

"Tom, listen, I —"

"Please, Al. You know we've always been friends, and I've tried to be just your friend, but I've always thought about you differently. You introduced me to my Savior, Al, the night you went forward. I have so much to thank you for."

He looked at the spot where their hands met. "But I think you haven't come completely forward yet. You've read the Word. You've heard it. But it hasn't made its way to your heart yet. It hasn't made its way to your soul."

Al stared at the strange scar on his hand. "I'm not saying you're wrong, Tom. You believe exactly as my grandmother does. Sometimes I wish I could be like you two, but I can't. I want to please God, but...I need more time. There's just too much going on right now. There's just too much in me."

He nodded, his pain visible. "I felt that way when I saw you go forward. I heard the message. I wanted to respond, but I didn't want to give anything up. That was part of it. The other part was, I felt ashamed, unworthy." Tom sat back in his white chair, and their hands separated. "When you're used to rodeoing, you think you have to earn everything. You do. But that's not how it is with God."

Al listened, even though she wanted to tune out his words.

"I know you're familiar with the Cowboy's Prayer, Al. Everyone who's been in rodeo ends up having it memorized, just from hearing the announcers say it so many times. But have you ever stopped to really listen, to really think about it? The last lines talk about coming to life's final go-round. The writer prays that when he reaches heaven, the Lord God, 'as our last judge, will tell us that our entry fees are paid.' Jesus paid the entry fee, with his death on the cross. We don't earn salvation. We can't."

He looked at his scar. "I thought about that a lot while I was still struggling. It didn't make sense that God would give us something we hadn't earned. I was riding high when Forrest and I won the world championship, enjoying everything that gave me. Took another year and the death of my daddy before I realized not even that was enough, till the emptiness settled inside me, and I knew it would never be enough. That everything I could even hope to do wouldn't be enough. You're one up on that, aren't you?"

Worth all and more than anyone can ever own. Al heard her grandmother's voice, and she lowered her head. "You're right, Tom. There is more that I want that doesn't have anything to do with racing. I'm just starting to understand that."

He smiled more with his eyes than anything. "Keep understanding it, Al. And please keep reading your Bible. Whenever we're in the same town, I'll keep looking you up, and we can talk about it." He touched her closed hand, and the cross on his skin rested near her thumb. "I promise you that any answer you ever need, you'll find in those pages."

"So what happened?" Forrest heaved his bag into the cab more roughly than usual, and from this Tom surmised that his partner was in a foul mood.

"With Al?" Tom had hoped for more time before Forrest probed that topic, but he knew he'd best face it. "We started out with a hot dog at the concession stand, then —"

"That's your business. What happened with your draw? Why'd you turn him out?"

Tom started the pickup and reached for the map as he considered a response. How could he explain to Forrest the reason he'd refused his mount? Tom didn't even want to acknowledge it himself yet.

"You finally giving up riding, Tom?"

"I don't know."

"Fine with me if you do." Forrest took the map from him. "Be the best news I've heard all night."

"Better than a first in roping?"

Forrest looked at him. "You're my friend, Tom. I'd like to see you live a while."

After they got out of the city, Tom steered the conversation back to what was on his mind almost as much as Al was. "So when do you know it's time to quit rodeo, Forr?"

"You getting tired of going down the road?"

"You know where I want to be."

"Let me guess. On a ranch somewhere near Mancos, Colorado?"

Tom let a semi pass him without increasing his speed to follow behind as he would have years before. "I'm here this season only. I can't promise anything after the NFR except that I'll be working the Circle H, if I can meet your granddad's terms. And I will, if I can just hang on." *I thought rodeo would be a spiritual battle, not a physical one. I feel like I'm fighting for my life.*

Forrest set his hat on the dash. "I'll be looking for a change in a few years, too, Tom. Sometimes I like the sound of what you say, having a place —"

"But?"

Forrest flipped on the radio before he answered, and Tom had to filter out the music to catch his partner's answer. "But is that kind of life any better than this? Lonely, both of them. Stuck in the foothills with nothing but cattle. I love the land. The evergreens, the lake. You know. But I need more."

"Jenny?"

Forrest let half a song go by before he answered. "What's between us now? I'm not seeing anyone. She's not. We know we still care about each other. Least I know I do." Forrest turned down the radio. "Now she lets me talk to her, go out, if it's the four of us. But she treats me like some old friend. It's almost worse than it was before."

"You were with her at the rodeo?"

"While you were with Al. Talked about our horses the whole time."

Tom thought out his words and prayed for wisdom. "Maybe she's angry at you, Forr, for what you did to Al."

"Al? I didn't do anything to Al."

"You used her. You tried to get Jenny back by dating Al."

"That's not how it started."

"But it's how it finished. Right?"

Forrest shrugged. "Jen acted like she never wanted to see me again. You should've heard what she said in Houston. And there was Al, suddenly. She started it, Tom. Whatever happened, she asked for it. I only gave her what she wanted."

"Maybe so. But you hurt her. You hurt Al and Jenny both."

"What did I ever do to Jen? She dumped me!"

"What about Felicia?"

"Nothing ever happened with Felicia until after Jen cut me loose. I knew what I had. I wasn't taking any chances with Jen. Not until I lost her."

"Maybe that's what's hurting her now, then," Tom answered. "Jenny's never dated anyone since you two broke up. Maybe she thinks she's been faithful to you while you've been faithless."

"She's had no reason to think that."

"Maybe she believes she does. Give her time, Forrest. If you love her, keep loving her. Keep showing her you love her. You've come a long way this season. When we first started, she was hardly talking to you, remember?"

"But I want it to be like it was."

Tom winced at the yearning in Forrest's voice. "Only God can wipe away the past, Forr. Only he can fully forgive. Let Jenny love you as she chooses. Don't ask her for what she can't give yet."

"You think there's a chance?"

"Definitely a chance." Tom saw relief come into his friend's eyes and wished Forrest longed for God's love and acceptance the way he longed for Jenny's. But there was time and hope for that, too. Wherever there was life, there was hope.

40

TOM AWAKENED JUST AS THE BULL in his dream reached with his massive head, driving his horn into Tom's stomach: a new ending to the recurring dream that until now had only involved hanging up.

Tom lay, listening to Forrest's breathing until his own steadied. He managed to salvage another hour or so of dreamless sleep for the night, and he felt at least partially refreshed when he arose.

He could still feel the burn of the bull's thrust during the day, particularly when he checked out his draw, a brindle that at least didn't look like the yellow-hided demon of his dreams. Tom said a prayer of thanks for that mercy and felt more secure about his upcoming ride. Though every bull grew progressively difficult to face, Tom hadn't turned out any of his draws since the rodeo at Colorado Springs.

He milled around the arena all day, working with the horses, studying his draw, trying to force the fear out of his system. When he ran into Suicide Sam a few hours before performance time, Tom took the bullfighter up on his offer to grab a bite.

Suicide lingered over what he called his only indulgence, a cup of coffee. "So, you getting over what's been gnawing on you, Tom?"

Tom could have denied anything was gnawing on him, but he

knew Suicide had been at Colorado Springs to see him refuse his mount. "No, Sam. It's...getting worse."

The bullfighter took a slow sip, then nodded. "Could tell. Seen it before."

"Any suggestions?"

"You thinking about quitting?"

Tom contemplated his empty salad bowl. "I asked Forrest about that. When do you know it's time to quit riding bulls, Sam?"

The bullfighter put down his cup, his eyes deadly serious. "When you start thinking about it."

The answer had force. Tom let several moments pass before he tried to speak. "So you're saying I should quit?"

"Up to you. But I've seen your riding lately. Not at Colorado Springs of course," Suicide said significantly. "I've seen other guys who ride when they know they should hang it up." He tapped his temple. "It's mental to get on a bull in the first place. But to get on when you think you might get hurt...you will, Tom. No question. Once the bull gets your mind, he'll get you, too. They sense that fear. They'll use it. They'll pin you down, Tom. I'd hate for you to be one of them that don't get up."

When Tom returned to the arena, he mulled over Suicide's words before tucking them away. Horse Heaven Rodeo had only five events, none of them barrel racing. As Tom began warming up for his event, he wondered if Al was packing up to leave the Wild Bill Hickok Rodeo in Abilene, Kansas, where barrel racing replaced team roping in the lineup. He and Al seemed to be doing alternate rodeos, and Tom couldn't wait until he reached Pueblo, where they would both ride. Maybe they'd have more time to spend with each other, now that September was near, the season's turning point. From September first on, most contestants would either slow down and save up for the NFR, or quit and go home.

The last time he'd seen Al was in Caldwell, Idaho. She'd barely placed in the first go-round, but that wasn't what made the rodeo memorable for Tom.

Al was beginning to ask the right questions, if there were such things. Foremost on her mind was the issue of works versus faith. Tom prayed that this was the barrier string holding her back from salvation. Once it fell aside, he hoped she'd be out of the box and into the Savior's hands.

This time a pizza parlor was the scene of their theology discussion. After consuming an Italian sausage thick-crust pizza with black olives, they had settled into their corner booth and ruminated on Scripture.

"So it's not what we do, it's what God does?"

Tom nodded, wondering if Al knew what a distraction she was to logical thought, even in such an important conversation as this. The *phileo*-friendship love he'd had for her before he was saved now had the added element of God's *agape* love, the limitless love that demanded nothing.

It was another kind of love that made her a wavering torture for him, however. Tom knew he could never have a lifelong relationship with a woman who didn't know his God. But he felt, too, that he wouldn't be able to endure a life without this woman: her gray eyes, ever in thoughtful meditation, her tumble of brownish-blond curls — only her heart was imperfect. And God could change that.

She smiled and folded her arms. "If that's how salvation is, why can't I just sit here and — presto — get saved? If it's nothing I do —"

"You must respond, with your whole heart. You must believe. Those are the only acts required, and the Bible doesn't call them works. What I'm getting at, Al, is that you don't have to try to be good enough. You don't have to attempt to please God. It's impossible to do it on your own, anyway. When you let Jesus be the sacrifice that covers your life, you *are* pleasing to God."

"Pleasing to God." She repeated the phrase, and Tom felt that at last the words had gone deep. They talked another two hours, and when they said good-bye, she was the one who hugged him.

"Thanks, Tom." The tangle of curls touched his ear and neck softly. "I know you're trying. I'll try too. I'll think about what you said. I'll keep on reading. And Tom?"

Speech had come hard for him, still holding her. She unclasped her hands and stood near, asking with her eyes what she wasn't ready to convert into words.

"Yes, Al?"

"Pray for me." She left then, suddenly.

Tom hadn't quit praying since that instant. She was close to salvation. He felt it. If not for his own struggles with bull riding, everything would've been perfect. He was near to meeting the final dollar amount for the Circle H, well within the time limit. If he could just ignore his fear, just hang on until the NFR, the ranch would be his. And maybe Al would be, too.

He tied his bull rope to the link fence and began scraping off old rosin, getting the feel right, then going on to his glove. He could hang on, just a little longer. That's all he had to do: just hang on...and bury his fear so deeply that not even he would know it was there.

Eileen crumpled the piece of stationery in her hands. A letter was not going to do it. She jotted down the number she was about to dial in the small notebook in which she kept track of all her expenses, then picked up the receiver and punched in the numbers.

The cry of a child answered her before her sister did. "Good afternoon, King's Kids Kare."

"Margaret?"

"Eileen! Just a moment, let me take care of Natasha here. I'll call you back. You're at Rhoda's?"

"Yes."

Margaret returned the call in several minutes, which gave Eileen time to compose herself. "Hello again, Margaret."

"Hey, Firebrand."

Eileen smiled at the old term of endearment. "Yes, that's me. I believe I've gone off on another spree of pyromania, too."

"What this time? I'm sure it's not so bad as you think." Margaret's voice resonated with love. "You're pretty hard on yourself, Sis."

"No harder than life is. I've decided to renew divorce proceedings, Margaret. I've got to get out of here, out of this town, away from Harvey —" Eileen charged on for five minutes before she faltered.

"Janette failing?"

"Y-es." Eileen said, like a child weary from crying.

"I'm so sorry." Margaret paused. "Would you object if I came and stayed with you for a while, until things get a little easier?"

"What would you do with your day-care business?"

"School is starting for many of the children. Even the smallest will soon begin preschool half days, and I've phased out the infant care. Until next summer, I'm looking at slack for the most part. I've always wanted to see Wisconsin this time of year."

"If you're thinking of seeing the maples turn, that's some days away."

"Well, then, Willy could join me come fall."

"But I've no place to put you."

"We could stay at the farm with Harvey."

"With Harvey? The man I'm going to divorce?"

Margaret didn't answer immediately. "You haven't divorced him already? I thought I misunderstood you the first time. Didn't you tell me months ago that the hearing —"

"I don't know, Margaret. I thought perhaps I should wait. That Bible reading Janette's forcing on me must be softening my brain. I withdrew the papers at the last minute. I didn't want to tell all of you until I had made up my mind. But I'm ready to go ahead with it now."

"Are you?" Margaret's words sounded refreshing as a spring of water. "Isn't it just the stress of Janette's illness that's pushing you now, wearing you out? How much of the past twenty-four hours have you been at the nursing home?"

"Well, I worked —"

"And then went straight to her. How long have you kept up this pace?"

"I've been trying to see her more since Saturday."

"At least a week then, although I'll wager that you were doing bedside duty long before last week. You're exhausted, Eileen. I can hear it in your voice."

"I am tired," Eileen admitted.

"As well you should be." Margaret turned businesslike. "I'm on my way, then, as soon as I can arrange for the children. Willy can handle them until my neighbor Gloria can take them. She's been wanting to break into the field. She'll be glad for this opportunity."

Eileen heard several seconds of silence. "There's something you aren't telling me, Margaret."

"It's just Promise. But Willy can attend to him, if it's not for too long. I expect Alison to trade him for her new horse any day."

"Have you seen Alison recently?"

"No, but she writes every few weeks. She's not doing so well as she was."

"I know. She's keeping the letters coming to us, too. Margaret, do you think I should let Alison know my fears for her grandmother?"

"Is it worth her rushing back? Janette isn't much worse than when Alison last saw her, is she?"

"More bad spells, but not a lot of change, just slowly deteriorating. She can be quite clear sometimes, as she was when Alison came. I never know what to expect when I enter her room. I never know if I'll be Eileen or Patsy..." Eileen tried to keep her tears from her voice, but Margaret must have heard them.

"I'll be up soon, Sis. You keep being faithful, but try to give yourself some care, too. No one, least of all Janette, expects you to wear yourself out for her."

Eileen lowered the receiver as she dabbed her tears with a napkin from the table. "I'll try, Margaret."

"And Eileen? Tell Harvey how you're feeling. Tell him you need him. I think he needs you as much and more right now. But tell him straight out. Don't try to make him do or say anything. I think you'll be surprised at his response."

"Yes, Margaret," Eileen answered doubtfully.

"And Eileen?"

"Yes?"

"I'll be praying for all of you."

Eileen paused. "I'd like that, Margaret," she replied, and hung up.

Al glanced up from her book as Jen walked into the hotel room.

"What are you doing? Reading again?"

"Still."

"Ever since I left?" Jen gave Al a look of disbelief before flipping on the television. "Must be good."

"It is." Al laid back on the bed. "Ever heard of Paul, Jen?"

"Saint Paul?"

"The apostle Paul, Tom calls him, but I guess they're both the right names for him. I've been reading a lot about him, his letters, his life. Did you know he was so much against Christians that he persecuted them? And one day, when he was going down the road to get more Christians to kill, Christ himself appeared to him and set him straight. Just like that."

"Pretty strange." Jen looked from Al to the TV.

"Isn't it? Paul was going to kill Jesus' followers, and Jesus saved him." Al let this thought rattle around in her mind. "Would you say Paul was worthy of Jesus saving him, Jen?"

"What?"

"A murderer. Is a murderer worthy of God's grace?"

"A murderer is worthy of death," Jen said, returning to the television.

"That's what I thought, too," Al said quietly. "Yet instead he was given eternal life." She looked at her cousin, who had risen from the bed to do some stretches but was still watching the screen. Then Al reopened her Bible and continued reading.

CHAPTER

41

THE WHITE FORD PICKUP TURNED A BEND that opened the view to another slope of multihued wildflowers, grasses, and trees. Al felt she must say something. "Thank you so much for talking me into coming along."

Forrest glanced at her, but it was to Tom that she directed her words, and he replied, "We have to meet up with Jenny later tonight, so we can't stay too long, but I really wanted you to see where Forrest and I grew up."

Tom pointed to the range ahead of them, and Al could see what looked like snow clinging to the peaks, though the lower foothills and meadows still celebrated summer.

"This is our backyard, Al," Tom said.

"What a backyard! I wish Jen could see this."

"She has," Forrest offered bleakly. They were the only words Al remembered him saying since they left Pueblo, where Jen had promised she would also go along on the day-trip. Later Jen reneged, saying her father hadn't wanted to risk his new rig on the winding back roads and that it would be better to meet them some-where closer to Ellensburg, Washington, their next destination.

Al looked at Forrest, feeling only a flicker of regret that dissipated under Tom's smile. "Jen may see it again, Forrest. Don't give up yet."

"Never give up," Tom said, with double meaning, Al thought.

The road ascended past oak brush, aspens, and high grazing lands dotted with cattle.

"Too bad it's not a little later in the year," Tom commented as he turned off the main road. "The mountains in the height of fall are really something."

"So is this." Al loved the landscape, full of pines. If not for the altitude, she could imagine that isolated flat areas were bits of Wisconsin uprooted and plunked down in the La Plata range. "Green is my favorite color."

"Mine too," Forrest said somberly, putting an end to the talk for some time. The scenery more than made up for any words, in Al's estimation.

After dropping off Forrest for a quick visit with his grandfather, Tom turned to Al, who sat near the open window. She was letting her hands fly through the air as the pickup rumbled along the dirt road. "You're okay with this?" Tom asked, sounding worried.

"You and Forrest are the ones who'll have to drive 'till dark to meet Jen on time." Al flashed him a smile. "If the horses don't mind it, I sure don't. Where are we going now?"

"You'll see."

"Uh-oh." Al waggled a finger at him. "I remember the last time you pulled something like this. I ended up at the Master Riders' show. What is it this time? Billy Graham?"

"No people. A place."

"What? An alpine brook? Roaring falls? The peak of that mountain? We only have an hour, Forrest said."

"It won't take an hour."

Tom said no more until they pulled up a rise and skirted two larger-than-usual rocks cropping up on the road, which had disintegrated into little more than a cow path.

"Good thing you left the trailer at Forrest's. What is this place?"

Tom rolled up to a group of weathered, broken buildings, obviously an old homestead. He hopped from the pickup and walked around to help Al out. When he took her hand, he didn't let go. "Al, this is where I grew up."

With the buildings and the pickup behind her, Al faced the rounded slope of an old pasture. Rangy yellow and white wildflowers climbed and ducked over fallen fenceposts, and pines made a trail to mountain peaks miles away. A stretch of water spread near the pines, and a few low-flying clouds made patches of the pasture a deep, deep green.

"Perfect."

Tom uttered a short, soft laugh. "I've been wondering since Durango what you'd say. Something about the majestic mountain grandeur or a joke about settlers being too stubborn to know when to call it quits, I thought. But not 'perfect'."

"It is, though." Al sat in the thick grass, which felt like a mat under her. She plucked a yellow flower at her knee and twirled it between her palms as she stared at the pond, the mountains, the pines. She looked at Tom, then back to the images before her. "You grew up here?"

Tom pointed at a small building behind him. "In that house. Used to be pale yellow."

"Like one of the first wildflowers, I bet. Or the first rays of dawn." She reached for his hand and pulled him down to sit beside her. "Now I sound nearer to what you expected, right? But I'm not joking. I really like it here, Tom."

"I'm glad."

Al filled her lungs with air and closed her eyes. "You were lucky —" She stopped herself. "Blessed, I mean. What a place, Tom! Looks like somewhere...God would live."

"God's country, Mama used to say. Daddy called it something else. He sold it to my uncle despite her, to pay for his gambling debts. She never got over that."

"What a loss it must have been for her. The first time I saw a real mountain, I wished I could take it home and plant it in our fields. Mountains are the only things Wisconsin lacks. We have beautiful hills, like the pasture here, but nothing like a mountain." Al passed her hands over her bare arms in wonder. "No mosquitoes. This place is heavenly." She sat a moment, feeling the sun on her skin. "Where does your mother live now?"

"She died three years after Forrest's dad."

"I'm sorry, Tom. I've been afraid to ask. Guess I know why."

"I don't mind talking about her, or my father." Tom looked behind him at the leaning stand of buildings. "Makes me miss them, being here. Mama especially. This was her place."

"If I had a place like this, I don't think I'd ever go anywhere." Al stretched her legs out on the grassy ground.

"No? What would you do?"

She stood and turned a circle, first examining her surroundings, then twirling, arms outspread, moving down the slope. "I'd...raise horses. Barrel racers. And every day I'd take them for a lap around the pond!"

Tom kept beside her. "Most people raise cattle around here."

"I'd raise them, too."

"Oh, of course."

"And milk cows. Holsteins, with a milking parlor. And Rhode Island Reds. Those are chickens," she added.

393

"I know they're chickens." He laughed.

She finally collapsed near a thick bed of flowers. "We don't seem to be much closer to the pond."

"It's more than a quarter mile from the house."

"Perfect for the quarter horses. Let's run there. I want to tell you something, Tom."

It was almost time to leave before Al got around to her announcement. Only the knowledge that soon Forrest would be with them made her say what she'd been saving up to tell Tom. The moment didn't seem quite right. *There should be a rainbow in the sky, or falling stars, she thought.*

"Tom," she began, giving him one more chance at guessing her news. She marveled that he hadn't noticed her transformation. Perhaps it was internal only, though she felt it must show all the way through. "I've been reading the Bible a lot lately..."

"Good." He was staring toward the mountains.

"And," Al said, "I've been doing some hard thinking."

"Very good." He still didn't look at her.

"Tom! Are you listening?"

"Sorry." He gave her his entire attention. "This is like a dream for me almost, Al...having you here. I've been planning this for months. Years."

His confession caught her off guard, but it pleased her. And scared her.

"I tried to figure out how to get you here when we were at that rodeo in Colorado Springs," Tom said, "but I figured it was still too far out of the way to ask you to come. This was far, too, but I've been praying about it and felt like the timing was right."

Al looked at Tom, sitting with his arms behind him, surrounded by his mountain pasture. This was where he belonged, if he only realized it. Even more than the arena, where his skill and love for the sport shone, he belonged here. Couldn't he see that this old, ramshackle ranch was better than any number of world championships? Why did he continue to risk his life for rodeo?

Over the past few weeks, Al could no longer avoid the knowledge that her feelings for rodeo and Tom Rawlings were reversing. Her romance with Forrest had paled in daylight, but her love for Tom grew in sunshine, in the "Sonshine" he had shown her. *Mom and I are just beginning to quit being opponents. How is she going to feel about me falling in love with a bull rider?* Al couldn't find an answer to this dilemma, and neither could she find an antidote to her growing attraction to Tom.

Her vision of Forrest, like the Ex, had seemed unattainable. That made them both safe. But Tom was a real man, a Christian man, with real love inside him, love that might fulfill her dreams...or shatter them.

Rodeo was still his world, while this mountain meadow, this deep, quiet peace was becoming more valuable to her than even the prospect of riding at the Ex.

Al looked again at the vistas, the visible signs of God's creativity, his love. *How can Tom give this up? Do I want to tie myself to a man who prefers roads and rodeos to a beautiful homestead like this, a place where real dreams, dreams of love and families and animals and wildflowers, could come true?*

"Al? I'm listening. What is it?"

Could she tell him now? Should she? Al knew that as long as she had been distant from God, she was also distant from Tom. *If I tell him, there'll be no barriers. No...protection.* This was part of the reason she'd been slow to share her good news, her unparalleled news, knowing it would open up a new realm to her, where she could find love or heartbreak, not vicarious sampling of these emotions.

"Al?"

Something about his gaze told her that he had finally guessed. He knew now, for better or for worse. "I'm changed, Tom. Changing. Same Al outside —"

"But inside, a new creation." Tom stared at her as if half afraid. Slowly, his hand stretched out, touching first her shoulder, then her neck, then burying itself in her thick curls, his fingertips brushing the finer strands along her nape.

She hadn't imagined his touch would have such power, restrained but unmistakable, irresistible. She hadn't imagined her own response would match his, utterly untainted by awkwardness as their kiss moved beyond a welcome to a bold, heady promise.

When it subsided, and he held her, Al tried to control her trembling. The swirling gulf of emotion was still too fresh, her breath and pulse too quickened.

Tom bent his head next to hers, cooling her cheek with soft kisses meant to ease the transition. But Al wondered if she would ever be the same. She looked at him with new respect, new wonder. The thought of comparing him with Forrest never entered her head. There was no comparison — to anything she'd experienced in her half-baked crushes, in her intangible dreams. This...was real.

CHAPTER

42

EVEN WITH THE CIRCUIT'S FALL SLOWDOWN, Al couldn't see Tom enough. After every parting, there remained questions they hadn't answered, words they hadn't exchanged. Rendezvous in one state after another fostered their relationship — and her fear.

They nearly always met after the rodeo in which they were performing. Before then they could manage only a quick greeting behind the chutes, fragments of conversation before and after the grand entry, then a good-bye until their events were over. While Al rode, she knew Tom was watching and praying. When he rode, she did the same, but it did little to abate her increasing anxiety.

The arena's atmosphere itself changed when the bull riding began. Generally the last event at a rodeo, bull riding often started with a gradual climb in volume of background music, the announcer's voice, the crowd's rustling. By the time the beasts were loaded in the chutes, the crowd had stilled, but the music and the announcer's din heightened. Sometimes a light show, sometimes a specialty act, sometimes an inflated monologue opened the bull riding, stressing the event's inherent danger — as if Al needed a reminder. She suffered as she saw Tom lower himself onto a heaving bull, withstand the animal's wrenching and stabbing, and finally, finally, reach to unwrap his hand from the bull rope and scramble to safety.

When she and Tom reunited, the sweet calm between them recompensed her for the horror of those eight seconds, and the pleasure of his touch helped blot out the terror of his bull rides. While they were together, it was enough. While they were together...

Her new Lord reigned over their relationship, and her Bible study and prayer times with Tom brought them close. With each Italian dinner, eaten in a restaurant or at the shore of a brook or in a city park if they could do no better, she felt Tom's love. With every discussion, exploring her new faith or their unknown future, she felt herself drawing nearer to him — ready or not.

He had told her how he'd watched her for so many years, and now she watched him, reckoning the odds of their happiness as she once had her chances of winning. If the Lord was answering her prayers about the outcome, she had not yet heard his voice.

"Tom, why do you ride?" she asked one evening as they sat together in a hillside park, the wrappers of their submarine sandwiches at their feet. Beyond and below the deli papers spread the lights of the valley city in which they'd just performed.

He kissed her before he answered, a shrewd tactic, she thought. She waited for him to speak, holding herself away from his arms.

"Why do you ride, Al?" Tom returned. When she didn't reply, he said, "It's hard to answer, isn't it? I suppose I could tell you why partly, but just as you'd have a hard time describing why you race, I don't think I'll be able to give you a satisfying answer." He bent for another kiss, which she deflected with her palm.

"I'll settle for an unsatisfying one, then."

"Okay." Tom's arms around her loosened. "Right now, I'm riding because I have to."

"That's it?"

"I told you you wouldn't like it."

"How could I?" She swiveled to face him. "What kind of answer is that?"

"My kind," he said, smiling, and Al knew she'd get no better response. He was so candid on every other subject, so nearly perfect in every other way; but bring up bull riding, and the guy became... a bull rider.

He seemed right for her. The Lord had seemed to bring them together. But was it only to bring about her salvation? Was what they shared enough to outweigh what they didn't? And how, how could she stand to see him lay down his life like it was some kind of routine?

A confrontation was coming. A choice had to be made. But for the life of her, and for the life of Tom, she didn't know what she'd choose.

San Francisco's Grand National Rodeo was the last big gasp in the race to the NFR. The Cow Palace could make a Cinderella into a princess or send her home with a broken glass slipper, and as Jenny spent the morning conditioning herself to give all she had, her mental vigil was interrupted by a visitor.

Jenny shifted from one foot to another, but she didn't shut off the flow of words coming from the man standing in front of her.

"I can't take it, Jen." Forrest finished. "I'd do anything for another chance with you. Not much else matters to me anymore."

Jenny stared hard. He looked sincere. The words sounded true; but that was unlikely.

"Another chance," Forrest repeated. "That's all I'm asking."

Jenny lifted her head, trying to keep her eyes locked on his without feeling a reaction of any kind. But how could she? Anger, hurt, resentment for the time they had lost, for the love she had wasted — all of it rushed over her as she looked into Forrest's face, where she saw a reflection of her own struggle.

Forrest took a step, reached out, touched her hands. "Jen?" He moved closer and she was next to him, her cheek against his riding vest, the scents of horse and dirt and rodeo on them both, her perfume mixing with his cologne. His hat brim rested atop her head, pressing gently against her hair. So familiar. So comforting. Those arms around her, like a strong wall.

Where had that wall been when she needed it most? Not protecting her from the relentless ache of losing her mother. Those arms had been around Felicia. Jenny knew it, just as she knew Forrest was lying when he said they hadn't.

And even if he wasn't lying, Jenny felt incapable of giving him the chance he wanted. *Too hard...to start again. Too much time gone by. Too much pain. Can't bet on the future....* Jenny pulled away, knowing that the few inches she drew back were putting miles between them, more years between them. Still, she retreated until a full pace stretched between her and Forrest.

His arms reached to touch her sides. "Don't Jen. Please don't."

"I can't help it. I'll be your friend, Forrest...but that's the best I can do."

"Now? Or forever?"

She felt unequal to answering. Both alternatives seemed too final. She had to put him off, get room to breathe, time to think. Why couldn't he admit his guilt? Why couldn't he just confess he had messed up with Felicia or used her as he had Al? Why couldn't he wait until Jenny knew and felt and believed his love? And if he really loved her, why couldn't he even say it?

Jenny moved until his fingers slipped away, until his arms dropped to his sides, until the last bit of hope drained from his eyes. He should have turned and walked away, but he didn't, so she did it for him, hearing his hushed good-bye with every stride she took.

"Please don't ride tonight, Tom."

He looked at Al from where he stood by one of the Cow Palace's catch pens. "I knew it wasn't a good idea for you to see my draw, Al." He walked toward her, partially blocking the yellow bull from her view.

"You don't have anything else to prove. You and Forrest are going to the NFR for roping. Do you have to make it for riding, too?"

Tom had been through the arguments himself just the day before, but Sterling Jackson Sr. had not been moved.

"We made a deal, boy," the old man had bellowed through the receiver. "Got me a paper here, real legal-looking too, that says if you don't make $100,000 in winnings by October thirty-first, I get the Circle H. Like the sound of that? I sure do. I was out there the other day, did I tell you? Mighty nice grazing lands."

"But we're in for the NFR," Tom had argued, "and I've almost got the hundred thou —"

"Almost ain't all."

Tom's protests only caused the old man to laugh. But Tom wasn't laughing, especially not now, faced with his nightmare beast and Al's pleas. And his own doubts.

"Al, I have to ride." The way he said it didn't even convince himself.

"You do not. Why risk it? Everyone's telling you not to: Forrest,

Jen...me. Don't you care? Don't I mean anything to you?"

"I'm not choosing to ride, Al. I have to. I can't explain it all now, but —"

Al pushed his arms away. "When? When can you explain?"

"After the rodeo."

"What if there is no after?" She fixed him with her gray eyes, and Tom felt his inner turmoil growing. "Tom, I saw Suicide Sam this morning."

Tom listened, wishing he'd never told his dream to the bull-fighter.

"Sam says you have no business riding. He says you're lucky you haven't been killed so far." Al touched Tom's shoulder. "I couldn't bear to see you...I know God is protecting you, has been protecting you, but don't you think you should quit pushing it? Please, Tom. I've heard about this bull. It's a killer, a hunter."

Suicide hadn't mentioned the dream, then. Tom felt thankful for that at least. "Al, I know watching me these past two months has been hard on you, but it's almost over. After this go-round, I'm done riding bulls. For good."

"That means more to me than you know." Al traced the scar on his hand. "But I'm still worried about tonight. Can't you retire a few hours early? This is the only scar I want to see on you. Ever." She kissed it. "Please quit, Tom. Please quit now."

He shook his head. "I'm sorry."

Al looked at him sadly. "'Fall in love with a bull rider, you get what you deserve.' That's one of my mother's favorite sayings. I'm beginning to think she's right. You won't quit riding." Al's voice sounded harsh. "Not until it kills you or hurts you so badly you can't do it or anything else ever again. Not until it kills me." She walked toward the doorway.

"I'll make a deal with you, Al. If you don't race tonight, I won't ride."

She did an about-face. "Racing is nowhere near as dangerous —"

"Ever seen a racing wreck?"

"That doesn't happen very often," she said, but Tom could see he'd scored a point.

"It happens often enough. What do you say, Al? We can hang it up together. You're thinking about getting out of rodeo anyway."

"But I'm so close to making the NFR, Tom. I'm here, riding, at the Cow Palace! After this, I'll know. With Promise, I have a good chance of placing. That would tip me into the number fifteen slot. You can't ask me to quit now. I can't give up my chance for the NFR, for the Ex. It was a dream of mine. I've put too much into it to quit."

"I'm not asking you to quit," he said quietly, moving to her side.

She sighed heavily as his meaning sank in. "And I shouldn't ask you to, either, right?"

"I wish you wouldn't." He held her, feeling the stiffness in her body. "At least until after tonight."

"All right. But I hope you meant what you said, Tom. You mean...so much to me. I couldn't stand to see...part of me wants to run away now, before I fall for you terminally."

"I was hoping you already had." His smile was subdued.

"I...can't promise anything right now, Tom. You're a bull rider. I still can't believe I'm even dating you. I swore to my mother I never would. I swore to myself."

"You're afraid I'll end up like your father?"

Al hesitated a moment. "That you'll end up dead. I worry about it more than you know."

Tom hugged her, trying to reassure her with his touch. "Tonight is the last, Al." He held her a long time, but finally his arms came away. "You'll be watching?"

She nodded, looking unhappy but resigned. "I'll watch the whole thing. And I'll be praying for all four of us." She kissed him as he lowered his head. "You especially."

"Then I know I'll win."

43

IN THE INTERIM BETWEEN THE CONTESTANTS' ARRIVAL at the Grand National and when it began, old friends traded tips and howdies, old rivals sharpened each other for the coming test. The boasts, taunts, and words of encouragement cloaked an underlying tension. As the seconds dwindled, ropes, reins, and riggings congregated behind the chutes, a cowboy at each one, trying them, becoming reacquainted with his lifelines. This was not merely ritual, but necessity. Particularly in the case of a rough-stock rider, a single frayed fiber might make the difference between a thousand-dollar paycheck and a cheap funeral.

Riders worked their equipment, ran through their events, considered their draws, and exchanged banter while on another level they determined their imminent performance.

This rodeo, the last big blow of the season, meant life or death. Every cowboy and cowgirl knew it, especially Forrest Jackson, who seemed to have little other purpose for existence these days.

When Forrest first unpacked his duffel bag, he saw Winky Blackmont practicing his throws at one end of the fence. As Forrest pulled and rubbed and rode his saddle in the dirt to properly stretch the leather, he also watched Winky.

The roper had shed years since the night at the Master Riders' tent. Winky was regaining his old toughness, the assurance of movement that had first made him a world-champion heeler and then header. Talent that had dissolved under the deluge of too many tequilas had recrystallized. In each throw, Forrest once more saw winning accuracy.

When Tom and Winky came over a half hour later, Forrest stayed on the periphery of the conversation, still watching, still analyzing. Close up, Winky looked dramatically improved. The redness had faded from his skin, replaced by a tan probably earned from hours of practice under the sun. And when Winky spoke, his words were no longer the slurred philosophizing of a drunk. Along with his new religion, Winky Blackmont had gained self-respect. Forrest could not deny the change, no matter how much he would've liked to.

"Goin' good, Tom," Winky said, answering Tom's inquiry about how his new venture of Bible study was faring. "Don't know if I'll ever get the hang of King James, but some of them other versions you showed me make a lot of sense." Winky cast a look at Forrest. "Should try readin' the Word, Forrest. Might fill up that ache you try to drown all the time."

Before Forrest could reply, Winky turned to Tom. "The bottle got me into more trouble. Remember that one night in Pendleton? Ended up in jail after that bout, and if Clem Lincoln wasn't the easiest-goin' bulldogger on the circuit, he would've taken me apart for stealing his horse and riding it all around town like I did. Even rode it into the bar, remember?"

"That's the past, Winky," Tom said. "You don't have to keep living it. You're free —"

"And then the women trouble," Winky continued with a groan.

"Not quite so bad as the high jinks, I think, but there were these two times I don't even know half of what happened. One time in Ellensburg, I woke up in your room, Tom, decked out in Forrest's hat and chaps, just in time to see Felicia putting on fresh lipstick and leaving. Gave me this wicked little smile that made me try so hard to remember what happened, I sobered up enough to sneak out. She's a bad one to tangle with. Guess you know all about that, Forrest. I told her just today that I was sorry for whatever I done and was goin' to tell you the same first chance I had. She nearly tore me apart."

Forrest stared at Winky. "Say that again."

"Easy, Winky," Tom said. "You know Felicia has problems. Let her and whatever past —"

Again Winky interrupted. "I'm not judgin' her, Tom. I was only too willin', probably. Felicia's just as lost as I was. I know that. Can't help it when you're tied up in sin. Only Jesus can untangle them knots. I'm just thankful he did. Wish I would've known years —"

Forrest seized Winky's shoulder. "Winky! You were with Felicia, in my room, in my clothes...when?"

Winky squinched up his eyes and looked toward the ceiling. "Quite a few years ago. Four, five, maybe. Wasn't keepin' track of time then, Forrest, just tryin' to find somethin' worth livin' for, never knowin' how God longed to give it to me, free for the askin'. I've confessed what I can remember, but how do you get forgiveness for what you don't even remember doin'? That's what's bothering me now, Tom."

As Tom was about to answer, Winky went on. "There was this other time in San Antonio when I ended up in Val's room with some rodeo queen. Val swore he was there most of the time, that we all just drank until we passed out. Like Ellensburg, I hope, only I had my own clothes on in San Antone." Winky shook his head. "What a life."

He patted Forrest, who had released him. "You were back wearin' your duds the next day that time in Ellensburg, Forrest, so I figured no harm done. Had a tussle undoin' those chaps of yours. Tied up in these tiny little knots. How I got 'em on in the first place I never did figure out. Hope you'll forgive me, Forrest. Just didn't know no better back then."

What anger Forrest felt toward Winky, he saved for Felicia, but regret choked out even much of that. *Four years, wasted. Jen thinking I'm some drunk like Winky was, running around on her, thinking I didn't care that she'd lost her mother. Me thinking drinking would take away the hurt of losing her...and my folks. Felicia.* Forrest closed his eyes wearily. *So much waste.*

"You don't have to keep confessing, Winky," Tom was saying to the roper when Forrest rejoined the living. "God forgives it all, then forgets it. The Bible says he separates the sin from you as far as the east is from the west."

"That far, huh?" Winky gave a low whistle. "Guess I didn't read that part yet. Yessir, that is good to know. But I don't want to forget all I did, Tom. That just makes the Lord's forgiveness even bigger."

When Forrest looked at Winky, the roper grinned. "You're wonderin' if this change in me is real, ain't you, Forrest?" Winky gave him another brotherly pat. "It is. No goin' back. What's there to go back to, anyhow? Tell me that. I got everything I need now. God's given me everything." Winky smiled at Tom and walked alongside Forrest as the bronc rider fought his internal battle. "'No one has greater love than the one who lays down his life for his friends.' That's from the Bible, Forrest, and it includes you. Got to tell you about Jesus, Forr. Got to tell you 'bout his love for you."

Jenny wandered around the Cow Palace's practice arena. Depending on her run, now only minutes away, and the outcome of this eight-day rodeo, she could go to the NFR in either first or second position. Felicia was fighting hard for the lead and would be riding Wellington tonight, just as Jenny would be riding Clover and Al would be riding Promise. The Grand National was far too important to rely on relief mounts.

Although her father was covering the performance, Jenny had not come near him since his telecast began. As she prepared to cloister herself in the dressing room, she saw him in the alley, interviewing Tom and Forrest. She waited until the camera had withdrawn and the three had moved out of sight before she approached.

"Hey, Jen."

Jenny gritted her teeth and kept walking.

"I admit it. I ambushed you," Forrest said, keeping pace with her. "But I'm not going to do anything else to mess up your ride."

Jenny threw him a suspicious look, but he disarmed her.

"I didn't come here to fight anymore, Jen."

"What, then?"

"Just wanted to wish you the best...and to give you this." He held out a small piece of folded paper.

Jenny shook her head. "I don't want it, Forrest."

"Please, Jen, take it. I need you to. I need to know you'll read it." Forrest lowered his head, addressing the ground. "I wish I could tell you, but I want to say it right, and I know I won't." He gave a self-deprecating laugh that made Jenny cringe. "You don't have to read it till you're ready. Just read it...someday." He raised his blue eyes until they looked directly into hers, and Jen saw new emotions in them, emotions she couldn't understand.

Her own insides were strangling. It couldn't be love that caused her to feel like this: It was something nameless, heavy, crushing that was devouring her, would keep devouring her as long as she let it. She had to make it end. "I'll take the note, Forrest, if you promise to leave me alone from now on. I can't handle this."

"I can't either." He handed her the paper. "You'll read it?"

"When I'm ready, like you said. All right?"

He opened his arms. "One hug?"

"Forrest —"

"Okay. It's all right. I can remember, anyway."

He touched the brim of her Stetson, moving his thumb as he had so many times before, across her cheek, down her neck. Jenny shut off her mind to avoid recalling more and tucked the note in her jeans pocket. "Good-bye, Forrest."

"I love you, Jen."

The words caught Jenny, pinned her in mid-stride. She turned to look at him, saw sincerity, vulnerability in his face. Not stopping to think, she gave him a quick hug and raced away, wondering if he heard all her heart had told him with the brief embrace.

"Are you going to check Clover before your run, Jen?" Al asked after completing Promise's most recent flight check.

"I already did."

Apparently the pressure of the Grand National was affecting Jen, too. Al laid a hand on her cousin's. "What do you have to be worried about? The worst you could do is lose to Felicia and go to the NFR in second place. I might not make it at all."

"You're going to make it, Al." Jen said the words unemotionally.

"If you want it bad enough. You can make it. That's what you have to think. That's what you have to believe."

"Thanks, Jen. I'll pray." Jen was responding as if she were on automatic, but so was everyone else, Al noticed, looking around the dressing room. Even Sarah Bower, known for her happy chatter since her conversion in Sallislaw, was subdued, and most other riders either paced the floor or had concentrated themselves into comas. Only Felicia, aloof as always in her corner, appeared not to mind the wait. She knew she was on her way to Las Vegas, win or lose.

But this would be the season's last rodeo for many riders, who would soon load up their tired horses and drive home, licking their wounds all the way. Some of the women sitting here might never compete again. Now that Al knew how much sacrifice went into finishing the season, she couldn't imagine ending it without a hope of the NFR. The prospect seemed grossly unjust.

Just then, Felicia crossed the room to stand before Jen. "I believe you should know I've only begun to fight, Jenny."

"We'll give you a run at Las Vegas," Jen answered, but her response lacked conviction.

"Are you certain about that? It took you years to get over Ellensburg, and if Winky hadn't spilled everything, you'd still be hung up. I wasn't even trying then. But I will now."

Al looked from Felicia's spiteful face to Jen's blank one. "Felicia, what are you talking about?"

"Alison, I don't waste my time with you. Forrest never cared about you, he used you."

"I know," Al said impatiently. "I've forgiven him. What about Ellensburg?"

Felicia's voice rose by degrees, attracting the attention she always demanded. "You've forgiven him!" Felicia brayed. "Now why didn't you think of that, Jenny? Think how much it would've saved you!" Felicia spun out of the room laughing.

"Felicia!" Jen found her voice and lunged after Felicia, pulling on the door before she got it open. "Felicia!"

Al was right behind her. "Over there, Jen. By Wellington." Al pointed and Jen made a beeline.

Several officials approached as Felicia saw Jen and began shouting. Felicia had mounted Wellington, and the high-spirited horse danced underneath her. Al pulled Jen back with the help of one of the officials.

"You can mount now, Miss O'Neill," the official said, turning from Jen to Al, "but you'll have to return to the room, Miss Austin. You're not up for quite a few runs."

"Jen, what is going on?" Al asked as she was herded away.

Jen turned toward the stalls, but Al was forced back into the waiting room.

"Jen, after the race, I want to know what in the world —"

The official cut off Al's words by closing the door.

As Al approached, Jenny knew there was no avoiding her, but she attempted it anyway. "Al, I've got to get Clover —"

"He's fine. I've already taken care of Promise. You've got to be done with Clover by now." Al hauled her toward the grandstand. "If we don't get to the arena, we're going to miss Tom. I promised I'd be rooting for him, but I want to hear everything while I do."

Jenny clutched at this alternate straw of conversation. "I bet Tom will hardly hear you out there. You better root harder than you usually do. I've never heard you holler once."

"That's because most of the time I'm praying. But I can yell, and I will if you don't tell me what happened with Felicia. I was thinking about it even before my run ended. I'm blaming you if I blow my chance for the NFR."

Al handed autographed programs to the two girls who were giving up their seats. "Thanks, ladies," Al told them as they giggled and ran away. Al raised herself, stretching to see the chutes. "Tom's up next. Just enough time to tell me what in the world Felicia was talking about."

"I'm not sure myself. Maybe she saw me hugging Forrest or something," Jenny blurted, realizing too late that she had dug herself deeper.

"Oh." Al blinked. "Do you think she was just trying to ruin your ride...what do you mean, 'hugging Forrest or something?' You hugged Forrest? Now what on earth is going on?"

"It was a good-bye hug."

"Those work?"

Jenny didn't appreciate Al's humor. "Tom's ready," she said. "Look, Al. Forrest is just standing clear. The gate's going to open."

With Al's attention diverted at last, Jenny tried to continue sorting out for herself what Felicia had said. It still didn't make much sense. What did Winky have to do with Ellensburg? Jenny thought hard, not hearing the whistle as she internally reviewed Felicia's words. It seemed impossible, but could he and Felicia have somehow arranged the scene in Forrest's hotel room, knowing how it would appear? In that case, it hadn't been Felicia and Forrest she had seen by candlelight, but Felicia and Winky, and Forrest really hadn't —

"No!" Al cried and leaped to her feet. "Tom! Dear Lord..."

Tom's body dragged from the side of his yellow bull. The beast ignored the bullfighters and thrashed close to the gate. Cowboys clung to the rails like frightened monkeys while Tom, his arm extended and hand clearly stuck in the rope, tried to avoid colliding with the metal bars, the hooves, and the horns so terrifyingly near him.

Despite their skill, the bullfighters were helpless in the face of the hunter's rage. The bull leaped toward the open gate, Tom breaching the gap between its heavy, heaving side and the thick metal railing. Jenny had seen riders in similar situations, and as she raised her hands to shield the sight of the wreck, she saw a cowboy leap from the nearest chute and land on the bull's back, snagging the end of the wrap as he went, freeing it.

As he landed, Forrest jerked Tom loose and pulled him clear, into the hands of a bullfighter. The robbed monster turned and lowered its horns for the thrust, ignoring the other bullfighter who hammered the beast to distract it. One horn ripped into Forrest's upper thigh, hurling him over the bull's own back and slamming Forrest against the chute. As the bull closed in to finish the job, Jenny covered her eyes.

CHAPTER

44

FORREST'S THIRD-FLOOR ROOM WAS ONLY TWO DOORS down from the nurse's station, but that made it impossible to slip in without being caught. Jen had tried it half a dozen times before buckling under to Tom and Al's pleas to wait in the lounge, a small room four doors farther down the hall.

"Do you think he's in his room?" Jen asked from her post at the lounge's doorway. She had asked the question repeatedly of the nurses but wouldn't accept their answer. "I think he's in there. Why won't they let us in? Why are they keeping the door closed?"

Al steered Jen to the corner of the lounge where a television set quietly babbled. "They'll let us know how he's doing as soon as they can, Jen." As Jen sat, Al flipped through channels until she found Jen's favorite station, Country Music Television.

When Jen leaned her head against the off-white plaster wall and closed her eyes, Al flopped into the seat next to Tom's, across the room. "Besides praying, what can we do? And don't say that's enough."

Tom's look said it for him. "I think we should give Forrest's granddad a call. He might want to come, depending."

Al shuddered. "Depending. I hate the sound of that." She held

415

Tom's hand and traced his scar, swallowing tears at the thought of Forrest's sacrifice. "What are you going to tell him? We don't know anything."

"I can tell him that and leave it up to him."

"Yes." Al sighed. "I guess that's all we can do."

Tom walked over to Jen and told her their plans, inviting her to come along. Jen shook her head without opening her eyes.

In the lobby, Al listened to the first part of the conversation between Tom and Forrest's grandfather at the wall phone, then walked over to the vending machines. She had finished half her Sprite before Tom hung up the phone. "He's coming?"

"Can't. He's sick."

"Not seriously?"

"Sick enough to keep him from traveling, he said, though it didn't affect his mouth." Tom stuck his finger in his ear as if dislodging words. "That old man can beller. He'd been notified about Forrest's accident and thought I was calling to gloat."

"About Forrest getting hurt?"

"About the Circle H. It's mine now, Al." Tom looked dazed. "Since this happened, I didn't realize that. Sterling thought I arranged Forrest's accident somehow so I wouldn't have to go on with the season, now that I've got the ranch."

"Could you explain this a little more?" Al fell heavily into her chair.

Tom did, and Al felt some of the knot in her stomach loosen as he told her of his dreams for the ranch. "It's all coming true. Only thing is, I thought Forrest would be around to take over the Cattle Company, too." Tom looked close to tears as he finished.

"You really are planning to quit rodeo," Al said slowly.

"I told you that."

"I know, but...what about the Ex?"

Tom touched her cheek with his good hand, his other shoulder and arm secure in its sling. "I'll be doing well to heal up in time for the NFR."

"You're still planning to ride?"

"Rope only," he said, kissing her, then falling silent. "I'll rope, but it doesn't look like Forrest will be able to," he said at last. "Sterling thought I found a loophole and made use of it. Forrest means so much more to me than the Circle H. I wish I'd never signed that contract. I wish Forrest —"

Al stopped him from rising. "Was it suicide, Tom? Was Forrest trying to kill himself? His last words on the way here, were about there being no greater love than giving up one's life for a friend." Al shook her head. "It sounds crazy. And this is another crazy idea, but could he have planned all this?"

"Planned me getting hung up? No way to plan that. On his own ride, maybe. The verse was something Winky had told Forrest. According to Winky, Forrest got saved tonight." Tom pulled her close, staring ahead of him. "I pray that's true. I'm not sure about Winky's spiritual sensitivity. He practically slammed Forr over the head with his Bible before the rodeo."

"Maybe that's what Forrest needed," Al murmured. "Maybe it was the only way God could get him saved in time —"

"Maybe seeing me hung up brought back memories of his dad," Tom said, rushing past her words. "That must be why he did it. Sterling Jr. died at the Cow Palace, Al." Tom paused and looked at her. "Forrest's tried to get me to quit riding for months. If I'd listened to him, he'd be okay now. But I had to have the Circle H. I sacrificed my friend to do it."

Al's head came up. "You couldn't know Forrest would jump in

like that! All you did know was that if you had quit riding, you would've lost the ranch." She halted. "And me."

"What?"

"I can't stay with a drifter, Tom. I need a place, some security. You don't know how relieved I am to know you've got the Circle H. That's my guarantee. I know someday you will quit rodeo because that land is there waiting for you. You love riding, Tom, or you did. If you didn't have this other love, this love for your land, do you think you'd ever give up rodeo?"

"I…don't know. Right now, I —"

"But later, when the fear wore off and you had no ranch. Wouldn't you go back to riding, to roping at least?"

"I…guess that could happen."

"Would happen. You belong in two places, Tom Rawlings: the rodeo and the ranch. But I can only belong in one."

Tom looked stunned, and Al wondered if she'd gone too far.

"So I would've lost more than the Circle H if I had quit. I would have lost you." He sounded desolate.

"But you didn't. I'm not saying all this to make you insecure about me, Tom, but to let you see the good in this. We have to see the good. You can't blame yourself for what happened." Al sighed, and a sob interrupted it. Tom held her until she could speak again. "I sure hope Winky's right about Forrest. Think he's really saved?"

"Only God knows the heart, but according to Winky, Forrest confessed his need for a Savior, and Winky led him in a prayer of faith. We have to believe that…especially now. I want to believe it. I choose to."

"So if Forrest doesn't make it —"

"Then…I'm going to trust the Lord that Forrest's found the happiness he always searched for," Tom said, but didn't meet her eyes.

Neither of them spoke for a long while.

"What about you, Tom?" Al finally asked. "Have you found your happiness? Are you finished with rodeo after the NFR, or are you going on to the Ex?"

Tom exhaled tiredly. "I'm never climbing on another bull again, Al, but if this shoulder heals, I'll rope in the Ex. Then I'm done." He studied her as he spoke. "What have you decided?"

"I don't know if I can walk away from the Ex, either."

"What about after the Ex? Vet school?"

"Remember that day at the Circle H?"

"You said you wanted to raise horses."

"Pretty idealistic, right?"

"Perfect." Tom smiled for the first time since coming to the hospital. "That's what you said when you saw the ranch," Tom continued. "Good grassland up there, Al. You could raise some fine quarter horses."

Al shook her head. "It's all just dreams, Tom. Notions. We haven't really settled anything."

"Do we have to, right now?"

Al stared at him, then a gradual smile touched her lips. "No," she said, laying her head on his good shoulder. "I guess we don't. Tom?"

"Yes?"

"Let's pray."

"For Forrest?" Tom asked, already dropping to his knees.

Al joined him on the floor. "For Forrest."

Jenny unfolded the note, almost wishing Forrest had never written it but thankful to have a scrap of him to hold in her hands. His small script barely covered half the page, but his words summarized twenty-four years of suffering and foreshadowed a future completely opposite: a future of hope.

What was he talking about?

She understood the part explaining Felicia's trick, but this reference to new life, to forgiveness and salvation, left her confused and cold. *If Forrest does live, will I know him? Should I even be here?*

Jenny shoved the note in her pocket as a nurse approached.

"Jenny O'Neill?"

"Yes."

"You may see Forrest now."

"He's all right?" Jenny's hand still grasped the note.

"Please come with me," the nurse said, showing the way. "He can only see you briefly."

Jenny stood and followed.

CHAPTER

45

EILEEN CLOSED THE COVER OF THE BLACK LEATHER BOOK and thought a moment about what she'd read before she took her coat from the hook and fished out her car keys.

She shut the front door behind her, zipping her coat to keep out the wind and the flakes of the first snow. Several white patterns dotted her sleeve before she could get into her car.

Instead of going to the nursing home, Eileen found herself on the familiar route to the farm. The hand-painted red letters of Harvey's "for sale" sign were dimmed by swiftly falling flakes by the time she turned off the road and onto the driveway of Elder Valley Farm. She made her turn and pressed her foot on the accelerator when she released it and backed up to give the sign a second look. The phone number on the sign was now covered by another board that said "sold" in small block letters, as if ashamed of the fact.

When Eileen reached the house, she didn't stop to take her keys out of the ignition but strode into the entryway, knocking only as an afterthought.

Harvey stood by the sink, a cup of coffee in his hand. "Eileen! I was just getting myself some java. Like a cup?"

"You sold the farm?"

"Last night." He set down his cup, pulled another out of the cupboard, and placed it on the kitchen table. "Here okay? Or would you like to go into the living room?"

"This is fine." Eileen sat woodenly, taking the cup with both hands but not drinking from it.

"Getting cold out, isn't it? The coffee should warm you up."

"Why didn't you tell me, Harvey? Why didn't you say the farm had been sold?"

"Didn't want to until I was sure." Harvey sipped from his cup and pushed the sugar bowl toward her. "I'll get you a spoon." He pulled the drawer open before she could move. "Closed the deal late last night. I'm going down to the bank tomorrow afternoon to sign the papers, if that's a good time for you."

"You got what we were asking?" Money was hardly the issue, but the whole thing seemed so unreal. If Harvey began quoting figures, she'd know it was true.

"Got more than what we decided to ask. I've been fixing the place up and thought I could go a few thousand higher. They were glad to give it to me." Harvey handed her the spoon and closed the drawer with his elbow. "One o'clock okay with you? I know you aren't working tomorrow —"

Eileen reached out and touched his arm.

"Something wrong?" He laid one big hand on her shoulder. "Coffee too hot?"

"Selling the farm. I never thought it would happen."

"Solid buyer, too, your boss says. Lloyd doesn't think we'll have any trouble collecting. He should know."

"We're not selling it outright?"

"Did a little research on that. Better to stretch it over a few years. Taxes won't gouge us so much, and the buyers have already agreed to it."

"Selling the farm." Eileen rubbed a small chip on the kitchen table. "Now where will Alison come to when she comes home?"

Harvey's hand slid from his wife's shoulder as he sat next to her. "I'm thinking of getting a place above the hardware store..." He peered at her and touched her again. "Eileen, don't you want to sell?"

"I'm not sure..."

"Couldn't ask for a better, firmer offer, Lloyd says. But if you want to wait, we can wait."

Eileen moved her forefinger over the brim of her cup.

"Eileen?"

"I just heard from Alison this morning." Feeling numb, Eileen made another revolution around the brim. "She's still going with that young man, though she's not saying much about it. She hasn't even told me his name. Maybe after the National Finals Rodeo is over."

"And what about the Ex? She decided about competing in that?"

"She isn't sure, but I think she will, if she makes it. And Harvey," Eileen said, lifting her finger and putting it on her husband's hand, "she's coming home for Christmas."

Harvey pushed his cup of coffee out of his way and leaned over the table. "The farm will be here for her, Eileen. I'll be here for her." He remained close. "Bet she'd like it if you were here, too. Would you think about coming home for a few days? I'd stay in the spare bedroom, and you could have our room," he hurried to say. "I don't mean to push you, but if you want to stay on any terms, nothing could make me happier. I'm ready to give farming...and our marriage...a real go."

Eileen turned to look him full in the face. "What?"

"I've...missed you, Eileen. I don't want to...be apart."

Eileen's smile came tentatively, but it stayed. "Give me some time to think about that, would you, Harvey?"

"You'd consider coming back?"

"I'd consider it."

"Thank you." Harvey stood and gave her an awkward hug before pushing in his chair. "Let's have our coffee in the living room, honey. We can watch the snow coming down. I remember how you always liked to watch the first snow."

He carried their cups into the living room, setting them beside the new oak coffee table and the new blue love seat which stood in place of his old ripped recliner. The love seat matched her favorite throw rug.

Eileen had just taken her first sip of coffee when Harvey spoke. "Radio says we could get a blizzard. Cows are all set. Got done patching the barn last week. It'll be the warmest, driest winter they've had since Al was little. She'll be pleased when she comes home."

"I'm sure she will," Eileen answered, relaxing into the soft upholstery and resting her feet on the blue rug.

"Going to see Mom tonight?"

"I was on my way when I decided to come here."

"That's right. You always see her around four each day, don't you? Regular as clockwork." Harvey looked steadily at her, and when he spoke, Eileen could not mistake the emotion in his eyes and words. "I…love…all you're doing for her, Eileen. For me, too. You've been so good…to us. Put up with so much." He gave his wife a quick kiss, then broke into nervous chatter. "Mind if I come with? I've been trying to pick up the slack since Margaret and Willy left, but I haven't seen Mom since yesterday morning. Can't see her enough lately."

Eileen took another sip of coffee, then placed her cup on the table and slipped her hand into her husband's. "I hope your mother doesn't mind if I'm a little late today." At Harvey's surprised look Eileen added, "But somehow I think she'll understand."

They held hands and watched the snow float down, the flakes curling in a gentle western wind. Harvey refilled their coffee cups and brought in some freshly microwaved store-bought cinnamon rolls, steaming and drenched with melted butter.

Eileen took one and had peeled away the first gooey layer when the phone rang. She popped a portion of the roll into her mouth and lazily surveyed the accumulating snow. Her mind drifted randomly over pockets of time in her life, milestones: meeting Harvey, marrying him, giving birth to Alison.

The telephone rang again, and Eileen heard her husband's low voice, his words muffled as if by a thick winter scarf. Her attention shifted to the snow, coming down heavily. The yard light flickered in short bursts of decision until it finally shone steadily several minutes later. A thin coating of snow now covered the grass, the tree trunks, the mailbox, transforming all colors into white.

Come now, let us reason together, Eileen thought, remembering the words from Isaiah she had read at Janette's request the day before and read again to herself before leaving Rhoda's. *Though your sins are like scarlet, they shall be as white as snow; though they are red as crimson, they shall be like wool.*

Red, white: so at odds. The one so full of anger, the other so calm and pure, covering all wrongs completely. *Let us reason together.* No condemnation. An invitation. Could there be a God like that, who did not accuse, but merely offered?

A crucifix filled Eileen's mind, the large wooden one that had hung in her grandmother's living room. The cross was rough and splintery, and nails were driven through it, through the hands and feet of a painted porcelain figure. The figure seemed so real that once Eileen had climbed the back of the couch to see if the blood on its feet was wet.

Scarlet. Blood. Snow. Salvation? More pieces of Isaiah invaded her mind: *Turn to me and be saved, all you ends of the earth; for I am God, and there is no other.* It pierced Eileen as suddenly as one of those nails on the cross. *Turn to me and be saved. Be saved. Saved!* Not foolish by any reckoning, but urgent, all at once. To be saved…to resign all cares and worries to those outstretched, blood-stained hands, to let them turn everything white as snow! Eileen pondered the paradox, this time with eyes that could see, a mind that could reason, a heart that could feel.

The months and years of her mother-in-law's teaching bore the first tender buds of fruit, and the Word that had so long lain in Eileen's heart came to life — eternal life, as she prayed. How absurd that she hadn't understood until now! How tragic. And how faithful of the Lord and her mother-in-law to stand by and wait, holding out what she had scorned to touch.

"Eileen." Harvey's voice. She looked up, seeing him through tear-smeared eyes. He did not appear to think it strange to find his wife kneeling before their coffee table, crying. She began to explain, but he helped her up and spoke quietly, cutting off her profession.

"Mom's had another bad turn. The doctor's been in to see her. It doesn't look good this time. Not at all. They're transferring her to the hospital in Eau Claire, and they say we should come if we can. Now."

"Alison —"

"Called a second after I finished with the nursing home. She's flying home right away."

Eileen was glad he was holding her, for she felt so unsteady. Her new joy was mixed with old grief. The balance helped sustain her, as did her husband's arms. She shot up a simple prayer to the Lord of her fledgling faith, and together, she and Harvey went out into the blizzard.

Al made it as far as St. Paul before her connecting flight was postponed. She sat in the airport, praying for a break in the weather. But the snow outside the observation window swirled across the dark airfield, and the last plane that taxied in had frost on its windows. No more flights would be allowed until conditions cleared, the loudspeaker repeated, and Al went to find a phone.

She knew better than to try home, and called information for the Sacred Heart hospital in Eau Claire. She was transferred to her grandmother's room, but it was her mother who answered.

"How is she?" Al wasted no time.

"Not...well. Where are you, darling?"

"St. Paul. I don't think I'll be able to fly any farther. The airlines have quit running, and I was supposed to take a twin engine to Eau Claire." Panic hit Al as she spoke, and though she prayed through her fear, she felt her words tumbling out wildly. "What do I do?"

Her mother didn't seem to notice that Al had regressed to near-infancy. "I'll try to come and get you, darling, but the snow is supposed to be bad the whole way." There was a pause as she probably looked out the window.

"It's snowing hard there, too?"

"Yes, but I believe I can make it."

You believe? Why did the words sound so strange in Al's ears, create such a tingling? Wondering if she had completely lost control, Al took a deep breath and sent up an arrow prayer. "I think I should try to make it from here. Maybe I can rent a car —"

"I doubt they'll let you take one in conditions like these."

"But I'm not even two hours away!" The strain of the past few days swept over Al, and her unspent tears for Forrest and the untapped ones for her grandmother spilled down her face. She wiped at them as she willed her voice to quit wavering. "I've got to get there, Mother. I've got to see Grandma. I've got to talk to her!" Her voice spiraled, and Al stopped speaking, knowing her next words would be off the auditory scale.

"Grandma's all right," her mother said gently.

"But she's dying!"

"And she's already in a coma, darling. I'm so sorry for your sake, honey. She may be able to hear us, but she can't respond. I wanted to talk with her, too. But she doesn't need us. She's at peace. You can see it in her face. She's going to meet her Lord."

"I want to see it in her face myself!"

"We'll do our best to make that happen. You just stay put, and I'll meet you. You're at the downtown airport?"

"Yes, but —"

"I'm coming now." There was a short pause. "The Lord keep you until I get there, darling."

The Lord? I must be losing it. Al simultaneously nodded and shook her head. "I'll wait at the entrance with my baggage, if it got here."

"I'll be there as soon as possible. I love you."

Al repeated the phrase and hung up the phone.

46

"YOU DON'T SEEM TOO TICKLED TO SEE ME up and at 'em," Forrest said to his former team-roping partner who half-sat, half-leaned on the hospital heating register and kept firing glances out the window. "Surgery wasn't enough for you? Wish I was in critical, maybe? Then you could've gone with Al."

Tom was about to demur when he saw his friend's grin. "Sorry, Forr. I guess I'm not much company."

"Got that right. Good at reading, though. We'll stick to that. Ready for another hour or two?" When Tom didn't answer, Forrest aimed his remote at the mounted TV and turned up the volume. "It's okay. Keep saving your vocal cords. Jen's up next. Should keep me occupied for fourteen seconds or so."

Tom sat in the chair next to Forrest's bed, and the two watched the redhead on the black horse smoke through the barrel-racing course of the Cow Palace.

"That's one woman who can really chase cans," Forrest said after the standings had shown. "Still in first, but Felicia's close. Jen'll be in Vegas next. Wish it was us, too, Tom. All four of us." He switched off the television. "Sure surprised me when Al up and quit. Guess I'd do the same if I heard Granddad was getting any worse. I'd sneak out of here in a second."

Tom looked at him skeptically. "How do you figure to travel with a fractured arm and collarbone? Not to mention the puncture in your leg and the fact that even your face doesn't look so great anymore. They'd never let you out of here."

Forrest craned his neck but he still couldn't see his face in the mirror above the set of five drawers across the room. "Thought I didn't look too bad this afternoon, when Jen was here. And I feel fantastic."

"No pain?"

"Maybe you're kidding, but that bull wasn't. I'm talking inside. That hunk of beef didn't touch what really counts."

Tom picked up the Bible lying on Forrest's bed table. "I still can't get used to you talking like this. You're sure that bull didn't scramble your brains?"

"No guarantee. But if he did, it's permanent. So get used to it, and read me something. About the Lord." Forrest let his tongue roll over his last two words, so new to his mouth. So wonderful.

"Psalm Twenty-three again?" Tom asked, paging through the Bible and balancing it on his knees, his sling no help at all.

"Read something else for now. I know I'll go back to Psalm Twenty-three often, though. It's always stuck with me, since your mama read it to us during one of her cookie breaks. I kept thinking about it, the part about the valley of the shadow of death. Think I spent most of my life there, Tom. Once I heard a cowboy version of that psalm. Something like, 'The Lord is my Trail Boss, he gives me all I need.' You ever heard it?"

"I don't think so. And I don't remember Mama ever reading Psalm Twenty-three. I was more interested in the cookies then. Wish I'd listened more."

"Guess you listened enough, anyway," Forrest said, groaning as he tried to roll on his side. "Time for me to. Just start at the beginning and keep going, Tom."

"I'll read until I go hoarse."

"Fun-ny."

Tom chuckled. "It's so good to see you doing all right, Forrest. And to see you saved..." The former bull rider's eyes grew shiny. "I'm amazed. Amazed and humbled. And very, very thankful. I'll never forget what you did for me, Forr."

"Hey, now, don't go getting soft. Just read, cowhand. Don't skip a word."

Tom cleared his sight and throat, then he spoke. "'In the beginning God created the heavens and the earth...'"

Forrest's eyes closed. In his mind, he could see the heavens forming, the waters and stars, the sun and moon, as Tom read about their birth. Gladness washed over him as it had when he'd given his life to Christ, and despite his broken body, Forrest's spirit soared. Only one thought kept him bound to earth. *Jen. Jen. You've got to understand, too. You've got to,* he thought, and suddenly he heard Winky's priceless words, the words that had brought him from death and shadow to lightness and life. *Got to tell you about Jesus,* Forrest heard, but substituted Jen's name for his own. *Got to tell you 'bout his love for you.*

In his time, Forrest thought, paraphrasing some verses Tom had read earlier in Ecclesiastes chapter three. *It'll all come about in his time.*

Jenny drove to the ocean before she went to see Forrest. As she dragged her boots through the sand, she remembered him racing with the waves as he had so often. She didn't have the heart to do it herself, even though her latest win assured her of going to the NFR in first place. The victory over Felicia had not been quite so satisfying as she had hoped. They were still closely matched, and after Felicia's Ellensburg revelation, Jenny wanted to make the blond suffer as she had. She wanted to, but she lacked the energy. Even revenge didn't seem worth the effort.

Racing. It was Jenny's only anchor in the radical changes her life had so swiftly undergone. The racing course was always there, always the same, though the size of the arena or the town might vary. She and Clover. And three barrels. How Jenny wished the rest of the world were as reliable.

She sat on the sand and rubbed it between her palms, gritty and granular. *Forrest...* Why did she feel as if she'd lost him? Felicia posed no danger now, but this new religion did. Forrest was so different, almost like another person. Those words she'd longed to hear now fell regularly from his lips. He loved her, he said, and when she held his hand or searched his eyes, she almost believed him. The pained look she had associated with their love was gone, replaced by an inner light. It was...eerie.

Was it an epidemic, this personality change that had first affected Tom, then Al, then Forrest? When would her turn come? Jenny felt as if she were being stalked.

Detecting someone's approach, Jenny suppressed the urge to run. She turned her head and saw Sarah Bower bounding over the sand with her usual exuberance.

"Hi, Jenny!" Uninvited, Sarah plunked herself down.

"Hi, Sarah." Jenny faced the waves. "Looks like you'll be taking Al's place in the Ex," she said dully.

"Maybe, if everything goes all right at the NFR." Sarah twirled a strand of her blond hair. "You're going to do the Ex, Jenny?"

"Yeah." Part of her brightened at the thought: she and Clover in the Professional Rodeo Exposition. Who'd ever have thought it would really happen? *Al, she answered herself. Al always knew, and she always wanted to ride in it. Then her grandmother becomes so sick she can't. So much for getting religion. Doesn't look like it helped Al out any. Or Forrest. Doubt either of them will ever rodeo again.*

"Jenny," Sarah said, "Al's not coming back, is she?"

"I don't think so." *And I don't understand why. Why did Al get her dream snatched away when it was so close? Why?*

Before Jenny could take off on another round of questioning, Sarah interrupted. "I don't think so, either. So I was wondering: When the Ex starts, would you consider us traveling together? I know it's kind of sudden and all, but if I make it as the Ex rookie, I'll need a partner. This might sound crazy, but I was thinking maybe you do, too. Need a partner, that is."

Jenny stared at her. Sarah was direct, that was for sure. And confident, too. *She thinks I'll say yes. Taking it for granted, just like Al did, figuring I'll agree even before I say it.* Sarah's smile, however, didn't look anything but friendly — and wide enough to include Texas.

She doesn't look a bit like Al, not with those brown eyes and freckles. She talks like her, though. Free and easy, like a Dakota wind.

The young blond wasn't talking now, but waiting. Holding her breath, it seemed. *She's got to learn not to be so open,* Jenny thought. *She reads like a book without a cover. No wonder her horse overdoes the course. If I did travel with her, I'd probably have to teach her a lot.*

Jenny contemplated the racer. She knew Sarah's racing style, but she didn't know the person. It might be challenging to take her up, to train her as she had Al. With the thought came renewed purpose. There was nothing like directing raw talent toward success. Jenny had always been proud of Al's accomplishments, even when they threatened her own. When Al had given everything up so abruptly, Jenny couldn't help feeling that her investment had earned a no-score. And more than that, she felt lonely. Although Al had been spending a lot more time with Tom, the two women still traveled together. Going down the road seemed so quiet now. *It might be fun to have...someone to talk with again.*

"Okay, Sarah. I guess that would work out all right."

"Great! Do you want to use my truck or yours?"

Jenny glanced at the nearly empty parking area and saw a new-looking blue pickup next to hers. "If yours runs okay, how about if we use your truck and my trailer? It's a double. Guess Al won't need it anymore, and Clover's used to traveling in it."

"Yes! Jenny, that's perfect! Thank you so much." Sarah flung her arms around Jenny. "I've always wanted to know you better. I was just sure the Lord would bring us together someday!"

The Lord? Jenny's eyes widened. She'd forgotten about Sarah's other side. All the blond bubbles had blinded her.

"I am so excited!" Sarah hugged her again. "This is great. It's wonderful! I just praise God!" She popped up, stretching her arms upward and twirling her body, her beaming face raised toward heaven.

It struck Jenny as something Al would do.

Al decided the aqua-green vinyl chair had been designed neither for looks nor for comfort — and certainly not for sleep. It was over-stuffed and protruded where it should recede, and the thing was so slippery it often bucked her off during the night.

Every time she landed on the floor, she hoped the thud would awaken her grandmother. But it didn't. Grandma lay, plugged in and monitored, her breathing assisted with oxygen, her heartbeat enforced.

"Is she even alive?" Al wanted to ask, to scream. The only thing about the figure in the hospital bed that seemed remotely familiar was the old woman's face. Worn and ravaged, its folds and creases were set in deep lines of peace. She did look ready to meet her Lord. Or perhaps, as if she had already met him.

Her mother's new faith helped bolster Al's. If not for their daily prayers and Bible studies, Al knew she would have gone berserk. She couldn't bring herself to watch the Grand National, and though she called to congratulate Jenny on her win, even to her the congratulations sounded hollow.

What if Grandma never wakes up? Did I give up everything for nothing? Al hadn't thought out her decision, hadn't prayed about it, had simply done it. At the time, no other response occurred to her. Rodeo, the NFR, even the Ex seemed so small in comparison with the thought of losing her grandmother and the chance to share the moments of life she had left.

But the longer Al stayed at the hospital, taking turns watching over her grandmother's body, the more she wondered if she'd been foolish. What if Grandma passed away without a word?

"Don't come home until you're finished with rodeo. For good." Al could still hear how her grandmother had said it.

Should I have stayed and raced? No one had said anything against her going, but Al had seen the disapproval in Jen's eyes. Forrest had looked shocked, but Tom seemed to agree, and his daily calls were practically the only food she lived on. She wanted him with her more than she ever had before.

Now what's going to happen to us? He'll probably make the Ex, even if he doesn't make the NFR. A whole year without him! I can finish my degree then, but I can't face four years of graduate school afterwards. I don't want to put that much time between us. She often thought of asking him to come but sensed this was something she had to go through with her family. With every second away from Tom, however, she realized she never wanted to be separated again. She hoped he was reaching the same conclusion, but worried that her decision might have wedged them apart indefinitely. Maybe irrevocably.

Dear Father in heaven, was I mistaken? Shouldn't I be here?

"A...Al-li-son." The voice could have been the Lord's, so still and small it was. Thinner than a whisper.

Al moved her chair closer so she could hold her grandmother's hand. Grandma's eyes were closed, and her mouth half open in the dreadful relaxed manner that signified total acceptance of death.

Lord God, I —

"Al-li-son."

"Grandma?"

"My bless-ing," Grandma wheezed. The hazel eyes opened a crack. "No rodeo?"

"No rodeo," Al answered, leaning nearer. "I came to see you, Grandma. I've been waiting for you to wake up. I love you!"

"Don't cry." The old woman attempted to lift her hand, and Al raised it to her cheek. "You...bought...your...field."

"Field? I —"

"Trea-sure," Grandma squeaked. "For joy." Her eyelids closed. "Love..."

"I love you, too," Al said, fighting the silencing power of her tears. "I love you, Grandma. I love you!"

The beeping, humming machines were her only answer, and as Al wept and clung to her grandmother's hand, she felt something inexpressibly precious leaving her. "Grandma. Grandma!" *Lord, please don't take her away. I'm not ready yet!*

When her mother and father came in, Al was still holding the hand, but the only warmth in it was her own.

47

TOM LAY ON THE WEIGHT BENCH, forcing all his strength into his weak shoulder. The bar rose, then lowered; the cool steel touched his wet neck. He grunted and pushed up the weights until they sat in the rest.

He let his arms stretch to his sides, lengthening the muscles and relaxing them. As his arms approached the wood floor, his elbows locked, and within inches of drawing them in, Tom felt his shoulder give and explode in flames of pain.

"Better quit pushing it," came a voice from the doorway.

Tom released his grip on his shoulder and looked at Forrest through wincing eyes. "I can't. Only two weeks left until the NFR. You know that, Forrest."

"Yeah, I do. And I also know how long ligaments like yours take to heal. They said at least six weeks, didn't they, Tom?"

"It'll be almost that by the NFR." Tom reached for the bar and felt the same angry throbbing.

"Almost." Forrest crutched closer. "You planning to go for surgery after they blow? How long you think recovery'll take?"

"Those are happy thoughts," Tom said, sitting up and burying his face in his towel. "Haven't you got any faith in me, Forr?"

"Nope. All my faith's in God. Thought yours was, too."

"Forrest." Tom threw his towel down. "Are you sure we haven't traded places? I thought I was the one who gave all the advice."

"I learn fast. Good thing for you, too. You're going off half-cocked, Tom. You could do yourself some permanent damage if you don't ease up. Think Al wants an invalid for a husband?"

Tom grinned. "As long as it's me, she might."

Forrest laughed. "Well, maybe she would. But you won't be able to handle a ranch if you ruin your body."

Tom looked up and down the length of Forrest's frame, crutch and all. "Are you sure you're the one who should be giving this sermon?"

Forrest tried to get at an itch somewhere below the edge of his arm cast. "Somebody's got to. I don't figure you're thinking too clear right now. Love's got you loco," he said, his mouth breaking into a smile that quickly straightened. "I know you want to compete, Tom. I do, too. Neither one of us's got a chance."

"A prayer. That's all I want," Tom replied, telling himself that the next time he reached for the bar, the pain would be gone. It wasn't.

"Buddy, you've got my prayers, but without a miracle, you're not competing at Vegas. Or in the Ex. I hate to be the one to tell you —"

"Then don't."

"Got to. You're doing just what Carl did. Remember how he made out?"

No, but I'm sure you'll remind me. Since his conversion, Forrest had become steadily more verbal. Sometimes, Tom didn't appreciate everything about Forrest's new birth. Especially when the babe in Christ started lecturing his older brother in the faith.

"Carl and I didn't win any buckle, Tom. We didn't even end up in the top five. Carl finally had to go under the knife, and from what

I hear, he's still having troubles." Forrest placed his hand on Tom's good shoulder. "Hate to see you end up like that."

"Me, too." Tom tried to let the warning slide off him, but it stuck, like a thorn in his side. "I've got to do this, Forr. I want to get the ranch fixed up for Al, get her going with her horses. It's not for me."

"Think that'll make any difference to your ligaments?"

Tom reached for the bar, and even before his arms came off the bench, his shoulder ached. "So what am I supposed to do?"

Swinging his injured leg slightly back and forth, Forrest assumed an attitude of either intense thought or prayer. "What about that money you said you had saved up? And what about the extra thousands you won this year? Still got 'em?"

"It's not enough —"

"It is if you've got a partner. What do you say, Tom?"

"I don't get it. Partners in what?"

"Something I've been praying about. Still in the planning stages, but I've started calling it 'Jackson and Rawlings Stock Company, Incorporated.'"

"A cattle company? What about your granddad?"

Forrest launched into a spiel he'd evidently been preparing. "Soon's I'm okay, I want to start. At first I'd just be a silent partner, putting up the ante, but later on I'd like to get into building. Like a fence line, then a house or barn. Take it easy for a while, then expand into, say, quarter horses and cattle. Just until Granddad realizes I have enough sense to help him run our ranch. You know anyplace I could get work like that?"

"As a silent partner? Silent?"

"Well, pretty much. What do you say? We could be out of here and home tomorrow. I've got my rehab down. So do you."

Tom reached for his towel. "I want to do some praying and thinking of my own, Forr, but I like this idea." He could see the Circle H with a freshly painted ranch house, barn, and stable. He could envision cattle and horses drinking from the pond. "I want to let it ride, run it past Al before I'm sure, but you're right about one thing: I'm not helping my shoulder any, and I don't think I can make it for the Ex, let alone the NFR. Think she'll be disappointed? She's had so much to deal with already, losing her grandmother and her chance to ride in the Ex."

"Only one way to know, Tom." Forrest swung ahead, and Tom resisted helping him when the crutch tip caught on the doorway, knowing Forrest wanted to be as independent as possible. Tom understood that, and as he rubbed his shoulder, he felt better about his future than he had since getting hung up. Without competing in the Ex, he couldn't offer Al the mansion or the gorgeous spread he'd planned to surprise her with. But maybe they could get married sooner, after he built a decent house and respectable ranch, something he felt Al would like and his mama would approve of. Something that might even be closer to a Circle of Heaven than a twenty-room home or a state-of-the-art ranch. And maybe Al would like it better that way, too. He hoped.

The two men watched the big-screen TV as if captivated. Spread out on opposite sides of a soft leather couch, they ate from the snacks on the end tables at their elbows.

Sterling Sr. wandered in and out of the room as he had since the NFR began nine nights earlier. Since Forrest was no longer competing, the old man said he didn't care to waste his time gawking. He'd stay just long enough to catch a run or two from each event, make a pointed remark about quitters, and pilfer a piece of his grandson's jerky.

"Tom, give me a handful of yours, will you? Granddad just cleaned me out."

"Out of what?" Tom asked, intent on the screen though it showed a commercial for Stetson hats.

Forrest stood and stretched carefully, then hobbled over to Tom's horded pile. "Jerky," he said, leaving his friend with three pieces.

"Hey! We've still got roping, barrels, and bulls to get through."

"One piece of jerky for each." Forrest regained his seat as the commercial ended and Las Vegas's Thomas and Mack arena hit the screen. The announcers began their work, but Forrest spoke over them. "Wish it'd been us, Tom."

"Team roping?"

"Anything." Forrest put his boot on his footrest. "Not so much for the competition. Just to be there for Jen."

"You could have."

"She said she didn't want me." Forrest chewed on his jerky. "I'm trying to respect what she wants this go-round. She seemed pretty set on cutting me loose."

"Maybe you were a little hard on her. Maybe you didn't start respecting her soon enough."

"You keep saying that. I only told her the truth: I love her, Christ loves her. We both just want her to give us a chance."

"That's tough to choke down for someone who's not ready. Remember how you were whenever I tried talking to you?"

"No. And I don't want to remember. For the first time in my life, I'm not struggling, not weighed down by anything. For the first time, I'm free. That's what I want for Jen." Forrest held up his palm. "I know. It's not my timing that matters. It'll happen in his time, right?"

"Right."

They watched the rest of the roping between conversation and Sterling's regular interruptions. When the barrel racing began, however, Forrest quit speaking. He watched without interest as Felicia turned in a score of 14.30, but when Jenny beat it, he threw his hat to the rafters and stomped the carpet with his boots.

"Easy, Forr," Tom said. "We've got work tomorrow. I don't want you hurting yourself and giving some excuse in the morning. I'm not getting a whole lot out of you the way it is."

Forrest recovered his hat and lengthened his body, testing the muscles of his leg and arm. "She did it, Tom," he said, sitting down but still elated. "She's a champ. For the third time. I was hoping, but I wasn't sure. She and Felicia really kept on each other's heels."

"A contest all the way. If Jenny keeps going like this, she'll match your record for broncs."

"I hope she does." Forrest turned to the screen, waiting for Jen to get her five seconds on prime time. After she had her interview and the action cut to bull riding, Forrest munched his popcorn. "Wish I was there with her."

Tom watched the last of the bull riders, then finished off his juice. "I'm glad you're here. We're getting more work done on the Circle H every day. Should be ready by spring."

"You going to tell Al that?"

"Not yet, in case we run into problems. But when I go to see her and meet her parents, I'm going to promise something I know I can do."

Forrest tried to enter into his friend's happiness. "When's the date?"

"I'll let Al decide that, if she wants to make any more decisions. She's still grieving, and with running around and trying to get readmitted into college, she's had a lot to schedule. She wants to finish her degree, then get married, but she hasn't said how soon it could happen."

"You're sure about all this."

"We both are. Being apart gave us time alone to think, pray, plan. Like it says in Romans eight twenty-eight, God worked good out of it, in spite of the pain. Marriage is a big commitment, but one we're ready to make now."

"And her folks see things the same way?"

"That's something I'll find out more about over Christmas when I go up there. Al hasn't told them we're planning to get married, but she's making it clear that it's a good possibility. So far, they've had no big objections, and Al said she thinks her grandmother gave us her blessing just before she died."

"Must be nice."

"It is. Keeps me warm when we pound nails out there," Tom answered, pointing to the window. Even in the darkness, the glare of snow reflected the moonlight. "Forr, does it bother you to hear this? I've tried to keep it to myself, but it's getting harder and harder to do it."

"You had your years of suffering while Jen and I were going strong. I guess it's fair. I'm glad for you, Tom. I just wish there was something I could do about Jen."

Tom traced the scar on his hand. "It's pretty tough to do much of anything when she won't let you near her. I thought maybe she'd change her mind. At least she's traveling with Sarah now. She's bound to hear a lot of Bible with that little chatterer."

"I thank God for Sarah. And you know what else, Tom? Jen did say she didn't want me to come for the NFR, but she didn't say anything about the Ex. I'm thinking about taking a few days off this

January for the first show."

"You're going to Houston? What about tickets?"

"Got those months ago. Three of 'em. Thought you and Al'd like to go, too."

"We'd love it, but I don't know if Al can, if she gets into school." Tom let out a sigh. "Sometimes, it's difficult to think that maybe I could've roped in the Ex if I'd pushed a little harder. But the Lord is giving me peace about that, and he's doing the same for Al. I don't know. Maybe too much fame would've been a trap for us. Or too much money."

Forrest looked around him at the thick log beams and walls, the silver and gold objects of wealth adorning them, making the ranch house a testimony to power. On one wall hung his buckles and trophies. Forrest would have torched the whole building without a thought if it would've meant Jen's or his granddad's salvation.

"I know this place never brought me a hair of happiness, Tom. The Lord gave me that." Forrest touched his buckle, where underneath the pictures of his father and grandfather were joined by a beautiful woman with red hair. "I'm trusting him to give me a whole lot more, too. In his time."

CHAPTER

48

THOUGH JENNY HAD GROWN USED to the Hollywood-like splendor of Glitter Gulch, she hadn't expected the Ex's opening rodeo to outdo Las Vegas so utterly. The NFR had been more star-spangled than usual, but the transformation of the Houston Astrodome left the Thomas and Mack arena in the dust.

Painted Wild West panoramas, a mile-long parade with enough tinsel to decorate every leftover Christmas tree in Texas, a western cookout, dance, auction, exhibition, bazaar, and fair complete with a midway were only a few of the festivities tacked onto the Ex's first rodeo. Texas, the world soon learned, knew how to rodeo right.

But even with the highfalutin veneer and inflated paychecks, the Ex circuit, whether in Houston or in Honolulu, was just another circuit to Jenny. The premier performance, with its myriads of rough stock, best-of-the-best announcers, top riders and ropers on earth, wasn't the climax of her career that she expected. The flashiness and flaunting grew tiresome. With each week's hoopla, Jenny saw less of the glamour and more of the grind. It was Sarah who kept her spirits up — Sarah, and Forrest.

After surprising her at the Houston performance, Forrest appeared every few weeks or so. The first time he had come, Jenny met him with reservation. What would he dump on her this time? But he had quoted no verses, given no testimony, asked no impossible questions, forced no note on her. He had simply invited her and Sarah to join him and Al and Tom after the show to celebrate Al and Tom's engagement and to sample what Carrabba's claimed was the best pizza in Houston. The pizza had been good, but better yet was the company. Even with Sarah's added presence, Jenny felt she'd gone back in time, when no worries infested her world and Forrest's arms were the answer for everything.

Maybe he hasn't changed so much. Except that now, he prayed before their meals. He listened to her, made no demands. He came to see her purely because he loved her, and loved to be with her. Though he rarely expressed it in words, Jenny saw his love in his actions, and gradually, a small part of her dared to love him back.

He wrote her weekly, telling her about the progress he and Tom had made on the Circle H, their plans for acquiring and eventually selling stock, the experiences he was having that made his life richer than ever before. Though he mentioned God often, this didn't rankle Jenny. She had always believed in a Creator; that much of her mother's teaching she had accepted. The hard part was whenever Forrest wrote something about Jesus Christ. She would continue reading, but guardedly, until she was sure Forrest had gone on to another topic. Why that name should bother her so much, she didn't know. And that in itself kept at her.

One day, several months before Al and Tom's wedding date, Jenny gave Sarah free rein to explain why this Jesus was so special. "But today only, Sarah. As soon as we hit Georgia, I don't want to hear any more, okay?" Jenny asked, calling herself a curious fool.

At first, when her traveling partner explained Old Testament prophecy and the Four Spiritual Laws, Jenny felt justified in her distrust and nearly ended the interview with some country-western. But when Sarah quit talking and opened her Bible to the gospel of John, Jenny examined each stroke of the emerging portrait of Jesus.

He was not adored by all, as Jenny had mistakenly remembered from her mother's instruction. Actually, he was an outcast, scorned and spurned by even some of those who followed him. Sarah hadn't finished reading the whole book of John when they reached the state border, and the next time they hit the road, Jenny didn't argue when Sarah continued the story. Jenny was almost glad she did, for certain phrases and parts of the book troubled her, like a poor score, and kept her thinking. When they went on to the book of Matthew, and then Acts, Jenny started realizing why prophecy was an important part of comprehending this Savior, this God-man who owned the whole earth but had nowhere to lay his head.

Homeless, just like me. But that was where any resemblance ended. In love, he endured hatred. In peace, he confronted anger. And in righteousness, he destroyed sin. As a result of only half-listening to her mother, Jenny still had many misconceptions, but through Sarah's patience and the unbroken stretches of highway, Jenny started to understand a piece here, a parable there. And with her understanding grew a hunger to understand more.

When she and Sarah took a detour to Colorado in early summer to attend the Rawlings-Austin wedding, Jenny had not yet discerned the spring in her own heart, the thawing and greening of her own soul.

Taking Forrest's hand at the outskirts of the Circle H, Jenny felt a lightness of spirit that had nothing to do with the fragrance and beauty of the wildflowers and neat ranch house ahead, decked with wedding bouquets and nuptial finery. Although Forrest's near presence did quicken her breathing, it was another Presence who quickened her heart, preparing her for the biggest victory ever: the marriage supper of the Lamb.

Forrest took care with his regulation best-man's suit. His was a darker version of Tom's white long-sleeved shirt and pinstriped vest, draped with a gold watch fob that looped into the hip pocket. A world champion buckle and filigreed belt held up his tailored slacks, and finely tooled leather boots encased his feet. The whole outfit was a gift from the bride's parents, and Forrest wanted to show his appreciation by keeping it clean at least until the late-afternoon ceremony. No easy matter, since he had a gift of his own that needed tending up to the time of its unveiling.

Rubbing a patch of dirt from his vest as the guests' vehicles trailed up the steep gravel road and found parking spots, Forrest didn't see Jen until she and Sarah were hiking toward him. Sarah carried some huge gift, but Jen's hands were empty. Forrest took Sarah's load with one arm and filled Jen's small hand with his, hoping his carpenter's calluses didn't bother her.

After seeing her gift safely stowed, Sarah ran off to hail another wedding guest, and Forrest led Jen to a holding pen hidden behind a stand of aspen fifteen minutes from the house.

"You're looking beautiful," he whispered to her as they walked. Jen's outfit, a rose-colored blouse and split skirt set, resembled what she had worn at the notorious Ellensburg rodeo and again at Tex Williams's benefit. Forrest hoped the memory of their former closeness and not their breakup had inspired her to wear it today.

The hand that didn't hold hers rested in his pocket on the photograph of a partially constructed white ranch house enclosed by a picket fence. Forrest didn't withdraw the photo. When the time was right to show it to her, he would know. With each of the miraculous letters she wrote him, with every post-rodeo supper date, he felt she was drawing closer to the Master. Forrest prayed that he had only to wait a little longer.

"They ready?" Jen asked, smiling as she let go of Forrest's hand to pull herself up on the fenceposts, closer to the brood mares in the makeshift corral.

"As soon as Tom and Al are standing in the reception line, I'll drive the whole mob past the canopy. Canyon'll be in the lead, and he'll bring 'em right on through to the paddock. It'll be a pretty sight, those mares racing across the pasture to the pond."

"Al doesn't know?"

"Or Tom either."

Jen laughed softly and jumped down from the fence. "You did a good job, Forr. Every time I call, Al's trying to figure out how she can afford to buy her mares and get her training business going right away...when she isn't talking about the wedding."

"I know. I hear about her horses all the time, too. Tom was hoping to get them next spring, but I figure this is a good investment for us. Al'll come through, Jen."

"Yeah, I'm sure you're as worried about that as I am." Jen chuckled. "I'm glad we did it. How did you manage to keep the mares a secret for so long?"

"Brought them over here yesterday evening, so I haven't had to hide 'em long. Kept them at my place before that, working them with Canyon." Forrest felt the edges of the photograph against his fingertips.

"And I 'spose Tom and Al have been too busy to notice them today? Or much of anything else besides each other?"

"Got that right. Al said something about hearing some horses this morning, but Tom figured Tamarisk and Promise were loose. He asked me to go catch them."

An unnatural silence fell. Forrest almost broke it, and was forever glad he waited it out.

"You mentioned your place. How's it coming?" Jen asked, toeing the ground with her boot.

"You want to see?"

"I don't think there's time now. We should get back to the house. I haven't even seen Al yet."

"I've...got a picture of the place."

"With you? Show me."

Jen took the snapshot from his hand and studied it. Forrest lived and died with her every breath, but he ordered himself to keep still.

"Looks like it'll be a nice place to come home to. Reminds me..." Jen's voice grew distant, "of something we saw once." She glanced up sharply. "You know what I'm talking about?"

"We'll have a ranch, just like that one," Forrest answered in a tone years younger. He pulled her nearer, as he had once done so often, so unthinkingly. Now he felt every inch of space between them, and closing it gave him exquisite pleasure.

"With miles of fences for you to paint?" Jen tucked the photo in his vest pocket and looked up at him, her lips trembling with a smile of shared love and memories.

"Miles. Miles and miles and miles..." He bent to kiss her, halting just as the brim of his Resistol touched the first waves of her hair. He forced himself to step back. *In God's time*, Forrest reminded himself. *If we're meant to be, she'll meet him. But soon*, Forrest prayed ardently. *Please make it soon, Lord.*

He took her hand and walked with her back to the house, watched Al greet Jen, joined in laughter and small talk with Tom and some other ropers he knew, but he kept Jen in sight throughout the afternoon, continuing his request to the Lord as was his habit.

When the music began and the guests filtered under the canopy, Forrest took his place by Jen. The joy of walking the aisle with her gave way to the pain of releasing her hand before the altar. *Just for now,* Forrest told himself. He focused on Tom who stood near him, and then Al, approaching on her father's arm. *Bless them, Father. And someday,* Forrest prayed, looking across the aisle at the redhead in rose, *someday, let it be us.*

Behind the gauzy veil, Al saw the world differently. There was her father, at her side, but giving her to another: a handsome cowboy in a western suit of white. She saw in Tom's eyes such beauty now, brown like a sturdy tree trunk or the solid earth. And all that love in them besides. Al wondered how they could hold it all in.

She had noticed many people during her walk down the aisle: Sarah, waving and holding a video camera, Uncle Barney in a garish green ensemble, Aunt Marg and Uncle Willy in matching white and red. Among the faces were shadows of those who should have been there: friends from the circuit who were now gone, Tom's father and mother, Forrest's father, Jen's mother, Grandma.

Your blessing. Your last gift to me, Grandma. Thank you. As Al left her father's arm and took Tom's, she felt God's blessing on her, too. She heard it in the music, voices and fiddle strains blending to praise the Lord for the union and to ask his favor. She heard it as her father and mother publicly gave their approval of the match. She heard it in the text she and Tom had chosen, a passage from the Song of Songs. And most of all, she heard it inside her, a song without note or measure, surging like white water, thundering like hoofbeats.

When she and Tom exchanged their vows and faced the guests as a wedded couple, Al leaned hard on Tom's arm. It was all too much, too good. *Worth all that anyone can possess,* Al thought, *and more. The love of God and of this man, whom the Lord has given me, in addition to his greatest treasure.*

As she and her new husband stepped into the reception line, Al heard a disturbance and looked past the people to see a herd of riderless horses coming up the drive and heading straight for the open paddock past the canopy, Canyon in the lead.

"Tom? Do you know anything about this?"

He shook his head, and as Al stared, she saw Forrest at the rear of the horses and Jen riding beside him. When Forrest reined in before the canopy and astounded guests, Jen raced past without benefit of saddle or bridle, astride one of the brood mares, her red hair a stream of roseate light. She rode with effortless grace, gripping the mare with her legs and lifting her arms over her head as she repeated the pastor's benediction from the Song of Songs.

"Blessings to you!" Jen shouted, eliciting smiles and laughter from the newlyweds and wedding guests alike, "On this 'day of your wedding, on the day of your gladness of heart!'"

And then she was gone, one rider among a living river of horses, flowing to the meadow pond.

A beautiful woman...a beautiful woman on a fast horse, Al thought, seeing far beyond her cousin's external beauty. Al pressed her face to Tom's vest to hide joyful tears for herself, Tom, Forrest, Jen — for the future that lay ahead of them, shining like the sunlight glinting off the shimmering manes of their wedding gift. More than the gift, Al thanked the Lord for the work he had performed in them all. For so long they'd been dream riders, racing in an illusory, self-centered pursuit of bucks and buckles. Now she, Tom, and Forrest were free,

free to serve and live and love, and to witness Jen's waking to the reality of an existence and God as old, and as new, as eternity.